SPECIAL MESSAGE TO READERS

This book is published under the auspices of

THE ULVERSCROFT FOUNDATION
(registered charity No. 264873 UK)

Established in 1972 to provide funds for research, diagnosis and treatment of eye diseases. Examples of contributions made are: —

A Children's Assessment Unit at
Moorfield's Hospital, London.

•

Twin operating theatres at the
Western Ophthalmic Hospital, London.

•

A Chair of Ophthalmology at the
Royal Australian College of Ophthalmologists.

•

The Ulverscroft Children's Eye Unit at the
Great Ormond Street Hospital For Sick Children,
London.

You can help further the work of the Foundation by making a donation or leaving a legacy. Every contribution, no matter how small, is received with gratitude. Please write for details to:

THE ULVERSCROFT FOUNDATION,
The Green, Bradgate Road, Anstey,
Leicester LE7 7FU, England.
Telephone: (0116) 236 4325

In Australia write to:
THE ULVERSCROFT FOUNDATION,
c/o The Royal Australian and New Zealand
College of Ophthalmologists,
94-98 Chalmers Street, Surry Hills,
N.S.W. 2010, Australia

Susie Kelly emigrated from London to Kenya with her parents at the age of seven, and endured a convent education — until she was expelled for refusing to devote her Saturday mornings to making doll's clothes, as she preferred to go horse riding. In 1975 she returned to live in England.

Home now is an ancient farmhouse, in the process of renovation, in south-west France, shared with a menagerie of goats, horses, dogs, cats, parrots and fish.

A PERFECT CIRCLE

Keen to discover some of France's lesser-known attractions, Susie Kelly, her husband Terry and their two dogs embarked on a 10,000-kilometre journey, where they encountered exploding gherkins, killer waves, and sinister submarines. They crossed the historic paths of Charlemagne, Vauban and William the Bastard, and the battlefields of two world wars. The camper van's exhaust falling off and one of the dogs trying to eat the vehicle and its contents did nothing to spoil their magical trip. A cornucopia of sights, legends and history, their journey was enhanced by the kind, charming and quirky characters they met on the way.

Books by Susie Kelly
Published by The House of Ulverscroft:

BEST FOOT FORWARD
TWO STEPS BACKWARD

SUSIE KELLY

A PERFECT CIRCLE

Complete and Unabridged

ULVERSCROFT
Leicester

First published in Great Britain in 2006 by
Transworld Publishers
London

First Large Print Edition
published 2007
by arrangement with
Transworld Publishers, a division of
The Random House Group Ltd
London

The moral right of the author has been asserted

Copyright © 2006 by Susie Kelly
All rights reserved

British Library CIP Data

Kelly, Susie
A perfect circle.—Large print ed.—
Ulverscroft large print series: non-fiction
1. Kelly, Susie—Travel—France
2. Large type books
3. France—Description and travel
I. Title
914.4′0484

ISBN 978–1–84617–862–7

Published by
F. A. Thorpe (Publishing)
Anstey, Leicestershire

Set by Words & Graphics Ltd.
Anstey, Leicestershire
Printed and bound in Great Britain by
T. J. International Ltd., Padstow, Cornwall

This book is printed on acid-free paper

ACC. No.	
CLASS No.	914.40484
B. N. B. No.	
B.N.B CLASS	
BOOKSELLER	Ulvers.
PRICE	£16.99
DATE RECEIVED	1.8.07
	CN

To KitKat, Jamie, Jasmine and Leonie
— four very special people.

ACKNOWLEDGEMENTS

Without Vivien Prince, this book couldn't have happened. For her dedication to the welfare of our menagerie, her zeal in keeping our garden under control and alive under the most contrary climatic conditions, and her rigorous reorganizing of my tumultuous housekeeping, we can never sufficiently thank or repay her. She shines like a diamond.

Carole Morrow somehow found time, in between caring for her mother, catering for her husband and tending to several dozen cats, to help us with planning our journey; she also proofread the manuscript and checked the facts, and I thank her profusely.

Mary Perkins and Liz George thrust an envelope into my hand just before we departed, with a note to say that if we had a bad day, we were to treat ourselves to a good meal with the enclosed. For that very kind gesture, thank you both. We did.

Thanks to my agent Maggie Noach, and Camilla Adeane for their continued encouragement and valued advice, and to Francesca Liversidge at Transworld who was kind enough to contract the book. Nicky Jeanes has been a diplomatic and skilful editor.

En route, many people helped us, offering advice and supplying information. They are too numerous to mention individually, but thanks especially to Fabienne Kiebel at the Office de Tourisme de la Communauté de Communes du Rhin; Stéphane Giraud at the Groupe d'Étude et de Protection des Mammifères d'Alsace; Maud Valla, Agent de gestion du patrimoine culturel Tignes développement; Mr Colin Bruce at the Imperial War Museum; Mike Werner, and those kind folk who dug and heaved Tinkerbelle out of the sand, and the patient people who gave us directions on the many occasions when we were so lost that we feared we might vanish for ever.

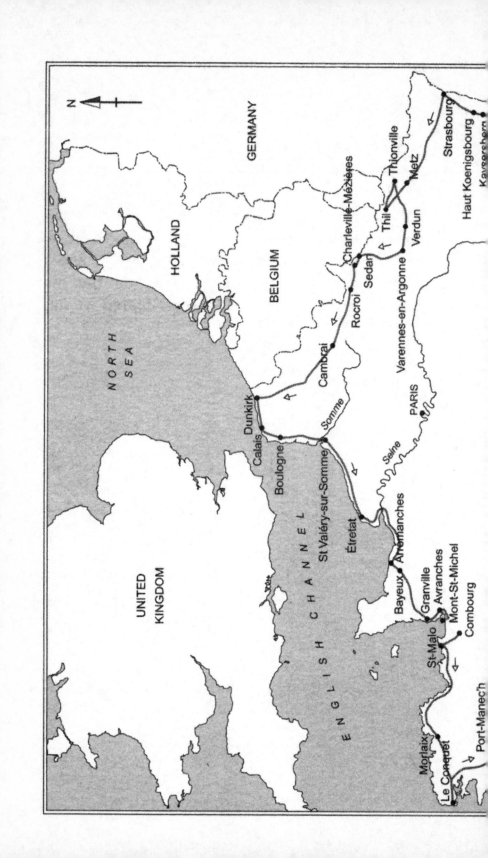

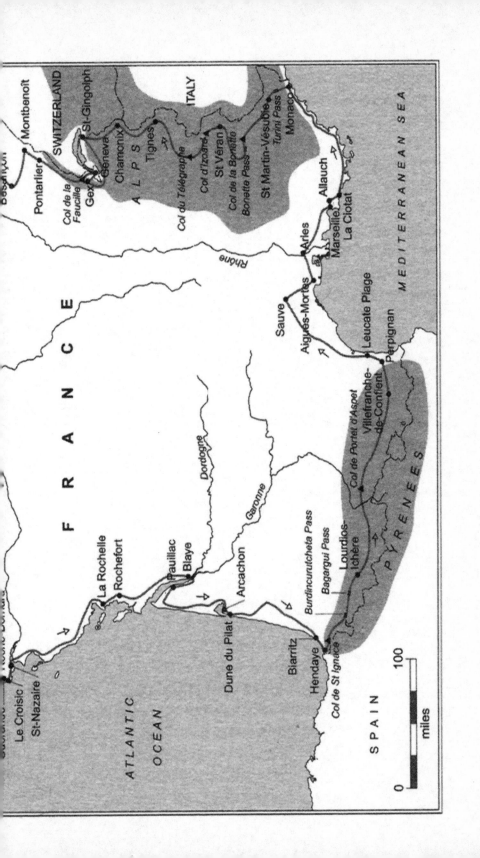

PROLOGUE

For the nine years we had lived in France, almost all of our time had been occupied with working on our property, leaving little opportunity for exploring the country outside our immediate area. Consequently we were embarrassingly deficient in first-hand knowledge of the history, geography, gastronomy, customs and peoples of our adopted land. The tranquil atmosphere and scenic beauty of the Poitou-Charentes have a tendency to keep us in a state of heavenly torpor, but there had always been a vague feeling that we should make more effort to investigate some of the quarter of a million square miles making up 'l'Hexagone', the largest country in Western Europe.

We devised a simple plan, which was to pack a tent in the car, take the dog, and spend eight weeks or so driving around the 'outside' of the country. We would not have any fixed itinerary, but would simply take each day as it came and enjoy what we found. Jennifer Shields, our American friend who had first come to look after all our animals when I walked across France in 1998, agreed to come back and oblige once again. Our route would take us through 41 *départements* and 17 regions of France bounded by the Channel, the Atlantic and Mediterranean coastlines, the Pyrenean mountains and the Alps, the Rhine and the frontiers of Andorra, Spain, Italy, Switzerland, Germany, Luxembourg and Belgium, each distinctly different from the others in its landscape, culture and cuisine. Our only worry was whether, in the most fervently carnivorous *départements* that we would visit, there would be some sort of vegetarian alternatives to regional delicacies like tripe, cassoulet, or frog soup.

As it was such a simple plan, it was inevitable that it would go wrong, and it very quickly did.

Several months before our departure, we decided that our dog Talisman should have a companion. He's a sociable soul, and very active, too. A small dog could keep him entertained while we were travelling, and help him disperse some of his abundant energy. And it would not take up a great deal of room in the car.

There is, in the Dordogne, an animal rescue organization called the Phoenix Association, run by a heroic couple called Richard and Sheila, whose tireless efforts save the lives of many desperate animals. When I phoned to ask whether they had any small dogs in need of a home, who might be suitable as a companion for Tally, Sheila mentioned a litter of puppies recently abandoned on their doorstep in a cardboard box. She was fairly certain that they wouldn't grow much bigger than a spaniel, based on some formula of her own involving the ratio of leg length to body length, or something like that. Spaniel size was perfect for us and would fit comfortably in the car. Off I went and collected a small black bundle that we named Dobbie. He and Tally became best friends as soon as Dobbie learned that in their relationship one of them was the boss, and it wasn't him.

As the months before our departure ticked away, our small bundle swiftly grew into something approaching the size of a calf. Much as we loved him, we watched in dismay as he outgrew the car and we realized that we were going to need a much larger vehicle for our journey. We started looking for a camper van.

Time continued to march onwards, as it does, and our departure date loomed. When the telephone rang one morning at just after six o'clock and I heard Jennifer's voice, I knew straight away it was going to be bad news. She'd damaged her Achilles tendon and was going into hospital for an operation; she'd be virtually immobile for three months. As looking after our animals normally involves a great deal of running about trying to catch them, or mending fences they've pushed down, or extracting them from inaccessible places, it requires somebody fleet of foot and fully fit. It was no job for a convalescent.

I had a friend in Kenya, Vivien Prince. We'd known each other since we were both pony-mad schoolgirls, and she'd said casually that if anything happened to prevent Jennifer's coming she'd be glad to step in, so I wrote and asked if she was serious. While we were discussing the feasibility of Vivien's fitting us into her already over-loaded schedule, destiny intervened. She bought a charity raffle ticket, without even knowing what the prizes were, and won the first prize, which was a return air ticket from Nairobi to Paris! She was on her way, and so would we be once we'd found a vehicle.

With only a week before we were due to leave, we were still without suitable transport. A camper van was turning out to be far more expensive than we had imagined, so when a friend introduced us to some people who were selling an ancient but still robust model we snapped it up. We christened the

4

fifteen-year-old Talbot van *Tinkerbelle II*, in memory of the charismatic Citroën 2CV I'd owned when I first came to France in 1995. The new Tinkerbelle was equipped with cooker, loo, hot and cold water, refrigerator and heater, and numerous knobs, buttons and switches which we didn't have the slightest idea how to operate.

Vivien's journey from Kenya to France was traumatic. The airline took her as far as Milan, where it disembarked her without apology or explanation, and from where she phoned me indignantly to say she was stranded. While I was wondering if I could possibly drive across the whole of France in my elderly car to collect her, the airline found her a flight to Paris, where she wandered around for several hours towing the four largest, heaviest suitcases I've ever seen, before finally arriving at Poitiers railway station at just after one o'clock in the morning, still smiling, a petite person whose fragile appearance disguises a titanium will and boundless energy.

The next morning I expected that she'd want to sleep at least until midday after her gruelling safari, but she was up at 8.00 a.m. bright-eyed and beaming, making one of her overpoweringly strong cups of tea, and ready to start an inspection of her temporary empire.

She wasn't impressed.

'My God,' she whispered, seeing the chaos in the hay barn.

'Oh, my Lord! What is *this*?' when she saw the stable and goat shed. 'What on *earth* have you been *doing*?'

It's quite true, the place was a simply dreadful mess, because I'd let it all get out of control and was no longer capable of cleaning it up. I'd just been putting more mess on top.

In the few days before we left Vivien familiarized herself with her new command. She made our meals and tidied up after us, chivvied us along and generally took control of our lives. I got the feeling that she couldn't wait for us to get out of the way so that she could start bringing order to the place. In her charge we were leaving Leila, our 37-year-old mare; two goats called Tuppence and Thruppence; two hens; two cats; two parrots; and a whole load of fish and frogs in the pond. Vivien is not only an expert horse-woman, she's also absolutely devoted to animals and their welfare, and apart from Jennifer there's nobody with whom we could have been happier to leave our pets.

So everything was falling satisfactorily into place: we had Vivien, and we had a vehicle. Nothing could go wrong.

With the van packed, and the dogs loaded,

we were preparing to climb aboard when I noticed a geyser of grey scummy water spouting skywards in the garden. Instead of evacuating itself to the soakaway, the used water from the kitchen had broken through the pipework and was disporting itself all over the lawn. Terry was forced to excavate a large area of the garden to rectify the problem, and then he needed a shower.

As he slid back the shower door, it casually abandoned its attachment and clattered to the floor. By the time it was fixed it was nearly nightfall and too late to set off, so we deferred our departure until the following day.

The next morning, with a definitive 'Bye!' to Vivien, we merrily swung the gate to behind us. The gatepost collapsed and the gate fell off its hinges. Were the spirits trying to tell us we shouldn't go? Or that we *should* go as soon as possible, before anything else went wrong? We decided upon the latter, and drove away. In the mirror I could see Vivien, who had watched the series of minor disasters in disbelief, waving us off with a gleeful expression. I suspected that as soon as we were out of sight she'd jump up and down punching the air and yelling, 'Yippee!'

1

BRITTANY — BUTTERY CAKES AND GALLOPING VALKYRIES

For no particular reason, we had chosen to begin our travels in Brittany, and to steer an anticlockwise course using the excellent Institut Géographique National's *Atlas Routier France*. En route to pick up the coastline we were going to follow, we arrived in Combourg, which looked so romantic, with the château's turrets peering over the rooftops, that we felt we must stop there for refreshment. Terry likes a good cup of coffee, while I'm a hot chocolate addict. The waiter recommended, in fact almost insisted, that we visit the château — it's always open, he said. The main entrance was locked but we found a small gate in the wall and pushed it open, and started strolling along a gravelled path flanked by perfectly mown lawns. In the distance a man on a tractor, mowing more lawn, changed course when he spotted us.

He dismounted and walked to where we were standing and now feeling rather guilty.

'*Non, non,*' he said politely, sweeping his

arm towards the building. '*C'est fermé!*'

When is it not *fermé*, I asked.

Every day, he replied. It's open every day except for today when it's closed for some unusual, undisclosed reason. *Tant pis*, maybe we could visit it on our return journey.

We reached the Brittany coast at le Vivier-sur-Mer, and followed a '*camping*' sign to a sublime location at the Pointe du Grouin just north of Cancale where we spent our first night. From a slight incline the campsite gives a dramatic view of the bay of Mont-Saint-Michel to the east, and the gulf of Saint-Malo on the west, and from a pathway along the cliff top the dogs had their first astonished sight of the sea glistening in the afternoon sunshine. Just offshore, the Île des Landes was a babbling mass of gulls and cormorants flapping and hopping about on the rocks. If a fairy had popped up and asked us to wish for a perfect beginning to our travels, we couldn't have hoped for a better one.

All our fellow campers were French, and at least half had dogs that they paraded around introducing to each other. There was a cheerful, relaxed atmosphere in the early morning; people in dressing gowns and slippers wandered in and out of the showers, or carried plastic bowls of dirty dishes to the communal sinks, and everybody greeted everybody else with remarks about how perfect the weather was on this day in mid-May and how long it might last. This instant camaraderie is one of the reasons we enjoy camping so much. Immediately next door to us in an odd little camper like an overgrown egg on wheels with a pop-up roof was a small, lean, handsome, nut-brown Breton with cropped grey hair and a striped blue-and-white jumper. He told us he was a retired *matelot*, and that he'd recently spent a fortnight touring the Monts d'Arrée on his motorbike. We should go there, he said: it was a strange and interesting place, a lunar landscape unlike anywhere else in France. He laughed delightedly when I said he was my idea of the archetypical Breton. Yes, he said proudly, indeed I am!

Flat calm and oily still, the sea bore no resemblance to the familiar postcard scenes of manic waves attacking lighthouses and ships. This was the Brittany coastline at its most docile and beguiling. On the way to Saint-Malo we found a perfect sandy beach; the only other occupants were a couple with a small child and a golden retriever. Tally rushed over to make friends, but Dobbie was entranced by his first introduction to the sea, and lay down in it. He gulped mouthfuls of salt water for several minutes before galloping over to chase the other two dogs around the rocks; half an hour later the several saline litres he'd drunk had its predictably violent effect upon his digestion. After he'd recovered we continued along the coastal road towards Saint-Malo, until we saw a sign to '*les rochers sculptés*' at Rothéneuf, where we picked our way down a twisty, stony path to find a colony of monsters, smugglers and corsairs sprawled in the sun on a windy hillside overlooking the waters of the ragged Emerald Coast.

A nineteenth-century local priest named Abbé Fouré, who was almost deaf and dumb, used to pass his time here on this rocky face when he was not on parish duty. Over a 25-year period and an area of half a hectare, he sculpted out of the granite several hundred figures, based upon the legend of a powerful Rothéneuf family, pirates and smugglers who flourished in the sixteenth century. Amongst the sea-calves, serpents, stern watchmen and figures eroded past recognition, my favourite sculpture was a rectangular tableau showing what looked like a couple of dwarves against a background of palm trees. The male dwarf appeared to be simultaneously pulling off the lady's headdress and kicking her up the backside. You can find postcards showing the *abbé*'s handiwork in its heyday, before time and tide and the tramp of feet took their toll.

I wondered what he'd been thinking as he chipped away for all those years, and how long his lonely labour of love will last before the elements obliterate it. I found it a rather sad place.

Every turn of the road revealed another glorious beach of pristine sand tickled by silky turquoise water. We drove on to Cap Fréhel where the lighthouse stands in 300 hectares of beautiful moorland of heather and wild flowers, and where we were all but blown off our feet and off the edge of the 70-metre cliff by the ferocity of a wind that arrived out of nowhere, and which was not only ferocious but also freezing. The original lighthouse, built in 1687 and illuminated by three torches burning tallow and turpentine, was rebuilt after the Germans blew it up during the war and is now powered electrically.

Minihy-Tréguier, which we drove through, is a small place, but of some significance because it's where Yves Hélori de Kermartin was born in 1253. He became a renowned lawyer who devoted himself to helping the underprivileged, and was known as the poor man's lawyer. Defending a poor man sued by a *bourgeois* for having the impudence to stand outside his kitchen enjoying the cooking smells, for which the smells' owner felt he was entitled to payment, Yves the lawyer rattled a coin. The noise, he said, paid for the smell. I like that! St Yves not only became the patron saint of lawyers, but also shares the holy patronage of Brittany with St Anne, whose origins are distinctly vague but who may have been the mother of the Virgin Mary. Nobody seems to know exactly where she came from, or indeed whether she ever existed at all, but she takes some of the burden off St Yves who's probably kept very busy by the lawyers.

It was almost 7.00 p.m. when we reached Ploumanac'h where, according to a directory we'd bought, there were three campsites. The first two were closed despite their opening dates being clearly stated as two days earlier. We were both hungry, and Terry was tired and irritable after wrestling all day with Tinkerbelle's gearbox which had without any prior warning become exceedingly temperamental and was refusing to engage reverse, something which we needed to do quite frequently. Driving up and down and round and round in Ploumanac'h, trying in vain to find the third campsite in the hope that it would be open, Terry became really bad-tempered — something that happens when he's hungry. Nothing was where it should be; the roads weren't properly signed; the traffic was too slow and the drivers were idiots.

Traditionally in our family it's the wife who bears the responsibility for such problems. We were barely speaking by the time we found and breached the entrance to the third campsite. The dogs seemed callously unaffected by this domestic unpleasantness, and ate their dinner with enthusiasm. After being righteously frosty with Terry for an hour, I accepted his offer to take me out for a meal, and we drove down to the bay at Trégastel-Plage, where we saw why this part of the Breton coastline is known as the Pink Granite Coast. The huge boulders that populate the beach in a jumbled heap known locally as a '*chaos*', and are the result of 300 million years of erosion, are indeed absolutely deep blush pink. Terry enjoyed oysters followed by *moules* and *frites*, while I tried the prawns and salmon, which were excellent (unlike the service), and we washed it down with a carafe of very drinkable *rosé* that perfectly matched the colour of the sunset on the rocks.

The following morning we drove through Ploumanac'h and Perros-Guirec, past quaint stone cottages half submerged in clumps of rhododendrons and semi-tropical vegetation. With the tide far out and the sea flat calm, the sky pale blue, the boulders deep pink and the sand bleached white, and ranks of yachts clinking on their anchors in the marinas, it was a perfect day.

Because Dobbie had eaten Tally's collar the previous day, we stopped to buy a replacement in Lannion (twinned with Caerphilly), where the receding tide had left an inlet filled with slithery, sticky mud in which a large congregation of gulls stood ankle-deep, preening themselves. It seemed a little odd when with a few flaps of their wings they could have reached the beach and been standing on clean sand. Local place names beginning with Plou, Tré, and Lan reflect the fact that the Breton language is a sister to Welsh and Cornish. It was to Armorique, the land of the sea, that small groups of Christians led by monks and clan chieftains fled Anglo-Saxon persecution in England between the fifth and seventh centuries. Maybe because these exiles became homesick they began calling their new home Brittany, or Little Britain. That's why England, Scotland and Wales became known, in the seventeenth century, as Great Britain.

Until 1959 the *département* in which we now were was called the Côtes-du-Nord. The municipal council at Saint-Brieuc called for a change of name for the following reasons: that the name Côtes-du-Nord was inappropriate for a *département* which geographically was in the west of France; that the word 'nord' suggested cold, whereas the Breton climate is mild; and that the name Côtes-du-Nord was quite damaging to the efforts of the tourist offices to develop tourism which, after agriculture, was the main source of revenue for the *département*. The council also cited the fact that several other *départements* had successfully applied to modify their names. And so the Côtes-du-Nord became the Côtes-d'Armor.

As the day advanced the cold wind (yes, it was definitely cold despite the mild Breton climate) resurrected itself, and on an improbably green sea a lone yacht rocked on curly white-tipped waves. We crossed the *départemental* boundary into Finistère, literally 'the end of the earth', and followed a road lined with trees in virgin green leaves until we arrived in the town of Morlaix, which is dominated by a towering viaduct.

It wasn't this 62-metre-high edifice that had lured us there, but what was glowingly described in a magazine published by the Brittany Tourist Board as possibly the oldest chilli palm in Europe, even the world, standing 20 metres tall and with 4-metre leaves. Despite the palm's height we couldn't find it by driving around, so we headed for the tourist office, which closed for lunch as we arrived at the door. We found a small *crêperie* in a sheltered sunny square, facing a row of tall houses crowned with saggy slate roofs, with gulls dancing on the ridges and self-sown plants growing round the chimney pots, and sipped chilled golden cider and lunched on *galettes*, mine filled with *soubise*, the lovely onion sauce, and Terry's with tomatoes, onions and herbs. Lemon and apple *crêpes* rounded off our meal very satisfactorily. To walk off the effects of the cider while we waited for the tourist office to come back from lunch, we wandered down the quaint cobbled alley called rue Angle de Gennisac and into l'Echoppe Artisan, the hat shop to beat them all. Creations of straw and ribbons, chiffon and silk, flowers, artificial fruits and jewels, so light, so colourful, so absolutely delicious they'd have looked at home in a Parisian *pâtisserie*. If you want a beautiful hat, try this shop first. Take lots of money with you.

Back at the tourist office there was an odd lady ahead of me who asked innumerable questions of the only member of staff in the office: had the list of concerts for the following year been published yet? Were they printed in Morlaix? She kept plucking brochures from stands, flicking through them and asking peculiar questions that had nothing to do with them and dropping them

18

on the counter. I thought the girl behind the desk was very patient. After more than five minutes of listening to the lady's enquiries I prepared to give up and walk out, but as I reached the door the tourist-office girl finally untangled herself and asked how she could help.

'We've come to see the chili palm,' I explained.

'Ah yes, there are many chili palms. You can see them in Roscoff.'

'But we'd like to see the one in Morlaix.'

'You'll have to go to Roscoff.'

'But where is the palm in Morlaix?'

She shrugged. 'There are many big palms in Roscoff.'

I wondered if her brain had been addled by her previous customer, and showed her the magazine from the Comité Départemental du Tourisme du Finistère and the article mentioning the great palm that lived in Morlaix.

She read the article, looking nonplussed.

'I don't know where that palm is,' she said, 'so it's probably privately owned and not open to the public.'

'Are you sure? Could you possibly find out whether we can go and see it?'

'No, I'm afraid not.' She began rummaging through a pile of booklets on a shelf behind her, from which I deduced that she'd finished with me.

'We've come quite a long way to see the tree. Perhaps you could suggest how we can find out how to view it?'

'Yes,' she replied. 'Go to Roscoff.'

★ ★ ★

Having failed to find the chili palm, we climbed into Tinkerbelle and set off on the next leg of our journey, pleasantly mellowed by lunch, sunshine and the anticipation of whatever new experiences lay ahead. The traffic lights caught us on the red, and as Terry braked Tinkerbelle gave a horrible shudder and made a very bad clunking sound.

'Oh, hell,' I groaned, 'has somebody hit us, or have we burst a tyre?'

Terry climbed out and walked round to the back, where he stood looking perplexed. In the rear-view mirror I saw the driver of the car behind us waving to him, and pointing. Terry lay down in the road and vanished under Tinkerbelle. When he reappeared he was clutching something large. The lights changed to green, and cars behind hooted. Terry brandished the thing he was holding, and they overtook us, the drivers smiling and waving. The large item was part of Tinker-belle's exhaust system, which she'd chosen to discard in this embarrassingly inconvenient location. My heart sank; this was only the second day of our trip, and how were we going to manage without an exhaust? There was already the developing problem with the gearbox. Was the entire vehicle going to drop to bits? Our funds were very limited, with almost no margin for emergencies.

'Don't worry, it's no problem,' Terry reassured me. That's his usual response to any catastrophe. 'We'll just keep going for now, and as soon as we find a breakers' yard we'll pick up a used part.'

Oh, good. Off we drove, noisily. To our right in the beautiful bay of Morlaix the inshore waters were palest turquoise, darkening into the distance to a deep aquamarine. Everything about this area was reminiscent of Cornwall: the lushness of the vegetation, the narrow winding lanes, the pretty stone cottages and the Celtic road signs.

To compensate for shedding her exhaust, Tinkerbelle allowed her gearbox to become a little more cooperative and it was going more or less where Terry directed it. He mentioned casually that the brakes weren't quite what they should be, but added that I shouldn't worry about them, so I tried not to.

Beside us in a field was a tractor towing a device from which men were planting artichokes. Different men were picking artichokes in the next field. Then there was a field of potatoes. And then more artichokes. Artichokes covered the land right up to the horizon, and to the horizon after that.

Roscoff has a postcard-pretty harbour front lined with slate-roofed stone cottages, people drifting around in the sunshine through narrow streets, and a bridge going nowhere into the sea. It is quaint and picturesque, touristy but charming. We wanted somewhere peaceful and unspoilt to spend the night, and found it on the Coast of Legends at the Sainte-Marguerite dunes, a stunningly beautiful location in the Abers.

Gulls floated overhead, and a single fishing boat with its traditional Breton red sail skirted the rocks jutting from the sea. Patches of seaweed as red as the sail formed a playground for legions of sand hoppers, and all along the beach were nests of beautiful pebbles, so smooth, such subtle colours, so tactile — if only they didn't lose their soul and fade once taken from their natural environment; so we stroked them and put them back. The only other life form on the beach was a young man with a black Labrador tied on a rope, which gazed wistfully at Tally and Dobbie playing on the rocks. Making our way back from the beach at dusk we almost stepped upon a large green and buff-coloured toad camouflaged on the sandy path, and it scrambled clumsily out of our way making indignant tutting noises.

We went through the evening ritual of moving the dogs, together with their beds, blankets, toys and water, into their night-time accommodation in Tinkerbelle's cab. Before doing so we had to remove from there anything chewable: camera, maps, guide books, pens, mobile phones, ropes were all grist to Dobbie's insatiable mill. If he could get his jaws round it, he'd chew it. He'd already demolished the washing-up sponge and a plastic storage container screwed to the wall.

The night was absolutely still and quiet, and as the light faded away into darkness over to our right we could see the sweeping flashing white light of the Phare de la Vierge. Lighthouses are very competitive: they strive for the title of the tallest, the oldest, the longest beam, the widest sweep. At 82.5 metres the Phare de la Vierge holds the 'tallest lighthouse in Europe' record.

Next morning was announced not by the song of the larks, but by the persistent rapping of a woodpecker. As soon as Terry opened the cab the dogs leapt out and hurtled straight in through the open door of a neighbouring camper that had arrived during the night, to visit a tiny poodle who stood her ground and sent them packing. Shrugging off this antisocial rebuff they dashed down to the beach. This was the greatest freedom they'd ever enjoyed, and while we breakfasted they made the most of it, spending the next hour chasing each other along the sands and through the dunes.

We wriggled our way along the glorious coast, past a large flock of gulls standing in a field all facing in the same direction like some exotic crop, and villages with comic-book names — Ar Stonk, Kroaz Konk. Around every curve was a new paradise, the beaches of dreams, the beaches of childhood memories. No busy promenades, ice-cream vendors or deckchairs. Just fine sands patterned with birds' footprints and sprinkled with small, delicate shells, lapped by clearest waters and topped by cloudless skies. We stopped for a coffee at a superior beach-side restaurant. I needed to use the loo which was down some steep stairs in a sort of narrow basement. A large lady on crutches was being helped down by another lady, so I took the crutch-lady's spare elbow and we manoeuvred her to the bottom. While we waited for her to emerge, the other lady and I talked about the superb weather, and we wondered if it was too good to be true (it was), and if it would last all through the summer (it wouldn't). Down the stairs hopped the chef in his whites, and he went through a door next to the loo, reappearing a few seconds later with a large box of oysters. All the time we waited he popped up and down, collecting the oysters from their storage area next to the ladies' loo and taking them up to the kitchen. I hoped Brussels wouldn't find out.

Cascades of bedding dangled from almost every first-floor window in the villages we drove through, as folk took advantage of the sunshine and a nippy breeze that stirred the paddles of a cluster of windmills. We passed a hairdressing salon named Marine Hair, where the mermaids go when they need a new style, I think. There was little traffic. We followed two tractors, one towing a trailer loaded with new potatoes and the other a cargo of fragrant cattle-shed cleanout, and as we meandered slowly along the lanes several swarming platoons of cyclists in bright-coloured tight clothing whirred past, with sinewy arms and stringy legs. They were a scrawny bunch, I thought rather sourly. The hot chocolates and Breton food were already starting to wreak havoc: that morning I'd been unable to find a single pair of trousers which I could do up at the waist.

Across the sea to our right lay the Île d'Ouessant, a haven for lighthouses — it has five, including Créac'h, the most powerful in Europe, and another known as la Jument, which has an interesting history. In March of 1904 M. Charles Eugene Potron, who had survived a shipwreck, bequeathed the sum of 400,000 francs for the erection of a lighthouse of the highest quality, fitted with the finest equipment, to be built on a rock in some of the most dangerous waters of the Atlantic coastline, off the Île d'Ouessant. M. Potron's Will stipulated that if the lighthouse wasn't completed within seven years, the legacy would become void and the amount would pass to the Central Society for the Shipwrecked. One hundred square metres of rock, only accessible at low tide and during calm weather, was chosen as the site for the new lighthouse and construction began in May 1904, in diabolical conditions. During the first year only 51 hours of work were accomplished, but the la Jument lighthouse was eventually completed just within the seven years. Twenty years after it went into service somebody fortunately noticed that it wasn't anchored to the rock, but simply perched on top of it and maintained in place by its own weight! Since then it had been secured to the ground by four high-tension cables.

We reached picturesque le Conquet, or if you prefer its funny Breton name, Konk Leon, on market day; the town was jammed with vehicles and holidaymakers and numbers of strutting dogs. Shoppers at stalls offering strawberries, pillows, fish, cheeses and vegetables, fabrics and jewellery, and bread in every possible shape, turned to stare as we spluttered and farted, exhaustless, through the streets of the appealing little town. Once Tinkerbelle was tucked into a car park we set off with the dogs to explore the port. The morning's catch had been unloaded and despatched many hours earlier, and a few fishermen were picking out tiny crabs and small fish from the awful nylon nets which have replaced the traditional linen and cotton ones.

We bought two heavy, glossy slabs of the Breton cake known as *kuign aman* — literally 'butter cake', made with lashings of butter, heaps of sugar and a teeny sprinkling of flour just sufficient to bind the two together — and two slices of a cake with a layer of seaweed in it from Denis Lunvan's *boulangerie* in rue Clemenceau, and established ourselves at a table on a sunny pavement. Terry ordered coffee and I had a glass of cider. If ever we should go and live in le Conquet, I shall eat Denis Lunvan's *kuign aman* every day for every meal, until my arteries simply give up fighting a hopeless battle, which probably won't be very long. Oozing butter, *kuign aman* is lasciviously delicious and should carry a compulsory health warning. Terry couldn't finish his slice so I helped him, and he wasn't very keen on the seaweed cake so I had that too, because it would be a pity to waste it. We were entertained by a very small, self-important dog who was swaggering about bringing the traffic to frequent abrupt halts, uninterested in its own danger and the irritation of lunchtime drivers — or in Dobbie's frenzied attempts to join in the fun even if it did mean dragging our table and us with him.

Saturated with buttery cakes we drove on to St Mathieu's Point, where there's a monument to sailors who have given their lives for France, and a ruined abbey which has a lighthouse growing out of it. The abbey was built facing Jerusalem, in accordance with tradition, by Benedictine monks and dedicated to St Matthew, patron saint of tax collectors, accountants and other leeches (only joking), whose relics (a piece of his skull) were brought there from Ethiopia by

Breton sailors. Saint Matthew may have died naturally, or been martyred in the course of squeezing taxes out of people. Nobody knows how he met his end. If you examine a set of apostle spoons, you'll see that each apostle holds something in his hand. St Matthew holds an axe. Don't you think that's an odd tool for a tax collector!

The abbey's skeleton is very tall, with elegant arches in the old walls, and granite pillars reaching to the ceiling that isn't there. The church must have been spectacular when it was intact, and even in its current state of ruin is an imposing sight. Pigeons nest in the dark and dank dormitory with its bright-green mossy walls, and through the missing roof you can see up to the sky and the St Mathieu lighthouse which overlooks one of the world's busiest maritime crossroads, through which 50,000 ships pass each year between northern waters and the Mediterranean. If the lighthouse were not tucked up so close to the abbey it would topple on to the rocks below, because there's not an inch of ground between it and the edge of the cliffs. Beside the abbey is a walled field that was once the monks' garden, where they grew vegetables and fruit, medicinal plants and fodder for their animals, and which provided a threshing ground for local farmers. Now there were only buttercups, and a blackbird feeding her baby. There's a tiny simple chapel too, with a beautiful high vaulted ceiling and pots of agapanthus and arum lilies by the altar.

★ ★ ★

'Strawberry Museum' said a sign at Plougastel-Daoulas. Uncharacteristically Terry dug in his toes, and refused to visit it. That worried me: how could anybody fail to be attracted to somewhere that could create a whole museum out of a strawberry? The museum of bees on the Crozon peninsula also failed to arouse his interest, and so we drove around the bay of Douarnenez, hoping for a glimpse of the fabled sunken city of Ys, built by the king of Cornuaille for his daughter Dahut, an unpleasant person whose dissolute behaviour brought about the city's destruction. Every night Dahut took a new lover and forced him to wear a silken mask. At daybreak, the mask became a nasty thing with claws which killed its wearer, whose body was thrown into the sea. Dahut met her comeuppance when Ys flooded and she was drowned. It's said that in March, when the tides reach their nadir, the ruins of palaces are seen in the sands and on a quiet night you may hear the city bells tolling.

Having neither seen nor heard any sign of Ys, we headed towards inelegantly named Plogoff, and on the way found a simple campsite belonging to a dear old lady who keeps a small public bar in her front room, where she sells packets of biscuits, jars of coffee, tins of vegetables, and very old postcards. We had a drink of cider with two locals who wanted to know whether we were going to visit the Pointe du Raz. We asked if it was a long walk, or if we should drive there, and became mired in confusion when the two customers and the landlady all pointed in conflicting directions and gave walking distances ranging from half a kilometre to twelve kilometres, and times ranging from ten minutes to four hours. We decided to leave the visit to the following day and to drive there, because we didn't actually know where we were, and if we left on foot we might never find our way back. There was no road sign at either end of the hamlet, and when we asked its name they all talked at once and gave different answers, and we never did discover what the place was called.

Apart from a young couple in a tent, who looked suspiciously like a pair of school-children enjoying an illicit weekend together when their parents thought they were studying at a friend's house, we had the campsite to ourselves. The only sound came from a blackbird in the hedge, and the methodical munching of cattle in a neighbouring field.

Before we left the following morning, at the suggestion of our hostess we walked down the lane to admire the quaint little chapel, decorated with naïve paintings and a smart new timber ceiling, which it owed to the local community who had organized fund-raising events to restore the church from its previous ruins. If only it had had a name on it, we might have been able to discover where we were.

We drove to the Pointe du Van, a site of unbelievable, unspoilt beauty carpeted in grasses and herbs, heathers and wild flowers, pierced by granite boulders growing out of clumps of pink scabious that perfectly complemented the blues of the sea and sky. There were just the two of us and the dogs, and in the far distance three walkers with a dog on the path along the cliff top, at this enchanting place that seemed like the very end of the world. The Pointe du Van is magical; no words or photographs could capture the essence of its beauty. There are maybe a dozen different shades of blue between the sky and the sea below, where

Morgane the treacherous mermaid still sings sailors and fishermen to their death on the rocks. It's somewhere that has to be experienced to appreciate it. And if you stand at the cliff's edge looking out at the Atlantic Ocean, on a perfect early summer day when the sea is calm and there's not another human being in sight, and the only sound is of lazy waves tickling the rocks, you'll believe you can fly. Even the dogs seemed affected; instead of their usual wild galloping they wandered slowly, sniffing the air and staring around them as we followed the cliff-top path to the chapel of St They, mainland France's most westerly place of worship, also restored from ruins by its staunch congregation. Outside stands a granite pillar topped by two characters back to back, but the inscription has been worn away by time. Lizards scuttled round the stone window openings and over the lichen-covered slates of the roof. From its fourteenth-century Gothic belfry the bell is said to toll by itself to warn boats in danger to pray for protection. When, long ago, the French fleet was being pursued, the bell of St They rang out to guide the ships to safety; but when the enemy fleet followed a strong current appeared, dashing many of their boats on to the rocks and dispersing the rest out to sea. St They's altar is a splendiferous creation of columns and pillars and plaster saints, one of them pointing to a nasty wound above his poor knee. The curved wooden planks forming the ceiling are painted turquoise, and the walls decorated with coats of arms and shields. Model boats stand in front of each of the two minor altars, and there's a lifebelt on display washed up from a shipwreck. Behind the chapel, tucked into a hollow, is the tiny St Matthew's fountain.

Despite its forbidding name the Baie des Trépassés, the Bay of the Dead, is a wondrous sandy beach cradled between the Pointe du Van and Pointe du Raz, and it was from there that dead Druids were sent on their way to the gateway to the other world on the Île de Sein. In the sixth century the Breton Saint-Guénolé had the clever and ambitious idea of linking the Île de Sein to the mainland by a bridge of ice, but when the Devil walked over it he melted it with his hot little cloven feet. There are many macabre legends attached to the bay, all to do with death. It's easy to see why Druids chose this to be their final point of departure from the temporal world, because it would be difficult to find anywhere more naturally splendid. It's somewhere you can only stand and be in awe. We felt we might run out of superlatives in this part of Brittany. It's almost too beautiful.

Satiated with scenery, we went in search of lunch, which we found at a restaurant named le Doris, in a village called Kérity, between Penmarc'h and Saint-Guénolé. They served an excellent meal. The succulent salmon came with a generous selection of fresh vegetables, and not the customary uninspiring little castle of boiled rice. At the table next to us an English couple were treating their lunch very seriously, working their way through a five-course menu as if they might have to take an exam about it later, savouring each mouthful with reverent expressions, smacking their lips and not exchanging a single word. In an act of supreme self-denial I refused both the bread and a dessert, to counterbalance yesterday's cakes. Afterwards we walked along the small harbour front, with its bobbing flock of sailing boats, and stopped to read a plaque on the wall of Quai Général de Gaulle that told us: 'From this harbour, on 23 and 24 June 1940, in response to a call from General de Gaulle, our following compatriots sailed to England aboard *Notre Dame de Bon Conseil* to join French forces, and fought on all seas and all fronts for the honour of France and her liberty.' There are eight names listed, and we wondered whether they'd all safely returned to Kérity. Despite its startlingly bright orange walls and purple shutters, the local *crêperie* was rather attractive. A lady with a small dog perched in a basket on her handlebars cycled past waving to stallholders selling lacework and hot dogs, while on the rocky beach seabirds poked around in puddles left by the ebbing tide.

Saint-Guénolé, where we arrived a little later, had been the scene of something rather awful on 10 October 1870. The wife of Finistère's *préfet*, together with their daughter and a friend, was swept away from the rocks and drowned at the place known as the Hell Hole, or the Victims' Rock. Whatever was the *préfet* doing allowing his wife and child to get themselves into such a perilous situation? Even on this peaceful day the waves were heaving and crashing violently on to the rocks. A rather superfluous notice warned that this place was treacherous and claimed lives even in the calmest weather. You could see that just by looking at it. A sturdy iron rail ran protectively round the edge of the rock. On the other side of it, unbelievably, incredibly, ankle-deep in swirling foam on a small, wet, round rock stood a fisherman, seemingly oblivious of the waters churning round him and sometimes over him as he calmly cast his line at any fish foolhardy enough to venture there. When a couple of young men climbed out of a car and into wetsuits in preparation for plunging into the sinister waters for some strange purpose known only to them I began to suspect that this place robbed visitors of their common sense, and dragged Terry away before he could develop any crazy ideas.

★ ★ ★

In busy Concarneau just after 4.00 p.m. the temperature read 35°C, and the fortified walls were aflutter with flags. It all came as quite a culture shock after our last few days of deserted beaches and dozy villages. Crowded shops were selling beach balls, English and German newspapers, postcards and sun lotions; there were traffic jams, a funfair and shoals of squealing children swimming and splashing each other in the bay. Tally was surprised by this sudden change in our environment, and stood on top of the fridge for a better view. The town was bathed in an all-pervasive odour of fish, which seemed to be wafting into Tinkerbelle from every crevice and cranny of the town, not surprisingly as it's France's third largest fishing port. Seeking somewhere quieter and less scented, we kept going until Pont-Aven where we drove round in circles for a while, looking at the art gallery windows filled with seascapes and nudes, and similar art galleries, and more art galleries, until I was certain that it was the multitudes of nude paintings that kept us driving around, and nothing whatsoever to do with being lost.

We eventually escaped from the centre of Pont-Aven and found a breakers' yard where we might be able to get an exhaust system to stifle Tinkerbelle's roars. The yard had closed a few moments before we arrived, but that was fine, we'd return in the morning. At nearby Port-Manec'h, by sheer chance and great good luck we discovered a small, pretty car park in a grove of trees just a few metres from the beach. There was another camper van there, and the French owners came over to tell us that it was permitted for campers to stay overnight. They'd been there four days, but were leaving today. We should be very careful, they warned, because a couple of nights ago a gang of drunken youths had attacked them. No damage was done, *mais quand même* . . .

Two dozen blue and white bathing huts stood, or in some cases leaned against each other, like sentry boxes in a row on Port-Manec'h's small bay of pepper-fine silver sands. A few yachts were anchored in the aquamarine water. No wonder that for

Gauguin and his friends this was a favourite holiday spot — it's easy to imagine them sitting on the sands at their easels, catching their pipe smoke with the brims of their straw hats, and dabbing idly at their canvasses.

I put a couple of salmon steaks in the oven, and Terry and I strolled along a footpath through a copse which led to a cumbersome stone building standing on a small headland. As we were wondering what its purpose was, a lean, lanky man came out, wearing a checked shirt and faded blue jeans halfway down his snake-thin hips. Large spectacles magnified his bright-blue eyes, and an unlit but aromatic pipe jutted out from beneath a walrusy moustache.

He wanted to know what we were doing, but without waiting for an explanation he offered us a glass of wine, and would we like some oysters? We hadn't any money with us, and I don't eat oysters if I can possibly avoid them, so we declined. Nevertheless, he introduced himself as Hervé, and vanished inside the building, returning with two glasses of wine, a fistful of oysters and a sharp knife with which he pointed us to a table. A deafening noise came from the building — I think it was the Ride of the Valkyries, playing at thunderous volume on a radio that wasn't precisely tuned to the station. Hervé wouldn't have a drink himself, but expertly stabbed open an oyster and held it out to me, obliging me to graciously accept the vile thing. Terry happily finished the rest, because he loves them. Hervé and his pipe sat down between us and started talking. Quite what he was talking about we weren't sure, because all his tales tapered off before reaching their finale, and he was very much given to meaningful stares whose meaning we could not grasp, and elbow digging, and all the while the Valkyries were galloping louder and louder through the radio's static crackling.

I was thinking about the salmon in the oven and made getting-up-to-go moves, but Hervé was regaling us with a story featuring Admiral Dönitz, some English submarines, and the barbarity of the Ukrainian soldiers who'd massacred the Port-Manec'h locals.

'When the Resistance — you know about the Resistance, don't you?' He jabbed me with his elbow, and I nodded — 'when the Resistance caught the Ukrainians, you know what they did to them?'

'Killed them? Shot them?'

He put his wide blue eyes close to my face, and said slowly and clearly: 'They cut out their tongues, and dug out their eyes, and filled the holes with wire netting!'

'Why?'

'And you know the reason why oysters are so expensive in England, don't you?'

No, I didn't, and was still waiting to learn about the wire netting. At the same time Terry was trying to keep up with the conversation and I was trying to fill in the parts he couldn't get, without really understanding them myself.

'Well, I'll tell you.'

There was a long silence, while Hervé stared at me. I was beginning to panic in case the fish caught fire, and the dogs were locked in the van.

'You want some more oysters, don't you?'

No, I said, thank you very much, we really didn't want any more oysters; in fact if I never ate another oyster again for the rest of my life I'd be perfectly happy. Further, we didn't know what our relationship with Hervé was, if we were his guests, or his clients and going to be presented with a bill that we didn't have the means to pay. But he went and brought back another fistful of oysters and put them in front of Terry, who raised his hands in a gesture that said no thank you. Hervé pushed them at him forcefully. Terry opened and ate them.

Hervé wanted to arm-wrestle with Terry.

'Well, what a pity we must leave,' I said. 'We have a long way to go.'

This was patently untrue, but I was worried that if he knew we were staying in the nearby car park, he might spend all night, to the accompaniment of the furious Valkyries, telling us stories that didn't end and we couldn't understand, and forcing upon us oysters I didn't want and we didn't have the wherewithal to pay for. And I was seriously anxious about the salmon, the oven, the dogs and Tinkerbelle.

We all stood up, and Hervé kissed me six times; Terry received one kiss and another arm-wrestle. Hervé wrote his and my name on a piece of paper, and gave me six more kisses, and Terry asked him whether we could pay for the oysters. Hervé casually indicated a battered box on his table, and Terry emptied into it all the loose change from his pocket, which in England wouldn't have paid for one oyster, let alone a dozen, and we never did learn the reason why oysters are so cheap in France and so expensive in England.

We marched swiftly back to the car park, and found the salmon steaks very well done but not quite beyond redemption. Hervé, we agreed, was quite a character. Possibly barking mad, but definitely a character. We sat outside reading and watching a mixed group of blue tits, robins and chaffinches hoovering up the charred pieces of fish we discarded, while a small green caterpillar humped itself ticklishly up my leg.

★ ★ ★

During the night we were not attacked by intoxicated adolescents; the only thing we had to contend with was a pervading odour of burned salmon. We had agreed to forsake our cooked breakfasts each morning, because by the time we'd prepared and eaten them, washed up and stacked everything away, half the morning had gone. In future we'd have a quick cup of tea and wait until we found somewhere for a hot drink and a croissant. When we drove back to Pont-Aven to the breakers' yard the next day, we were surprised to find that although it was almost 10.00 a.m. it wasn't yet open. Nor, strangely, were any of the factories on the industrial estate. The only sign of life came from two noisy German shepherds hurling themselves at the fence. We rattled the gates and roamed around looking for human life forms, before realizing that it was the third of the four bank holidays France enjoys in May. So off we roared, following a large herd of cyclists who were a rather charmingly podgy crowd, particularly the lady at the back who looked like a madly pedalling piglet and made me feel a little better about the butter cake.

The countryside became tamer, more sophisticated; grander houses in tropical, jungly gardens replaced the chocolate-box cottages of northern Brittany. On the roundabout leading into Guidel stood a weird metallic creature, a surfer with the head of a monster; the church bells were thundering, the market was lively, and there was a show-jumping competition on the beach, where we sat watching horses bouncing over obstacles, or sometimes knocking them down like spillikins. The riders cooled their mounts down by walking them about in the sea, and before we could catch him Dobbie charged happily up to a rider already teetering on the edge of control, whose horse nearly turned a somersault at the sight of the slavering black creature with the foot-long floppy tongue galloping towards it through the waves. We watched for half an hour, and drove on, past le Fort Bloqué where the Atlantique golf course is bisected by the road, and on to Lorient to visit the submarine base there.

Because it was a public holiday there were no guided tours of the base, but the young man at the gate said we were free to wander around and explore.

This is a truly unpleasant, profoundly horrible conglomeration of submarine pens, sinister concrete buildings with walls several metres thick. Even the few plants struggling for life in cracks in the concrete had a depressed air. From here German submarines had sneaked out to attack Allied shipping in the Atlantic during the Second World War. I broke out in a sweat when I thought of men locked inescapably in the ghastly vessels. A single submarine sat at the dockside, a shiny black capsule reeking of stealth, death and claustrophobia. I wanted to escape from the awful place, but Terry was in his element, fascinated, ready to clamber into a submarine, submerge and sail off in it if he got the chance. Then something attracted his attention away from the submarines: a trimaran up on a trestle, with a man working on it. Terry commanded me to ask the man to invite him aboard, which I obediently did, mentioning that Terry had navigated a winning British Admiral's Cup team yacht, and also an Italian contender.

Soon Terry is up on deck with a charming and handsome Portuguese gentleman called Miguel, who speaks fluent English and tells Terry the trimaran once belonged to France's greatest yachtsman, Eric Tabarly, who sadly fell overboard and disappeared at sea in 1998. Although Tabarly's boats were usually named *Pen Duick*, this trimaran is called *Côte d'Or*

II, because it had been sponsored by the chocolate manufacturers. *Côte d'Or II* has an unfortunate history, having been dismasted and overturned twice, but Miguel has rescued her and for the last year, whilst living in a container at the submarine base he's been working to rebuild her. Terry is absolutely enraptured for the next two and a half hours, while I'm stranded on the cracked and sweltering tarmac. But soon I have a friend, a beautiful Spanish girl wearing a bikini and a huge smile, who rides up on a bicycle.

Rosa speaks no English and very little French, and I speak virtually no Spanish, but mostly due to her enthusiasm we find a way of communicating. In between bouts of conversation she cycles round and round beside the boat, looking up at Miguel, and I think she's in love with him. She talks about him a great deal. He's her friend, and she comes from Spain to visit him several times a year. She stays at a flat in Lorient. Miguel is in love with his boat, she tells me. Rosa is outgoing: she tells me about her mother, who is from Asturia, and her father who is from Galicia. They're retired and live in Asturia. She has a sister named Anjelica, who is a talented artist, and is looking after Rosa's golden retriever while Rosa is visiting Miguel. Rosa comes from Corunna, a word that always takes me back to my schooldays and giggling rather heartlessly as we recite Charles Wolfe's 'The Burial of Sir John Moore after Corunna', emphasizing heavily the words 'The sods', which at the time had seemed extraordinarily entertaining:

We buried him darkly at dead of night,
The sods with our bayonets turning,
By the struggling moonbeam's misty
    light
And the lanthorn dimly burning.

Rosa used to work in tourism, but since the devastating oil spill on the Galician coast in 2002, when the *Prestige* went down carrying 20 million gallons of oil, the tourist industry is in decline and she's currently jobless. She doesn't mind, though, because she hates working in an office anyway.

Terry and Miguel are talking obsessively about sailing, and Rosa is cycling round in her bikini with her beautiful, tanned, slim body, gazing up at Miguel. She looks eighteen. She spots the dogs in the van, and insists we take them for a walk. She loves dogs, she says, and so we get them out of the van and they tow us around the beastly concrete place for fifteen minutes; then they're gasping for water so Rosa cycles off and brings back a bucket for them.

I ask how old she is, and she astonishes me by replying that she's thirty-three. I laugh and shake my head, and on a piece of paper write down *23?* No, she laughs, writing down *33*. Then she tells me her boyfriend lives in Madrid. He used to be an engineer, but now he has become an actor, which pleases her because it's a far more interesting career than engineering. Is Miguel married, I ask tentatively, because he wears a wedding ring? Yes, she beams, his very beautiful wife is at home in Portugal, expecting their second baby in December. They're both very happy. So is she. I'm bewildered.

She cycles away and returns with a digital camera, with which she takes a photo of the two of us with our arms around each other.

Finally I manage to tear Terry away from Miguel and *Côte d'Or II*, and Rosa gives me a great hug, and I give her the bracelet that I'm wearing. I'm totally charmed by this lovely girl, and absolutely confused as to why she's content to spend weeks cycling around this strange area while Miguel works on his boat, her boyfriend is acting in Madrid, and Miguel and his wonderful wife are joyfully expecting another baby in Portugal.

Terry is very excited about this meeting; he hopes Miguel will launch the boat in July, when Terry will be welcome to sail with him. There's talk of sailing her across the Atlantic. Mentally Terry is already packing his ditty bag. As we drive away Rosa whizzes past on her bicycle, and indicates one of the submarine pens. Terry goes over and looks inside, and takes a photograph of the monstrous thing that is in there.

*   *   *

We drove on to the Quiberon peninsula, resisting the lure of the elegantly named Schitter's Antiques; the peninsula was absolutely crammed with traffic on this fine sunny day, as was Carnac where we simply couldn't find anywhere to park, which was rather a shame as we wanted to see the church of St Cornely, who wasn't only the patron saint of Carnac, but also of horned animals. We wanted to see Carnac's famed megalithic alignments, which are said to be legions of soldiers petrified by St Cornely to stop them chasing him after they'd driven him out of Rome. Defeated by the impossibility of parking, however, we carried on to Larmor-Baden, which was similarly traffic-ridden. From there we'd planned to explore the two islands of the Île aux Moines and Île d'Arz, just a kilometre apart, and once linked by a

49

narrow causeway. Their respective inhabitants detested each other, because one group were sailors who considered themselves superior to the others, who were mere fishermen. When a boy from the Île aux Moines fell in love with a girl from Arz, his parents imprisoned him with the monks. Every day, the lovesick girl crossed the causeway to sing to him beneath the walls of the monastery. The girl was so beautiful that the inhabitants of the île aux Moines stopped breathing, and seeing this as the Devil's work the prior called upon God's help. His prayer was answered: the sea rose and submerged the causeway; the girl was drowned; the two isles were separated for ever. No word on what happened to the lad.

Everywhere overflowed with people celebrating the public holiday, so we drove round the gulf of Morbihan, the inland sea that was formed, as everyone knows, by the tears of fairies driven from Brocéliande, the enchanted forest, home of Arthur and Merlin. Flower garlands tossed into the waters by the fairies became the islands of Houat, the duck, Hoëdic, the duckling, and Belle-Île, the Isle of Beauty. When we arrived in Vannes, with its sensationally pretty timbered buildings and really quaint old-fashioned cinema, whose fading fascia was bedecked with plaster roses, we decided to stay the night. The municipal campsite provided spacious lawned areas for tents and caravans, but camper vans were confined to a bleak and crowded tarmac patch with no charm whatsoever; but we did have some friendly neighbours, a Dutch couple who kindly loaned Terry one of their bicycles, a Dutch-manufactured Giant, so he could pedal off to the nearest shop and buy something for us to eat.

I greatly admired the Dutch lady, who was very strong-willed, and who knew exactly what she did and didn't like. She most particularly didn't like cooking, so she didn't cook. Ever. No ifs. No buts. She simply didn't cook. Instead she sat doing what she did like, which was mostly reading. Luckily and wisely for her she'd chosen as a partner a man who loved cooking, so she could sit and relax while he happily took care of the food department. The previous year, when she was working in a casino, she had had a terrifying experience when three armed robbers held up the place and put a gun to her head, and she was greatly underwhelmed by the failure of the Dutch authorities to bring the men to justice.

Next day we decamped from the tarmac and drove to Berthelon-Plage, a beach of pebbles and rough sand, where we stopped to give the dogs a run. Several giant beige-tinted jellyfish lay dead upon the beach, looking like transparent bowler hats. Dobbie was fascinated by them and would have liked to eat them if only he could have found a way of getting one, or even part of one, into his mouth. Tally, being a great deal more discriminating, found a dead seagull and chewed on that, generously allowing Dobbie to share it once he'd abandoned the jellyfish-eating attempt.

From France's biggest estuary dam at Arzal we watched the yachts and motor boats negotiating the lock, then drove to the historic Viking town of la Roche-Bernard. In the quiet square is an exciting depiction of somebody about to be guillotined. A life-sized silhouette of the victim kneels expectantly on the block, in a reminder of the bloody Vendée rebellion when the revolting peasants and Chouans engaged in civil war against the Republicans. La Roche-Bernard was once an important naval shipyard, well sheltered far up the estuary of the Vilaine river. Nowadays it's a quiet and lovely small town of cobbled streets, medieval buildings with brightly coloured shutters, and stone walls whose crevices offer accommodation to clumps of poppies and other wild flowers. A most pleasant place to visit on a summery morning. Yachts relaxed in orderly ranks in the river, overlooked by two rusting cannons; relics from the great seventeenth-century warship *La Couronne*, they point at a row of beehives sitting across the river in a field of cornflowers.

2

ATLANTIC COAST — ASSES' MILK AND EXPLODING GHERKINS

Leaving la Roche-Bernard basking in the sun, we crossed into the Loire-Atlantique, and it was almost a relief, because we were becoming punch-drunk from an abundance of magnificent scenery, beautiful towns, intriguing legends and history. That is not to suggest that we thought the Loire-Atlantique wouldn't be equally wonderful, of course, but Brittany, which we had seen at its very best, in perfect weather and out of season, really does overwhelm the senses.

In marshy fields of buttercups herds of horses gambolled, with their wobbly foals tottering around their heels, in the Brière Regional Natural Park. Our destination was le Croisic where, according to a brochure we'd picked up somewhere, there was a splendid aquarium with an attached restaurant where the food was served by divers. That is exactly what the brochure said. When we arrived the aquarium was closed for lunch. The attached restaurant was open, but we were disappointed to see that the waiters and waitresses were ordinary terrestrial creatures, and not divers at all. We'd visualized them swimming to the tables somehow bearing trays of food and drink without its getting wet or floating away. Terry was particularly irritated and insisted that I ask the manageress where the aquatic servers were. She looked back at me quite blankly and plainly hadn't the least idea what I was talking about. Terry was hungry and, as I mentioned earlier, is never at his normally good-natured best when he needs feeding. He would have liked me to cross-examine the lady, and try to force her to produce waterborne staff, but I was already sufficiently embarrassed by the strange looks she was giving me, so I said that he'd have to speak French if he wanted to get involved in that kind of contretemps. I should explain that because up until very recently he had worked in England and spent only a few days each month in France, he hadn't had a great deal of opportunity to learn very much of the language. Although he'd recently begun studying it seriously, he hadn't yet reached a level where he could discuss swimming waiters.

Anyway, despite being served by mere earthlings, our meal was excellent. We had *moules* with *frites*, instead of the salad I'd intended. Having broken the rule with the *frites*, there was no reason not to top off the *moules* with a nice calorie-laden *crêpe à la caramel fleurs de sel* (the addition of a pinch of the local salt really does something very special to the caramel) and wash it all down with cider served in teacups. Suddenly the restaurant was plunged into semi-darkness, followed by much shouting and yelling, some laughter and a worried conversation. The power failure, for such it was, had put the credit-card payment machine out of action, and the person who was trying to pay for his meal had no cash, or claimed to have no cash. The electricity showed no sign of returning imminently, nor the manageress of letting the diner escape without paying. Finally the customer admitted that he had a chequebook, and settled up just a little reluctantly, I thought. I was worried about the fish in the aquarium if the electricity was going to be off for long, but our waiter assured us that there was a generator for such emergencies.

The aquarium conveniently reopened as we finished eating, and we entered a fabulous underwater world populated by infant oysters and baby lobsters (quarrelsome characters, who'll have their claws bound as they mature to stop them mauling each other), infinitesimal plankton and young sturgeon with tip-tilted noses. Sea anemones as brilliant as herbaceous borders wafted their tentacles dreamily at spider crabs and the fearsome-looking but harmless wolf fish. A small fish called a spiny lumpsucker, with Brigitte Bardot lips and big eyes, appeared to be talking to us through the glass. Sunflower stars, the world's largest starfish, spanned a diameter of ninety centimetres, and cheerily waved their numerous arms or legs. I'm not sure which they were, but they can have up to two dozen.

Crossing a walkway to visit the Australian sharks and manta rays, we were shocked to see, in a large ground-floor room at the back, white-coated people busily chopping up fish! We stared in amazement for a few seconds, before realizing that we were witnessing not the massacre of the inhabitants, but the preparation of lunch for the mob of penguins swimming around excitedly in their pool.

The gurnards lined up in an orderly row to watch us with their sad, expressive faces and funny legs all round their heads. Ethereal jellyfish floated around in a glass cylinder, and we learned that they are related to sea anemones, composed of 90 per cent water, and extremely fragile, and have a short lifespan. Not much going for them, really.

There was a very large spider crab standing upright and rubbing together what looked like little hands, like Uriah Heep, while odd things in its mouth went up and down like piano keys. Next to the yellow feathery corals, spotted dogfish eggs were incubating, huge things like stag beetles; they undergo an eight-month incubation period (nearly as long as a human being!) and we could clearly see the embryos moving inside the casings. Sea horses pranced around and hooked themselves to coral branches with their curly little tails, and everywhere we went it seemed as if the fish were watching us as much as we were watching them.

It isn't only the spectacular who live in the aquariums, but also more mundane denizens of the deep, the type usually destined to end up encased in batter and surrounded by fried potatoes. Swivelling small eyes on the floor of a tank betrayed flatfish like turbot and plaice camouflaged in the sand. We learned sadly that the iridescent shoals of mackerel, twisting in a perfectly choreographed aquatic ballet, are such sensitive souls that they cannot survive longer than ten seconds out of water, or being touched. And all cuckoo wrasse are born female, and pink, but as they mature some of them change into males, and turn blue! Pink for a little girl, blue for a boy, in the words of the song. Amazing.

Once we'd seen everything and agreed that le Croisic aquarium was every bit as excellent as it claimed to be, and that it might be a while before we could eat fish without feeling uneasy, we tried to go somewhere else. On the map the town looks fairly small, but when you're actually there it's quite large, and it was very busy that afternoon. Once inside le Croisic you spend so long trying to find a way out that you contemplate buying property there. The road signs go just so far, usually to a junction, where they entirely disappear. We circled round and round in slow-moving traffic until finally escaping to Batz-sur-Mer a few kilometres away, where we drove straight into a monumental traffic jam and were trapped for fifteen minutes outside a clog shop. This was an interesting interlude because it gave us a chance to see that clogs are manufactured in more different colours and designs than you would believe possible. The award for the most tasteless went undisputedly to the purple snakeskin pair.

During the Middle Ages, Guérande was an important producer of fine salt, and during the last twenty years a new generation of *paludiers* has been working to revitalize the industry. We passed them cultivating their precious natural crop in the time-honoured manner, using traditional wooden blades to delicately scrape up the precious grey crust formed by evaporation on their murky-looking salt pans, and went to see what else the town of Guérande had to offer. Enfolded by a mile-long granite wall we found an attractive well-preserved medieval city, throbbing with holidaymakers and gift shops. We'd taken the dogs with us for a walk through the town, and when Tally spotted a cat in an alley and almost jerked Terry off his feet as he tried to follow it, a cluster of camera-laden Japanese scattered in squeaking panic. We bought a bag of *fleurs de sel* in a gesture of support for the local industry.

Leaving Guérande with our little bag of damp grey salt flakes, we spluttered along in noisy Tinkerbelle to the very fine beach at Pornichet on the Côte d'Amour. Tally, whose manners are normally as impeccable as his breeding, ran down the sands to where a couple were peacefully relaxing; the man lay on his stomach, propped up on his arms reading a newspaper, and his wife lay on her back soaking up the sun. Tally stopped no more than a metre from the newspaper-reading man's elbow, adopted an unmistakable posture, and proceeded to defecate copiously. Yes, I know, it's disgusting, and I can imagine readers who think dogs shouldn't be allowed on beaches tutting and grunting. I understand. There was only one thing I felt I could decently do, which was to walk in the opposite direction and act as if Tally was nothing to do with me. That's what I did, and watched from a distance as Terry assessed the situation and how to deal with it. As he talked to the man I tried to tell from their body language how difficult the man was going to be. He handed Terry a sheet from his newspaper, and stood up. While Terry made a neat parcel, the man started making a fuss of Tally. Dobbie joined the party and the sunbathing lady played with him. I felt it was safe to venture over and join them.

They were breeders of German pointers, and had fallen in love with both our dogs. Although Tally is the aristocrat, and Dobbie of unknown origins, it's often Dobbie who attracts the most attention, and people frequently ask what breed he is. I once heard Terry describing him as a '*braque noir*', a most excellent description, because Tally is what in French is called a *braque hongrois* — a Hungarian Viszla. I tell people that Dobbie is a '*chien de carton*' — a cardboard box dog.

Anyway, our new friends couldn't stop stroking the two dogs and making a fuss of them and saying how beautiful they are, which is quite true. They are beautiful dogs. While we were talking and watching them play, Dobbie ran back and spent a seemingly never-ending penny all over the lady's white fluffy beach towel. Mortification just doesn't describe how we felt, but they roared with laughter and recalled situations where their own dogs had similarly embarrassed them. Their daughter arrived with her boyfriend, and they were sent back to the family house a few metres from the beach, to bring their own dogs out to play with ours.

The man was a journalist for the local newspaper, and told us they'd spent the day sailing on a three-masted replica sailing ship which was departing from Saint-Nazaire that evening. If we watched the headland we might see it passing. He warned us seriously not to consider parking in isolated places for the night; the days were gone when it was safe to do so. Now times were dangerous: that morning the body of a young boy abducted some time previously had been found in a lake in Guérande.

We wished them *adieu*, and drove on to Saint-Nazaire, to the harbour where the three-masted square-rigger named the *Stadt Amsterdam* was readying to sail. People scrambled about on her decks amid a jungle of ropes and blocks; they climbed rope ladders and edged out on to the spars of her three masts like circus performers, loosening the sails in preparation for departure. From her stern flew the Dutch ensign, and from her standing rigging, as a courtesy, the French *tricoleur*. Both flags are comprised of red, white and blue stripes; many old sailors will say you can tell which is which because the Dutch do it lying down, and the French standing up. There was a surprisingly small crowd watching, maybe a dozen people at most, the men all enthralled and the women politely bored and visibly cold as the sun went down and a nippy wind came up.

We waited in the wind, and she waited for the wind. We waited, and she waited, until the tide had risen to match the level of the water in the harbour, and the lock gates opened. And Terry was totally spellbound as four of her squaresails unfurled, the upper and lower topsails on her foremast and main mast, and were then sheeted in to trap the wind; using nature's wonderful power, and slowly gathering momentum, she moved out into the Atlantic Ocean towards the sunset, driven only by the wind, and looking like something from the Onedin Line. We were watching a scene from a more romantic age, although how romantic life aboard was in those days of old I'm not sure. Probably hard and rather uncomfortable at times. Terry told me that it was from the most tall-masted of ships that the word 'skyscraper' originated, and that the old trading ships have left many of the words in use in our language today.

After the *Stadt Amsterdam* had disappeared into the distance we drove down to the docks to enjoy la Nuit des Docks, Saint-Nazaire's rather original idea of using clever lighting focused on various structures around the dockland to bring it to life at night. We watched as dusk fell and slowly the lights came on; giant gantries and cranes twinkled and the warehouse walls glowed green and red, the lights reflecting in the black waters. By the time we left the whole of the docklands were subtly illuminated, and it was very late and we had no idea where to find somewhere to stay. Had we not met the journalist that afternoon we might have found a deserted place at the back of the docks for the night, but we decided to heed his warning, and drove on until at the weirdly named Saint-Michel-Chef-Chef we found forty camper vans parked in a car park opposite the *mairie*. A notice announced that this was an area where camping cars were authorized to spend the night, so we joined them. It wasn't what we'd have chosen, had there been an alternative, parked wing mirror to wing mirror on a small crowded tarmac area without electricity or sanitary facilities, but at least it offered security.

In the morning, early, a wedding party arrived and parked in the car park before making their way to the *mairie* for the wedding formalities. The bride was like a galleon in full sail, enormous but pretty, with pearls in her hair and a full-length billowing white satin dress trimmed with pink rosebuds. Her bridegroom looked like a frightened string bean. A dozen cars full of friends and family accompanied them, the vehicles decorated with the traditional net posies and ribbons flying from their aerials.

Near us was a camper similar to Tinkerbelle, and Terry commanded me to ask the owner if he had any problems with his gearbox, because Tinkerbelle's gear lever had started flopping around and Terry was getting tired of fighting with it. The owner was a talkative little man with a weeny moustache and a worried-looking wife, and he looked like a second-hand car salesman. I explained that Tinkerbelle's gear lever was loose and difficult to engage correctly, and his spivvy little face assumed an expression of understanding combined with bad news. He put a hand on my arm, and with a serious gaze announced that the gearbox was absolutely *foutou*. It's the worst possible thing to happen, because it's impossible to repair and, worse still, impossible to find a replacement part. Very soon our gearbox would fail completely, just as his did in Angoulême last year. He asked his wife to corroborate the unfortunate episode, and she nodded briefly and looked away. Oh! what a horrible experience they'd had, he remembered: they had to simply abandon the vehicle and at hideous expense hire a car to get home to Saint-Nazaire, followed by the exhausting hunt for a replacement because nobody manufactures parts for these vehicles any more. He estimated we had perilously little time left before our gearbox gave up the ghost entirely. It was our *pinion baladeur* that had gone; he hoped we didn't have far to go, because he very much doubted we'd get there. I listened in terrible dismay, translating to Terry and envisioning us stranded on the road with no *pinion baladeur*, two dogs and several thousand miles still to travel. *Mais*, said the little man triumphantly, it was our lucky day, because when he'd managed, at unspeakable expense and with unimaginable difficulty, to locate the part for his own van, he'd bought not one, but two, and the other, which was in fact far the better of the two and virtually new, was in his garage at this very moment not twenty kilometres from where we stood. As you might guess, something of such rarity was worth a fortune, almost as much in fact as we'd paid for all of Tinkerbelle. His wife shuffled and looked anywhere but at us, and when we thanked him and told him that it was too expensive and we would have to take our chances with our *foutou* gearbox, he shrugged, said '*Comme vous voulez*', and climbed into his cab without another glance at us.

The stone cottages and slate roofs were behind us, and had been replaced by bright white bungalows with blue shutters and pantiled roofs, and the landscape was flatter, more open and Mediterranean, sunnier and warmer. Old gun emplacements squatted along the coast, neither beautiful nor useful, but a reminder of the past; the seaweed-carpeted sands of the rocky Jade Coast were peppered with people digging on the beach and poking things out of the sand. A chap waded into the sea in a wetsuit, while a couple paddled past in a canoe that looked about to sink, with barely an inch above the water. Two little boys were demonically pedalling their bikes through the traffic, almost knocking cars over. This was the seaside.

We skirted the Baie de Bourgneuf, where herds of fat ponies grazed the salt marshes, and crossed into the Vendée and the Marais Breton. The oyster- and mussel-producing port of le Collet was a muddy affair, trembling in a violent easterly wind that whistled and wailed through the masts of the boats in the harbour, and the flat windy area was reminiscent of Norfolk. Tally had started to become offended by cyclists, pedestrians and other dogs who came anywhere near Tinkerbelle, and yelled his feelings at them as we passed. As we approached Beauvoir-sur-Mer we noticed and followed a sign to la Maison de l'Âne. Some fifty donkeys, mules and horses live there along with various geese, ducks and other assorted poultry. They're the children of a dark, handsome man called Paulo Dieumegard, who when we arrived was perched on a three-legged stool in a cosy barn, milking one of the donkey mares. Donkey — or asses' — milk is pure white with a firm frothy head that any beer could be proud of. It tastes, Paulo said, similar to coconut milk, and is rich in vitamins and minerals. It's ideal for people with skin problems, but because of its low fat content it's no good for making butter or cheese. Transforming it into soap using traditional methods and ingredients is a very much more practical way of keeping the complexion up to scratch than trying to wallow about in a bathful *à la* Cleopatra. And cheaper, too — asses' milk sells for thirty euros a litre. While Paulo collected milk in a plastic jug from a donkey who stood placidly watching us watching, her foal ran up and down the next-door stall, indignantly yelling that his lunch was being stolen from him. The donkeys are only milked once a week, so their babies aren't deprived of their natural food. Paulo likes to feed his animals organically, and told us that the coarse grass on the salty marshes provides a perfect, nourishing food that they thrive on. They all certainly seemed to be in radiant good health. We walked around meeting the different breeds of donkeys and petting their furry, fluffy foals with their spindly legs and tiny jewel-like hooves, ears that were far, far too big and velvety muzzles that explored our fingers and clothing.

Then we bought a bar of lavender-scented asses' milk soap for Vivien (who, every time we spoke to her, was either cooking a meal for friends, bathing and grooming one of the animals, redesigning the garden or retiling a roof) and drove over the causeway, only navigable at low tide, on to the Île de Noirmoutier. The roads were lined with stalls

69

selling oysters, mussels and salt, and almost every centimetre of the twelve kilometres of the causeway was filled with parked cars and dried seaweed. More cars arrived, queuing to join those already there. Gulls and egrets shared the vast expanse of sand with scores of wellie-wearing people armed with buckets and plastic bags, all prodding around in the small pools of water to excavate the shellfish lurking there. A festive feeling was in the air, an atmosphere of excitement, and it was like a seaside scene from a century ago. Frequent signs warned of the danger of drowning when the tide came in over the muddy waste, but while we were there it was so far out that the sea was invisible, and at that moment it was difficult to believe it would start coming in soon to cover the sands and the road we were driving on.

After driving to the far end of the island we headed back over the causeway in the direction pointing to 'le continent', and on to find somewhere for our next over-night stop. Saint-Jean-de-Monts has a magnificent golden sandy beach, a long seafront where people stroll or ride around on bicycles or electric scooters, and wall-to-wall modern low-rise apartment blocks. A couple of hundred metres from the beach was a packed area allocated for camper vans to park, with about half a metre of space between each vehicle, and the campers already there doing their utmost to discourage any newcomers. One girl flailed her arms around at us and shouted 'C'est complet!' but Terry managed to squeeze in and still leave just sufficient space for us to get in and out of the door. It's a very nasty way to spend an evening, but it was free, and with Tinkerbelle critically in need of an exhaust system we had to make sacrifices where we could to try to establish the contingency fund we hadn't made allowance for.

We were up at sparrows' crack to take the dogs to the beach, which was being raked by a bitter wind and empty apart from a scattering of unoccupied mussel and razor clam shells, and two more of the giant beige jellyfish. Dobbie retrieved a dead seagull from the surf to run around with, and stared at Terry reproachfully when told he couldn't bring it into the van and play with it on our bed.

Even very early in the morning there was heavy traffic on the Corniche. This was a different world from the wild unspoiltness of Brittany; here it was full of new houses and buildings, highly developed and geared for tourism, filled with camping sites, play-grounds, quad-biking parks, giant slides and pizza stands, and a mini-golf park dominated by a giant green plastic frog, several plastic penguins, and three life-sized skewbald plastic cows. Most appealing was the family of coypus playing among yellow irises on the river banks; least appealing was a sign advertising a three-star campsite bizarrely named Pong.

At la Maison de l'Âne Paulo had recommended that we shouldn't miss a visit to somewhere called le Potager Extraordinaire, at la Mothe-Achard, a small town a little inland from our course. As we drove through the town we were very startled to spot a completely naked blonde trollop sprawled in a blatantly, lewdly suggestive pose in the doorway of a café. We drove back round the square for a closer look which revealed rather disappointingly that she was a life-sized plastic model; an equally realistic pirate was clambering down from an upstairs window with a swag bag over his shoulder.

We followed a sign to find out what was so extraordinary about the *potager*. Where exactly can I begin? There is, on two hectares of land, a collection of the most peculiar, intriguing, and truly weird plants we'd ever seen, felt, smelt or tasted, as the signs invited us to do: gherkins that exploded when we touched them, and plants that proudly declared they smelled of *crotte de chien* — dog poo. (They did.) Tomatoes that looked like sweet peppers; aubergines that looked like tomatoes; other aubergines that looked like boiled eggs; mile-long beans; and gourds in the most astonishing variety of shapes and sizes, including one rather rude one that Papuan males use to shield Big Jim and the twins, and another that was speckled, two metres long and curled round like a coiled snake. The colours of the vegetables and flowers were startlingly vibrant; there were purple stems and orange stems, hairy ones, smooth ones, shiny ones and spiky ones. Fruit that was long and thin, round or flat. Chocolate cosmos and After Eight mints which, if you smelt them with closed eyes, you'd stake your life savings were the real thing. There were plants with timid leaves that flinched and curled themselves up tightly when touched, and two labyrinths — one of flowers, and one of corn. We all know the difference between a maze and a labyrinth, don't we? In a sunny patch pumpkins relaxed and grew in preparation for the National Largest Pumpkin competition that would take place in October — the record stood at 354 kilograms. The Potager Extraordinaire is indisputably the most fascinating garden we've ever visited. Every space contained something to surprise and delight children and adults, gardeners or not.

★ ★ ★

Lunchtime came at la Tranche-sur-Mer at a pizza restaurant where, as a bonus, the Monaco Formula 1 Grand Prix was just about to start on the television. We are great fans of the sport, and were delighted when the restaurant's two owners asked whether we'd like to watch the start before we ordered, which was the gracious thing to do because they were glued to the set. Once the race was under way, Eric cooked us the most perfect pizza. He was an adorable person with a kind, gentle and rather sad face, who told us that his girlfriend lived in Mexico, where she had to look after her mother. Eric hoped to make enough money during the summer from his new pizza business to enable him to go to Mexico to visit her. He was very *sympa* and we desperately wanted him to be happy.

There's a pleasant campsite at Marans in the Marais Poitevin, France's answer to Venice, where we spent the night. I phoned Vivien to check that everything was well with her. She told us she was presently involved in a matchmaking venture, and had invited the pair for breakfast the following morning; all the animals were well, and by the way, a roof had collapsed at Charles de Gaulle airport killing six people, and wasn't it lucky she wasn't there at the time.

Tally managed to escape and disappeared to chase rabbits with Terry in hot pursuit, and while they were gone I discovered some odd fragments of plastic on the floor which, when I'd pieced them together, formed a thermo-meter and hygrometer which had been fixed to the wall of the camper, and Dobbie had destroyed. They didn't work any more. During the night we were woken by a rattling sound beside Tinkerbelle, and when we opened the door were entertained by a determined little hedgehog tipping one of the dogs' bowls over and helping himself to leftover biscuits, completely ignoring us and our torch.

Opposite us was a diminutive French couple in a caravan. They were on holiday with their dog and their canary, and told us that they came from the Cher *département*, right in the centre of France, and that he was eighty-two and she was eighty. Because they didn't find travelling as easy as they used to, they kept their caravan parked permanently on the site at Marans. It was much easier to drive backwards and forwards without having to hitch up the caravan each time, and they particularly enjoy the Marais. Had we been out on the water yet? If not, we really should. We said we would, and walked down to the river and hired a small, modern motor boat. Terry steered us through the thick green waters where moorhens and ducks fed amongst the yellow irises growing around the rustic jetties. The houses along that part of the river had pretty gardens filled with roses, and small orchards and fishing cabins. It was a peaceful interlude, floating along in the duck-weed, but when we returned to the jetty there was a drama.

The girl who'd collected the money from us for the boat, who was wearing a headscarf and a thick cardigan against the cold, was in earnest conversation with an anxious lady who was pointing upstream. We followed her finger, and saw a boat similar to ours, with several people aboard, stranded against the bank and apparently unable to do anything about it. The passengers were just sitting there looking embarrassed and glum. The girl wrung her hands together worriedly; she and the woman started walking towards the stranded boat, but then turned back, and the woman hurried off calling something over her shoulder. Shortly afterwards the girl's partner appeared, in yellow rubber trousers. He glanced at the marooned party, leapt down into a boat like a cowboy jumping on to his horse from a second-floor window of the saloon, and charged up the river, full throttle; came to an abrupt swirling halt like an ice-skater completing a routine; turned the stranded boat round, restarted the engine and guided them slowly back to the mooring, where they all disembarked in silence. Hey ho.

We drove through the Marais, where the maize was springing up, almost a foot high, the green and still water in the canals was filled with chirruping frogs, and a strong easterly wind was knocking plants and trees almost to the ground. In a fallow field a buzzard flapped as it tried to get airborne with a heavy load. Terry felt he must investigate. He found a newly dead rabbit and we watched as the buzzard kept trying to fly off with it, but could only lift it a foot before the weight was too much and it had to let go. Three crows sat calmly a few metres away, watching and waiting their moment.

On the map was somewhere called Pointe Saint-Clément, which looked as if it might be a wonderfully wide sandy beach, but when we arrived we found a large expanse of muddy scrub littered with dead oysters, fish heads and assorted dirty debris. It was the first time we'd found a beach anything less than perfect; the dogs thought it was wonderful. In la Rochelle we had our first and totally unsatisfactory experience of a cybercafé. As the pennies trickled away I tried without success to remember our latest password whilst also wrestling with a French keyboard which, as everyone knows, has the letters in the wrong place. Forty minutes and seven euros later, we'd achieved exactly nothing, so we consoled ourselves with coffee and hot chocolate and two massive toasted cheese sandwiches.

We made an early landing at Rochefort's *camping* 'Le Bateau', having decided to make our stops earlier than we had been doing so we had time to relax at the end of each day. Free condoms were available on demand in the reception area where a poster declared that the campsite was SIDA (French for AIDS) aware, and that they promoted safe sex. What a sensible idea. Inside the sanitary block, which was designed to look like a huge boat, a man sat cross-legged on a washbasin with a blissful smile on his face, plugged in to a CD player. It seemed quite an odd way to spend an afternoon, but *chacun à son goût* . . .

The site was next to the estuary of the Charente, and we spent several peaceful hours sitting in the sun watching boats and barges sailing past, and two handsome white geese standing on an upturned rowing boat intently watching children paddling canoes on a lake. A small bat swooped around us, as an ochre sunset split the ice-blue of the sky from the silver-blue of the river. During the night we heard the familiar sound of a dog's bowl rattling, and there was the hedgehog tipping it up and munching the leftover biscuits. It must have had to run like hell to get there from Marans.

★ ★ ★

There's so much to see and do in Rochefort that we didn't know where to begin, so we started by walking down to the Corderie Royale through an avenue lined with palms and tulip trees just coming into bloom. The classically elegant seventeenth-century royal ropeworks looks more like a stately home than a factory. Three hundred and seventy-four metres in length, the whole structure is balanced on oak beams to support it on the marshy land. The manufacture of rope ended there in 1867, and now the Corderie is a maritime museum and library, which has been faithfully and entirely rebuilt after being burned down in 1944. Just a few steps away a replica of the *Hermione*, the eighteenth-century frigate in which Lafayette sailed to America to join the fight against the beastly English, is being faithfully and skilfully reconstructed. One day, she'll sail to Boston. There are several museums in Rochefort, but we were saving the afternoon for something very special indeed, once we'd lunched.

The restaurant we chose was setting up tables on the pavement, and the manageress explained that for the past three days the wind had been too strong for outdoor eating, but they thought it would be OK today. There were some English people behind us with a little boy who banged the table loudly with his fork, sat on the ground and was generally being rather awkward, so one of the four adults hoisted him on to his shoulders and took him for a walk. Terry and I discussed why English children are unable to eat at table in the same well-mannered way that French children are, and why we English always seem to be so loud in restaurants. The French, even in large parties, keep their noise down to a level that doesn't interfere with other diners; the English don't. And we're the ones who are meant to be inhibited. We ordered grilled squid, which came in bleached rubbery sheets that were almost impossible to cut and skidded around the plate trying to outrun the knife. When we succeeded in catching a morsel, it was like chewing a piece of car tyre, and impossible to swallow, and made me gag, so we wrapped them in a napkin for the dogs. Behind us I could hear the English people in pidgin-French asking the waitress what *calmar* were.

'Fish,' she responded rather unhelpfully.

'What kind of fish?' they asked.

'White fish.'

'Oh, fine, that sounds OK.'

They all ordered it, while I wondered whether I should warn them, but deciding I'd appear to be eavesdropping I kept quiet. By the time their order arrived, we were just leaving, so we'll never know what they thought about the white fish.

After lunch we wandered around the pleasant wide streets of Rochefort. Somebody was moving house, and a removal team were packing a truck with paintings and pots of geraniums, and bringing out larger items of furniture through the window and down a ladder. In an unassuming side street, behind a very ordinary-looking front door, is an extraordinary and fabulous house. It was the home of Julien Viaud, born in 1850, a retiring, diminutive naval officer whose name might not mean much to many people. However, as the writer Pierre Loti, a *nom de plume* derived from an exotic blushing flower, he would become the youngest ever member of the Académie Française and one of the great names in early twentieth-century romantic French literature. His house is actually two adjacent houses, and the astonishing interior exactly as it was while he lived there. His father, a town clerk in Rochefort, was disgraced, accused of theft, and the family suffered the humiliation of being the targets of gossip in the town, living in two small rooms.

For the writer Pierre Loti, the description flamboyant is an understatement. He loved to dress up in exotic costumes, like an Arab prince, and from his travels around the world, mainly in the Muslim countries he loved and wrote about so romantically, he collected hundreds of artefacts, with which the house is crammed. The first rooms you enter are conventional enough, with family portraits and red velvet wall hangings, a piano and several uncomfortable-looking chairs where Mrs Loti could receive and entertain her visitors. The successful applicant for the position of Mrs Loti, by the way, had to have three specific qualities: she had to be rich, she had to be shorter than five foot four so that her little husband didn't have to look up to her, and she had to be a Protestant like Loti's adored mother. From her portrait she looks amiable, if not exactly beautiful.

It's after the drawing room that things start to become interesting.

The Renaissance banqueting hall is dominated by a vast chimney piece and two staircases, one timber and one stone; chandeliers hang from the ceiling, which reaches right up to the roof, and the walls are hung with heavy tapestries. Loti never forgot his family's early humiliation by the Rochefortais, and as he became rich and famous he enjoyed flaunting his wealth before them. This is the room where he held his lavish Chinese party, where the two hundred invited guests were paraded through the streets in rickshaws, and a young boy dressed as the Empress of China was carried into the room on a palanquin, the purpose of all this being to impress the locals who queued up in the streets to peer through the windows, unaware that the last Chinese Empress had died two centuries previously.

Climb another staircase to the second floor, past walls festooned with exotic hangings, and visit Loti's bedroom, which in contrast to the grandeur of the rest of the house is a small, simple room with a tiny bed, plain white walls, and icons of Hindu,

Catholic, Buddhist and Protestant persuasions. Loti was obsessed with death, and spent his life seeking a religion that he could believe in. The bedroom also contains a framed photograph of the writer performing as an acrobat, something he had learned to do with great skill.

The Turkish room is draped with silken cloths, the floors smothered in Persian rugs and tasselled cushions, the walls decorated with oriental weaponry. There are brass trays and hookahs, and an adjacent small room with a glass ceiling where Loti could sleep looking up at the stars and imagine himself in the desert. The *pièce de résistance* is the mosque that Loti brought from Damascus. It's a room of marble pillars, patterned tiles, stained-glass windows, a fountain, and five sarcophagi. Our passionate young guide told us that when Loti was entertaining young ladies (no mention of what Mrs Loti was doing at the time) a servant would hide in one of the sarcophagi and start moaning, in order to frighten the damsel into the writer's arms. In the mosque room is the headstone from the tomb of the Turkish girl whom Loti loved for years, and promised to return to one day. But when he finally did, she was long dead and buried, so he had a replica of her headstone made to secretly replace the original, which he brought home to Rochefort. If we had to choose just one place to visit in Rochefort, it would be Loti's magical house.

On our way out of town we passed a sign to the Conservatoire de la Bégonia, and popped in to have a look round. The man at the desk happily sold us tickets to join a guided tour that was just starting; the giant greenhouse was jam-packed with begonias of all shapes and sizes and colours, but all begonias and very many of them looking very much like the begonias all around them. The guide talked fast at enormous length and in unfathomable technical detail about the personal habits of begonias, and we couldn't understand very much at all. Almost nothing, in fact. Standing in the humid and incredibly hot tunnel was like being in a rain forest during a heatwave, and we tried to embark on an independent visit, but were abruptly stopped by the guide, who told us sharply that we must stick with the tour group. Nobody was permitted to wander around alone. We tried for another five minutes, during which time we progressed about six centimetres, becoming hot, sticky and bored, and beginning to feel less than friendly towards the guide in particular and the begonias in general. I attracted the guide's attention and apologized that time wouldn't allow us to stay any longer, and he shrugged his shoulders and turned back to his more appreciative subjects, and I was quite sure he made some disparaging remark about ignorant foreigners.

Our route took us past Rochefort's '*transbordeur*' bridge, the last remaining bridge of its kind in France, an unusual wrought-iron structure on which vehicles crossing the Charente drove on to a platform supported by steel cables hanging from the bridge; it was the platform that moved over to the opposite bank, with the vehicles stationary upon it. Nowadays it's an historic monument, open only to pedestrians and cyclists.

Crops looked weary and dusty in the overwhelming afternoon heat, except for the resilient poppies that lined the road. In Moëze there was a sign leading to '*la croix hosanniere*'. We didn't know what a *croix hosanniere* was, but apparently this one was unique in Europe, and while Terry entertained the dogs I went and found it in the centre of the town's cemetery, an enormous Renaissance structure of a tall tower set upon a collection of stone columns, which had been at one time an assembly point for religious processions. All around it the dead slumbered peacefully in the sunshine beneath flowers both real and ceramic, although a couple of headstones were tilted upwards as if their incumbents might be preparing to climb out at any moment.

After driving through countryside that was agreeable without being spectacular, we arrived in a small, attractive medieval walled town, whose restaurants were doing a cracking trade at tables spilling over the pavements of the cobbled streets. Despite being barely marked on our map, in its heyday before it became silted up Brouage was the salt capital of Europe, as well as an important arsenal used by Richelieu as a base for his merciless attack on la Rochelle. It was also the birth-place of navigator/explorer Samuel de Champlain, who established a trading post in what would become the city of Quebec. Quite impressive for a tiddly little place in the middle of pretty much nowhere, in this rather isolated area of flatlands and river courses, cattle, trees and bushes. Our journey being primarily impromptu meant we seldom knew what to expect when we set off each morning. We didn't know how far we'd go that day, nor what we'd find along the way: that was the whole idea, and the joy of it. Discovering little jewels like Brouage was a bonus.

At Marennes, at 4.00 p.m., the mercury on

the pharmacy thermometer had reached 40°C; the millions of oysters in their beds must have been close to cooking. We were. Outside a butcher's shop a happy, beaming wooden pig supported a blackboard advertising a long list of gruesome pork products. It's one of the things that has always mystified me about French butchers, how they came up with the bizarre concept of showing animals joyous at being killed and eaten. In the exhaust of an armoured fighting vehicle outside the military museum in le Gua a family of sparrows had set up home. We followed a sign from here to Caesar's Roman Camp, which sounded interesting. What we discovered was a flight of steep stone steps leading to a small cavern with several chambers leading off it, all displaying stacks of modern pottery for sale from the shop on the opposite side of the road. We didn't want or need any pottery, and rather disillusioned set off along the Gironde estuary to look for somewhere to stay the night.

There was a 'camping municipal' sign at Chenac-Saint-Seurin-d'Uzet, a delightfully unspoilt and typically French small town, one could say a one-horse town if there hadn't been a herd of about twenty horses in the marshes, galloping around like a shoal of fish, all turning and twisting in the same direction at the same time, excited by some event that we couldn't see. The *camping* had only opened for the season the previous day, and the *gardienne* was delighted to have her first customers. We shared the site with legions of large green mosquitoes, which overwhelmed poor Dobbie: his coat turned green as every inch of him had dozens of mosquitoes roosting on it. They swooped down upon us like wedding guests on the buffet, as if they'd been waiting all year for a meal to arrive. Every smack of our hands killed dozens of them and left us smeared with green and red smudges. Next to the campsite was a muddy, marshy inlet populated with sludgy-sided river boats and a decaying half-sunken catamaran. The church clock sounded the hour, twice, so that if you missed the number of rings the first time, you could listen and catch them a minute later. The mechanism of the bell was a kind of metal lollipop that created a rather feeble, tinny sound. It was because this little town was so unpretentious that we enjoyed it so much — it was France untouched by tourism.

Terry had forgotten to remove his slippers from the van that morning, and Dobbie had eaten part of one of them. Terry was rather sad and felt it was unreasonable for Dobbie to chew things that didn't belong to him when he had at least half a dozen of his own things which were specifically designed to be chewed.

By this time we'd mastered all of Tinkerbelle's gadgetry, but, distracted by the battle of the mosquitoes while I was cooking, I mis-twiddled one of the knobs on the cooker, and just avoided blowing us and the van into orbit, escaping with no more than part of my hair and my eyebrows being burned off.

After the mosquito-ridden interlude in Saint-Seurin we headed towards Blaye, under an overcast sky which offered temporary relief after the sweltering heat. Here in the peaceful and productive backwaters of the Gironde, in villages ignored by the advance of time, the countryside was at its very best: the gardens romantic jungles of roses and lilies, the sunflowers six inches high, the wheat starting its transformation from green to gold, the hallowed vines all of a uniform height and bushiness, and not a weed in sight. This was wine territory, and every few hundred metres a sign offered *dégustations* of wine and Pineau de Charentes, which we resisted because Terry was driving, I'm not a great drinker, and we both find Pineau rather too sweet.

Beside the harbour in Mortagne-sur-Gironde, priority on the road is given to the ducks: dogs must be kept on a lead, and vehicles drive at walking pace. It was Wednesday, half-day for the schoolchildren trudging homeward with heavy satchels. Standing in the road, foolishly, rather defiantly, was a hoopoe, a bird of great charm and apparently no intelligence whatsoever, which only bounced out of the way begrudgingly when Terry hooted it. In a region famed worldwide for its fish we anticipated a good lunch, and when we found a small rural restaurant I went in to enquire whether they had any fish on their menu. The man smiled and said, yes, we have roast pork, and beef, and chicken. I said we didn't eat any kind of meat, but we do eat fish, and did they have any fish today?

Ignoring my declaration, the man said encouragingly that they also had pork chops, and lamb, both of which were excellent. I gave up, and we drove on, failing to find any restaurants that served fish, or were open, or not full, or at which we were not too late. Driven by hunger and desperation we went to a large supermarket, and at 2.00 p.m. even there the restaurant was closing; the waitress was wiping the tables with a damp cloth as the leftover food disappeared back into the kitchens. We pleaded for something to eat, and after an initial refusal the manageress took pity on us and we had a meal of something that couldn't really be described as food, but for which we were grateful at the time. Afterwards we continued on to Blaye, where we explored the interesting citadel part of the town with its fortifications built by France's great military engineer, Vauban. We were destined to see many more of Vauban's works, but it was with Blaye that he said he was most satisfied. There's plenty of historic interest within the citadel — Charlemagne's nephew Roland, after his legendary death at Roncesvalles so romantically described in the great action epic *The Song of Roland*, was buried there. It was the birthplace of a twelfth-century troubadour and Prince of Blaye, Jaufré Rudel, who fell in love with a lady he'd never met, the Countess of Tripoli. On his way to the Second Crusade, he fell mortally ill and was taken to Tripoli where he met his lady-love and fittingly died in her arms. Not only was Blaye historically fascinating and aesthetically delightful, it was absolutely crammed with enticing restaurants that were all open, and all serving fresh fish.

Instead of driving down to Bordeaux to cross the Dordogne and Garonne, we took the ferry from Blaye, queuing up obediently and waiting for the whistle to invite us to board, as instructed on the notice. Beside us an old lady sat on a bench in the sunshine with her beautifully coiffed apricot poodle, watching a group of tanned men playing *boules* on a sandy patch of ground, waving their arms around and yelling, pointing and laughing.

There was a tariff for the ferry crossing: a horse cost €7, harvesting machines €58.50, and combine harvesters €84. Quite how a combine harvester would fit on the ferry isn't obvious, because it's a teeny-weeny little craft, and Terry wasn't certain he could even wrestle Tinkerbelle aboard and round the ninety-degree turn required at the bottom of the ramp. Following a horse-box he made the turn effortlessly, however, and the ferry chugged across the narrow estuary and delivered us to Lamarque on the opposite bank. It was the muddiest place we'd seen since the Essex coast many years ago when I held our daughter's hand and jumped off a jetty straight into three feet of slimy unexpected mud. She was only two foot six at the time, so it was rather a sticky moment.

Vineyards and châteaux were ten a penny here: Lamarque, Cartillon, Vauban, Haut Moulin, Clos de Relais, Lacour Jacquet, Château Beychevelle with its Viking emblem.

Every square centimetre not occupied with châteaux sprouted perfectly tended vines, each row ending with a rose, whose purpose we'd discover a little later. The town of Cussac is twinned with Mitsuse in Japan, and I think that's the first time we'd seen a French town twinned with a Japanese one. We settled for the night in Pauillac, where there were several other campers, amongst them a family with a little child that emitted an almost constant squeal like a whistling kettle. In fact twice I thought it was our kettle and had to go to check. Our immediate neighbours were a Swiss couple, retired bakers who'd sold their business and were spending their dough on touring France in their luxury camper van.

After a shower I was standing at a basin smearing on fistfuls of the exotic and extravagant face cream our friend Karen had so kindly given me. An elderly lady at the next basin pointed to the pot and said she used exactly the same cream. 'It's expensive, but at our age it's so important to take care of our skin,' she told me. She told me too that she was sixty-four, and asked my age.

I told her fifty-eight.

'Ah yes,' she replied, 'we're about the same age. And don't forget,' she reminded me, 'to pull back your fringe from your forehead sometimes during the day, otherwise you'll have a big white mark there.'

I promised to remember.

She toddled off, and her place was taken by the Swiss lady, who remarked that she and her husband were shocked and most disappointed with Pauillac.

'What a dreadfully scruffy place,' the wife said. I replied that we'd only driven round the outskirts on our way to the campsite. It didn't seem a very inviting town, but maybe, I said hopefully, the centre is more attractive.

'No,' she said, pulling a face, 'it's all horrible.'

We went off the next morning to inspect Pauillac for ourselves and agreed that the Swiss lady was absolutely spot on. It was awful, the most run-down town we'd seen since we set out. In fact, the only run-down town. The home of three *premiers crus classés*, Châteaux Latour, Mouton Rothschild and Lafite Rothschild, was dirty and unkempt and entirely unappealing. The restaurants looked insalubrious, the pizza parlours more so, and the unsavoury-looking characters hanging around in grubby alleys most unpleasant of all. On the main drag was a funfair whose tacky attractions included a giant purple octopus. The few elegant houses on the harbour front were shabby and in need

95

of a fresh coat of paint, apart from the *notaire*'s office which was spick and span. The whole place needed a great deal more than occasional pots of geraniums to endow it with any charm. The Gironde was a murky sandy colour; across the estuary skulked a nuclear power station, and just outside Pauillac a sprawling petrochemical complex. Ugh.

We drove round rather despondently searching for a restaurant that didn't look like a botulism-breeding plant, and ended up in Saint-Estèphe at a restaurant named le Peyrat, where we had a delicious meal served by an attentive waiter. Terry began with big fat oysters, while I opted for the vegetable soup, which tasted fine although it was strangely full of alphabet spaghetti. The main course salmon, the cheese and dessert were all impeccable, but the star of the show was the waiter's suggestion of a Château Canet *rosé*, an organic wine of a rich rose colour and strong raspberry flavour, which was absolutely delicious.

While we were in the Médoc, we felt we should visit at least one of the châteaux open for tours. With many to choose from, at random we booked a rendezvous at Château Pichon-Longueville, not to be confused with Château Pichon-Longueville, Comtesse de

Lalande, which is right next door and was once part of the same estate, but isn't any more. After our meal in Saint-Estèphe we drove to Château Pichon-Longueville and found it undergoing extensive building works, with bulldozers and heavy earth-moving equipment rumbling all over the grounds.

The château is an elegant building closed to the public, fronted by a large square lake embellished with water lilies and carp and flanked by two modern neo-classical style buildings, progeny of an American/French architectural collaboration to combine the old with the new. The reception area's terracotta floor tiles are expensive and squeaky, and from there you can look down through portholes in the curved white-painted walls on to stainless steel storage vats and python-like pipes running all over the place.

Our guide was a stunningly pretty and adorable girl named Aurélie, who struggled valiantly with limited English and against the noise of pneumatic drills and heavy machinery that rendered her almost inaudible. Every so often she turned to me and asked if I knew the English for a particular word. We started the tour outside amongst the vines, where Aurélie listed the grape varieties used to produce Pichon-Longueville's wines — Cabernet Sauvignon, Merlot, Cabernet Franc and Petit Verdot; she explained their chosen method of pruning (double Guyot), the pruning of the leaves and the harvesting by hand; and indicated the small brown plastic capsules attached to the ends of the rows, which contain a chemical that deters a particular pest from breeding and harming the vines. The roses planted at the ends of the rows fulfil a similar function by attracting harmful diseases that might otherwise affect the vines. The vineyard manager, Aurélie explained, favoured organic methods as far as possible.

With us was an Israeli family, mother, father, their son and his wife, who were doing a two-day tour of the Bordeaux vineyards. That morning they'd 'done' Château Lafite Rothschild and pronounced very favourably upon it. The mother was charming and would have liked to talk to us. We wanted to know about life in Israel, but her son, a heavy-set and ferocious-looking person, told her to shut up and listen to the guide. He's a wine fanatic, his mother confided, and we could tell that by the way he stared obsessively at the vines, the barrels and the bottles, and clung fervently to every word Aurélie said as if she was divulging the combination to the bullion safe of Fort Knox. Once inside the chai he posed in front of the stacks of barrels, with his chest outthrust and one foot on the bottom barrel, like a great white hunter with a kill, making his quiet, pale wife take photographs of him. Taking advantage of a brief moment when her son was out of sight, the mother told us that he was a solicitor. He overheard and barged back into the room, bellowing: 'Barrister, Mother, I'm a *barrister.*'

When the noise and language barriers overwhelmed her, Aurélie took a deep breath, blinked several times, smiled exquisitely and tried again. She explained something about corks — Pichon-Longueville's synthetic corks are hygienic, unlike Château Lafite Rothschild's traditional corks which harbour bacteria. She wrinkled her nose. By the end of our tour of the production line the racket created by hammering and drilling machinery made it impossible to hear a single word poor Aurélie was saying, although we could see her lips still moving determinedly.

The tour finished with a tasting. Terry's the wine buff in our family. I'm pretty much a wine philistine. Neither of us liked their premier wine, *grand cru* or not. The second fiddle was pleasanter, but more than we wanted to pay and we didn't really like it that much, and certainly not nearly as much as the *rosé* we'd enjoyed at lunch. Aurélie happily agreed that the wine we were tasting was not their best vintage. Our Israeli companion agreed it wasn't particularly good, but he still bought a magnum.

Driving away I reflected that without Aurélie's charm I'd have felt rather sour towards a château that offered tours that couldn't be heard, and inferior wines for tasting. Maybe, once the diggers and drills have finished their work, Château Pichon-Longueville will offer visitors some of the romance of the vine that we'd missed. Until then, I think they should postpone any more visits.

We were going to drive to the northern tip of land at the Pointe de Grave, following the N215. When we reached Soulac, for some reason we decided to pull off the road for a moment, and Terry steered Tinkerbelle on to the verge. We recognized instantly that this hadn't been a good idea as her front wheels sank down half a metre into sand. No amount of revving or reversing or using the gears in ingenious ways did anything apart from digging us deeper into the sand. We hunted around for branches and twigs and rammed them into the abyss beneath the tyres, which achieved precisely nothing, so Terry very crossly commanded me to go for help. Fifty metres from where we were trapped there was a small car park with several camper vans sitting in it, so I marched off there and decided to start with the only English-registered vehicle, next to which a gentleman was sitting peacefully reading his newspaper.

I said: 'Hello, we're stuck!'

He looked up from his paper, rather surprised at this abrupt introduction, and I continued: 'I'm really dreadfully sorry to bother you, but my husband has driven us into the sand, and we need some help.'

Up he jumped and climbed into his vehicle and drove to where Terry was trying to dig Tinkerbelle out. Our new friend, whose name was Mick, produced his tow rope and hitched the two vehicles together. At this moment a French gentleman arrived, and came to watch. As Mick climbed into his cab, the Frenchman, Thierry, took my arm and pulled me away in case the rope broke and swiped my head off.

Mick started his engine and nudged forward. Thierry and I watched the tow rope become longer and longer, and thinner and thinner, then start to fray, and finally explode. If Thierry hadn't moved me aside when he did, there was every possibility I'd have been decapitated.

Thierry said people were frequently getting stuck there in the sand, and the best way out was to jack up the vehicle, but Terry and

Mick were confident that towing it out was the solution, so Mick joined the two broken pieces of rope together and tried again, as Thierry and I watched the rope repeating its lengthening, thinning and snapping act. After the third attempt the remaining pieces of rope were no longer long enough to be joined together, but another French gentleman stopped. This was M. Miran, who had a heavier tow rope than Mick's, and it only broke twice. The road was covered in pieces of rope that looked like little fat plaited snakes.

M. Miran and Thierry were greatly amused by our predicament, and were not going to leave until by one means or another we were out of the sand. Mick's wife Hilary joined us, and passing motorists parked on the side of the road to enjoy the pantomime.

Finally, with Mick towing, using the remaining lengths of rope all tied together, and Thierry and M. Miran heaving, the sand let go and we were back on terra firma.

Thanking everybody vigorously, we drove on to Montalivet, a pretty seaside town with a 1950s air about it, with a splendid beach and lots of restaurants, bars, nightclubs and gift shops, but most of them were closed, because the holiday season hadn't really started. There was hardly anybody around. Terry said, wherever you look, there's nobody. Nearby there was a nudist camp, but after all that Breton food I was more into elastic waistbands and big prints than nudity. Gusty wind at Montalivet whipped sand all over us, so we drove further south until we arrived at a marvellous place called le Pin Sec, a surfers' paradise of crashing Atlantic rollers hitting a vast sandy beach hidden behind steep dunes. There was a simple rustic restaurant adorned with African and South American hangings and masks, and a large photo of Che Guevara. Le Café du Soleil had an appetizing menu of tapas and snacks, all freshly cooked, so we decided to eat there, and while we waited for our meal we talked to the proprietor Sergio, who is Spanish with dreadlocks, a deep tan and soft voice. He was playing haunting South American music on his sound system, and told us how he and his girlfriend had taken the restaurant for the season, but they didn't know if it would be successful because for some reason all the trees on the campsite had been chopped down so it would be very hot in the summer, without any shade for campers. During the winter they liked to travel, usually to Africa, but last winter they'd been to Mexico for a change. At le Café du Soleil they wanted to offer something a little different from traditional French fare.

His Old English sheepdog, a birthday present from his parents ten years ago, sprawled out in the shade of an umbrella on the terrace. Marie, Sergio's green-eyed girlfriend, served home-made potato tortillas, with a fresh green salad, and it was very pleasant indeed sitting there with the peaceful background music and a glass of wine. We asked Sergio and Marie whether they thought we could stay there for the night in Tinkerbelle, and they said that although the campsite was officially closed several people were staying there and we'd be quite safe.

Terry had done all the driving so far, saying Tinkerbelle was too awkward for me, but I wanted to have a go so I drove around the car park, and then headed over to the campsite to find a place under one of the very few remaining trees. I drove into what I thought was a perfectly good place, but Terry directed me forward twenty metres. I obediently moved to where he pointed, and Tinkerbelle sank gently down until she was up to the tops of her wheels in the sand. I put her into reverse and tried to back out, but all that happened was that sand showered everywhere and Tinkerbelle sank deeper.

Like white rabbits from a magician's top hat, four Germans materialized, laughing, and pushed us out, then disappeared back to their own patches, leaving us to discover that during the afternoon Dobbie had entirely destroyed the expensive little sleeping mattress we had bought for him. A yellow plastic object of unidentifiable origin and purpose lay chewed on the floor. He was obviously in need of distraction, so we hauled ourselves up and over the dunes to the beach where the dogs ran themselves into a pleasantly exhausted state. It was a perfect location for them because they could be left to wander at will without any danger from traffic or of getting lost.

After a peaceful night at le Pin Sec we awoke to the familiar sound of spinning wheels. Two of our German rescuers from the previous day were thoroughly bogged in the sand.

'We only went to buy a *baguette*,' laughed Silke, 'and we've been camping here for five days without getting stuck.'

Their vehicle was twice the size of Tinkerbelle, and really heavy. We all tramped about collecting logs and stones to put under the tyres. Jochen tried to drive out, but only managed to bury our offerings beneath the wheels. We tried using doormats, which the sand swallowed. Terry brought Tinkerbelle's wooden chocks and he and Jochen built a ramp for the van to drive up. Gradually more people arrived to help, until there was a jolly assembly of ten or so all heaving and digging and offering suggestions. Somebody else arrived with a powerful vehicle, and with everyone pushing, and the tug-van pulling, Silke and Jochen's camper finally escaped from its sandy prison. Dobbie hadn't been idle during this two-hour interval, and had mangled a kilo of tomatoes, leaving each one perforated with teeth marks and coated with sand; he had, furthermore, knocked over half a cup of tea on to our atlas so that all 250 pages were stuck together in a thick soggy lump. He'd also drowned the mobile phone with the tea, and ripped to shreds the remains of his mattress. Once we'd dealt with this devastation, we drove off with a wave to our German friends, quite forgetting Tinkerbelle's chocks, which are probably buried for all time beneath the sands of le Pin Sec.

The length of this part of the Landes coast is pine forest planted during the nineteenth century to stabilize the marshy land and keep the advancing dunes at bay: kilometre upon unending kilometre of pine trees growing obediently in straight lines and bisected by long, dead-straight flat roads. Tinkerbelle coasted along easily in the pancake-flat terrain, through Biganos, past a green-grocery whose display of vegetables was like a glorious shiny embroidery of vibrant reds, yellows, greens, oranges and purples, each vegetable glowing with *joie de vivre*, and into Arcachon's wonderful *ville d'hiver*, where the architecture changed abruptly from the white-painted, blue-shuttered houses of the Atlantic coast into wildly extravagant, over-the-top *belle epoque* villas in the form of palaces, temples and pagodas, with ornate twisty columns, curlicued wrought-iron balconies and intricately carved wooden fascias, sitting in sumptuous landscaped gardens. The *ville d'hiver* was conceived by two wealthy Jewish industrialists in the late nineteenth century, to provide accommodation for the wealthy from all over the world who came to benefit from the Arcachon basin's mild winter climate. There's still very much a 1920s feel to the town, and you expect to see bustle-bottomed, parasol-wielding ladies and gaitered, top-hatted men strolling around the elegant streets and through the exotic Mauresque public gardens.

We'd been expecting to reach the fabled Dune du Pilat sooner or later, but were really not ready for it. The signs were to Pyla, which I didn't connect with Pilat. The different spelling, we later learned, was because Pilat, in which the final t is pronounced, means in French a heap of sand, and the local estate agents didn't feel it was conducive to attracting house buyers, so the spelling was changed to Pyla. Maybe the estate agents hoped the alteration would prevent potential buyers from noticing the gigantic monster sitting there. In any event, our first sight of this sandy leviathan was breathtaking. It's an amazing work of nature, a sinister creature that's stealthily growing and eating its way across country from its lair on the Atlantic shore. It's the biggest sand dune in Europe, nearly 3 kilometres long, 600 metres wide, somewhere around 120 metres high and composed of 60 million cubic metres of sand.

Fed by the wind off the Arguin sandbank, it's calculated to be edging eastwards by some five metres each year, munching up anything standing in its unstoppable path. Somewhere in its belly are trees, tarmac roads, campsites and an entire hotel. It's a worrying thought that something composed of nothing more than grains little bigger than ground pepper can be so invincible and beyond the control of any means known to man. We started trying to climb the thing, but our feet sank into the sand and we slipped backwards faster than we could move forwards and were exhausted after a few minutes, so saying a respectful farewell to this titanic sandcastle we drove on to a beach a little way south, where the dogs could disperse some of their infinite energy. Although there were plenty of people on the beach it wasn't at all crowded, because it's so huge. There were still faint traces of oil from the spill on the Galician coast that had cost Rosa her job, but they were no more than dark shadows in small patches of sand. Three men were playing football, a game of which Tally appeared instinctively to know the rules. He joined in enthusiastically, to the delight of his new friends who passed him the ball backwards and forwards and cheered him as he leapt and pounced on it. Dobbie didn't understand at all, and annoyed Tally so much by interfering that Tally gave him a public warning, and he retired to sit and watch from a distance, his black brow wrinkled in puzzlement.

The weather had been uncomfortably hot and sticky, but by the time we reached Gastes the skies were gloomily grey, and a sharp energetic wind lashed the Biscarrosse lagoon into choppy waves that rocked the small motor boats. We found a municipal camping area beside the lagoon, and decided to stay the night. During our travels that day the door of the wardrobe had come open, and I found all my clothes scattered around the van, one pair of knickers chewed beyond repair. The campsite was very basic, with just loos and no hot water, so I boiled up a few kettles and washed our clothes and the dogs' spare blankets in a bucket, and hung everything to dry under Tinkerbelle's spacious wind-out awning.

* * *

I hadn't slept at all well since we began our journey. The space in the camper van was too restrictive after our very large bedroom at home, and even with the two roof ventilators open there wasn't enough air circulating. The privacy provided by Tinkerbelle's pretty pastel-blue curtains meant I couldn't see the sky, something I'm used to at home. A green light from the refrigerator to indicate it was plugged into a mains electricity supply, and a glowing red halo from the electric mosquito repellent, were like a set of traffic lights in my face. I was either too hot or too cold, and threshed around until I ended sprawled out like a disorientated starfish, with no idea where I was. I woke almost every night in sweaty panic, yelling to be let out of wherever I thought I was. Poor Terry was very tolerant, always managing to get the light on quickly, and never complaining at being woken by a screaming wife.

The day's heat dispersed during the night in a monumental storm complete with cracking thunder and sheet lightning, and next morning the awning had collapsed under the weight of rain water that had collected on it, its aluminium legs crumpled like a dead spider's. What had been our patio the previous evening had become a paddling pool for a cocky little wagtail. The tents around us were almost afloat, the canvas sagging down to a few inches above ground level. I vividly remembered the misery of such conditions from my hiking trip across France in 1998.

The clothes and dogs' blankets I'd washed the evening before were a soggy, muddy mass trailing in the grass, and we had to shovel them into bin liners and cart them off to our next destination, as we set off into the grey wetness all around. On the way out of Gastes we passed a newly built bungalow, a pretty building with garden furniture outside, sitting disconsolately in an ocean of thick mud. It was raining hard when we reached Mimizan, where the road was lined with exquisite pink and white dog roses growing from the sandy soil. There was a triathlon taking place through the town, with several marshals waving wooden paddles to direct the traffic.

The marshal who elected to hold us up was a tall, thin man with a damp moustache, wearing an ankle-length transparent plastic raincoat over his T-shirt and shorts, and we'd seldom seen anybody looking quite so miserable and embarrassed. He snapped his paddle irritably, signalling us to the side of the road, next to a bundle of spectators gently steaming inside their anoraks and waterproof clothing in the hot, wet air.

Once past Mimizan the landscape reverted to pine trees, an infinity of them in varying stages of growth, from little babies to great-grandfathers, whose foliage was all at the top so that they looked like big prickly lollipops, creating a huge canopy with millions of legs. Houses now were of brickwork and timber with a medieval appearance, beside roads lined with marguerites and bracken, and signs offering *foie gras* for sale. In Saint-Girons voluptuous groups of arum lilies clustered on the banks of the river, like a huddle of naked courtesans preparing for a swim.

As the road became more undulating we broke out of the pine forests, into deciduous trees glistening green and shiny in the rain. Beyond the sand dunes at Hossegor the sea hurled massive breakers on to the beach, and skimmed surfers through the wild waters; on

112

the sand people struggled with kites whipping in crazy spirals through sullen skies. Hossegor — Horseguards when the good old Duke of Wellington was prancing about in the area — is one of France's finest surfing beaches, where the Rip Curl Pro Competition is held every August. The waves along this stretch of coastline are the most powerful on the Atlantic seaboard, and I found the water particularly sinister and menacing that day, as it swished around hungrily as if looking for its next meal. Hossegor is heavy on barrack-like holiday apartments, and wherever you look every crack and crevice is covered in sand. It creeps over the pavements and into the roads, through gardens, along paths and up stairs. There's no doubt about it, sand is an invincible material.

Spanish restaurants and signs for paella and sangria indicated we were moving into Basque country. Leaving behind sandy, windy Hossegor we pushed inland to Saubusse to visit the ponies on the Barthes, marshy lands planted with oak trees and flooded regularly by the river Adour when it fills with melt waters from the Pyrénées. About fifty of the stocky semi-wild ponies, from which the modern Landais breed is descended, were going about their equine affairs. They looked well cared for and quite relaxed as we walked between them. A young foal with naïve eyes came to investigate us, shadowed by a small stallion who seemed to have appointed himself as the youngster's guardian. Two lads of about twelve arrived with bicycles which they loaded into a small wooden boat on a narrow waterway running through the fields. They climbed into the boat and started to propel themselves along the water, one punting with a stick and the other steering with a paddle, until they reached a low stone bridge, and we watched in admiration as they struggled and eventually succeeded in negotiating the boat underneath it, which they did by taking turns to curl up like dormice on the bottom of the boat, bending their bikes into strange configurations. From a few feet away a herd of ponies led by a grey stallion watched warily, ears pricked and tails high, necks stretched and nostrils flared, ready to flee. The stallion kept the herd a few feet behind him until satisfied that the boys, their bicycles and the boat were no threat, when he wheeled round and led his herd away. We could have been watching a scene straight out of *Huckleberry Finn*.

At the 500-hectare nature reserve at Orx we saw herons, egrets, crested grebes and ducks, and in the weedy water coypus swimming around like giant waterborne guinea pigs. We arrived early enough to spend a few hours relaxing in the sunshine at the campsite at Labenne-Océan while our laundry dried on a rope stretched between two convenient trees. The showers were good, too, with unlimited hot water. While I spent a blissful ten minutes under a cascade of steaming water, I could hear slithers, whispers and giggles from the adjacent cubicle. It sounded as though two people were in there together making some sort of carnal merriment. As I emerged the neighbouring door opened and out came a wet, red-faced young man, followed by a wet, chubby young girl. Neither of them carried towels or soap.

We went to have a look around Labenne, stopping to admire a house that was entirely painted dark lilac, and trying to visit la Pinède des Singes, which closed in our faces for lunch. There was a sign to a breakers' yard where we hoped to locate the elusive exhaust system for Tinkerbelle to silence her frightful roaring. It was two weeks since the original had so inconveniently fallen off, and every place where we might have been able to find the necessary spare part had been closed when we were there. Labenne was no exception, because it was yet another public holiday in France (the fourth that month), the yard was closed and we were condemned to keep attracting embarrassing attention.

From Ondres we had our first sight of the Pyrénées looming ahead, causing a *petit frisson* of excitement that quite soon we'd be exploring this hitherto unknown (to us) region.

We were beginning to feel hungry when we saw a roadside restaurant called the Roi de Gueux, where a measly €6.50 bought a very large grilled hake steak drowning in garlic and parsley, with potatoes and salad, and as far as I can remember it was the best-value meal we had on our journey, and the tastiest fish. Our waiter exuded toothy charm, and except for a red Basque beret was becomingly dressed entirely in black to show off his ballet dancer figure. He spoke English, learned when he used to travel to Dover and Folkestone from his birthplace in Boulogne, and assured us that we were going to simply *adore* the Basque region.

Oozing garlic from every pore and follicle, we strolled down to watch the surfers at Anglet, young men with long hair and earrings, faultless bodies and seamless tans, carrying their surfboards in cases, dressing and undressing uninhibitedly in the car park. Dogs were unwelcome on the beach, said a sign, the first we'd seen: a red circle round

116

a dog. This was a great blow to Tally and Dobbie, who'd enjoyed several hundred kilometres of unrestricted access to the beaches so far, and didn't highly rate walking on leads. A short distance from the beach, unromantically surrounded by topless clubs, tattoo and body-piercing parlours and fast-food outlets, is the Chambre d'Amour, a cave where according to legend a young orphan boy and the daughter of a wealthy disapproving father met secretly to pledge their love. One day a whopping great freak wave flooded into the love room and swept them both away, a valuable lesson regarding the importance of obedience to one's parents. When we visited the cave the only sign of life was a group of three pigeons nesting over the entrance.

Glitzy Biarritz is a confection of turrets and castellations, majestic, wildly ornate buildings, glorious gardens, and the superb hotel Palais, which was once the summer palace of the Empress Eugénie. Forget that the town started life as a nasty whaling port. When Napoléon III and Eugénie (more about them later) arrived and fell in love with it in the middle of the nineteenth century, Biarritz became the chosen summer playground of the royal, the aristocratic, the super-rich and super-famous from around the globe, who left behind a legacy of elegance and grandeur. It is still a place of architectural extravagance, but in the best possible taste, and at the same time there is a pleasantly egalitarian and relaxed feel to the town where blue-rinses and blazers sit side by side at the cafés with T-shirts and back-to-front baseball caps. Personally, I think that compulsory dress in Biarritz should be rustling taffeta gowns with bustled backsides, frivolous bonnets, top hats and tails, monocles and waxed moustaches. There was nothing genteel about the sea, though. It was wild and furious, smashing angrily around in the bay, swirling into a brown scummy foam, and looking thoroughly bad-tempered, as if it hated Biarritz. We sat for half an hour watching it hurling itself yobbishly on to the rocks, then crawled our way through traffic-jammy roads into Saint-Jean-de-Luz, and on to Hendaye, the last French town on the Atlantic coast before the Spanish frontier, where the ocean was calmer, the beach wide and golden, and the waves perfect for surfers.

Against the backdrop of the Pyrénées, Hendaye is a most appealing town. Its name comes from two Basque words — 'handi' meaning 'big' and 'baya' meaning 'bay'. It's two towns, really — the medieval Basque quarter and the more modern district comprising the beach and marina. Stuck as it is right on the Spanish border it's had a predictably turbulent history of war with that country. It was in Hendaye that General Franco gave Hitler his undertaking to keep Spain out of the Second World War. A little way down the road, in the river Bidassoa, is Pheasant Island, jointly owned by France and Spain; traditionally a place for exchanging hostages and prisoners, it witnessed the signing by the two countries of the Treaty of the Pyrénées in 1659, and the marriage contract between the Infanta Maria Theresa and Louis XIV — Louis the Godgiven, also known as the Sun King, who would so radiantly rule France for seventy-two years.

Pierre Loti came to Hendaye to die, so that his death wouldn't tarnish his wondrous house in Rochefort, and happily, from what we saw, it did nothing to spoil Hendaye either.

Everything was beginning to feel foreign and no longer French. Notices and sign-boards were in three languages — French, Spanish of which we understand very little, and Basque of which neither of us know a single word. Basque is not at all a helpful language; it's impossible to pick out even an odd word here and there to make some sense of it. There are no hints or clues as to its meaning. Unless the signs were also written in French, they might as well have been in Japanese or hieroglyphics for all the use they were to us. It's said that after seven years of trying to learn the Basque language, the Devil had only mastered two words: 'Yes, ma'am.'

We watched with interest as a female driver negotiated her car into a parking space, mangling an adjacent car quite seriously without appearing to care, then we parked Tinkerbelle by the port, and sat sipping sangria, reading in the sunshine for a few hours before nightfall, and then watching the lights come on across the bay and in the hills around us.

3

THE PYRENEES — CHILLI-FLAVOURED CHOCOLATE AND ADDERS IN HELICOPTERS

The next morning, in the same soft slow rain as had fallen all night, we set off to turn left at the bottom of France and into the mountains of the Pyrénées, via a pretty roundabout on the way out of Hendaye, where a giant terracotta pitcher lying on its side spilled out petunias and marigolds, like a stream of jewelled water.

Ten minutes later we were lost on winding roads in wooded mountains, in a heavy mist which parted momentarily to uncover valleys and vistas of rich greenness. Good fortune guided us into the village of Biriatou, which sits on a hill surrounded by similar hills and fields of hay bales, where nearly everywhere was closed, except for the one-Michelin-starred hotel Bakea. During our journey I had drunk many, and would drink many more, cups of hot chocolate, but I can categorically assure you that one would not, could not, find anywhere a more dazzlingly superior example of the beverage than in the hotel Bakea. Nothing about the drink had anything to do with a packet or powder. Just sufficiently sweet, the texture was thick and velvety, as if naked chocolate had been unhurriedly melted into fresh cream. It was a deep mahogany colour and had an indescribably seductive aroma. If the Michelin men were to return to the hotel and try the chocolate, I'm certain they'd award it at least one more star. On the wall of the restaurant there was a framed photograph of a *bouquet garni* of chefs surrounding Queen Elizabeth II. I asked one of the staff what it represented, and she fetched Madame, who told us that her husband Eric had been a chef at the Connaught for some years, and the photograph was taken when that hotel had celebrated its centenary in the presence of Her Majesty.

I could have happily taken root at the Bakea, but Terry felt we ought to continue, so off we roared, still exhaustless, past clusters of evening primroses and balconies crammed with geraniums, a tumbling crystal river and a long stream of trucks waiting to cross the border into Spain. The twisting narrow roads were wetly green; tatters of mist snagged the tops of the hills, and we passed occasional dank hikers and fields of donkeys and cattle whose coats were dark with moisture. This was Basque country, land of the mysterious people whose origins are unknown; who speak a language whose roots are equally unclear; and whose blood group frequencies differ from those found anywhere else in the world.

Ignoring the rain, workmen in the lovely village of Ascain were planting the flower beds around an old *lavoir* and fountain; the *logis* was smothered in wisteria, the banana palms were heavy with fruit, and an elderly lady was walking across the road towards the *boulangerie* in a startling cerise-coloured woolly dressing gown. The village has a disproportionately huge church dating back to the thirteenth century, and a fine pelota court, and Pierre Loti had stayed at the hotel de la Rhune while he was writing one of his novels, *Ramuntcho*. There's a more sinister aspect to Ascain, however. During the seventeenth century a number of unfortunate people, including the village priest, were charged with sorcery and burned in the village square.

We were so taken with Ascain that we decided to lunch there at the St Jacques, a typical Basque restaurant with a rose-pink wooden ceiling and smoky-blue painted beams, and heavy strings of wrinkled, shiny dried peppers hanging on the walls. A self-service buffet, followed by the main course and cheese board, was rounded off by a dessert buffet offering two dozen choices each as enticing as the rest. If I kept on eating like this I'd be in danger of exploding like the man in Monty Python.

Totally replete, we drove along a road with more twists and turns than a plate of spaghetti to the Col de St Ignace, to take a ride on the little cog train up to la Rhune, the mountain straddling France and Spain. At the ticket counter a notice advised that the top of the mountain was shrouded in fog and that the visibility was '*nulle*', but as the sun was shining and it hadn't rained since we finished lunch we disregarded this information, and waited as the train tiptoed down the track and stopped politely alongside the platform. Between the rails that support the wheels is a third rail, notched, operating on a rack-and-pinion mechanism to help the train haul itself up la Rhune's 900 metres. Except for the brass door handles the carriages, renovated to their original 1924 design, are made entirely of wood: local pine and chestnut, and African iroko. The slatted seats, highly polished and supported by turned wooden legs, reminded me of trams and the time the buckle on my new school raincoat slipped between the slats and could never be retrieved, after which I was the only girl in school without a raincoat belt.

The train has no windows, just spaces, with sturdy canvas curtains to draw over them if necessary. Our driver was a plump, lugubrious gentleman wearing a black Basque beret with a little stalk on top. Once the two dozen passengers had climbed aboard and the doors were closed, he sounded a whistle and we lurched off at the dignified pace of eight kilometres an hour, feeling as if we could at any moment stall and start to slither backwards. The countryside was heavenly, young oak trees and bracken splashed with purple digitalis and flat, lichened rocks with blue alpine flowers growing upon them. A flock of red-faced Manech sheep grazed beside the tracks until the train was only five metres short of them, when they decided they simply must cross to the other side, and the tail-end Charlie was within a millimetre of being bowled over.

We climbed the mountain in stately fashion, up the side of a steep ravine, looking out over remote villages and green mountains, and into thick cloud. The driver switched on the headlights. Vaguely through the clouds we saw white cattle grazing like wraiths, and then had our first sight of the scraggy little pottoks, the wild ponies living on the mountains. Generally grey at birth, the foals change colour as they mature, darkening to black or brown so they're camouflaged for protection from their traditional enemies, wolves and bears. Their dark colouring also helps to store solar energy to protect them from the cold, damp mountain air. They are necessarily hardy little creatures, adapted to survive their harsh environment. The foals were traditionally rounded up and sent to the butcher, but ten years ago a conservation programme was established in Bidarray to protect and preserve the breed.

The nearer we came to the top of la Rhune, the colder and cloudier it became, and by the time we disembarked it was raining and there was a bitter wind. We climbed up the steps to the cloud-shrouded summit, from where we could see absolutely nothing at all, and were within a few minutes blue with cold, so we climbed back down and sat in the little train, reflecting that we should have heeded the notice at the ticket office. The carriages soon refilled with our fellow passengers, the women with damp flat hair, dragging small, grizzling, anoraked children by their arms, and men with their hands jammed into their armpits. The children didn't seem to be enjoying themselves: 'Boring, boring, boring,' chanted a fat boy.

Clouds floated in at will through the glassless windows, but through gaps we caught glimpses of spectacular scenery, and herds of pottoks, the mares with bells round their necks, with their foals at foot and the next crop of babies well on its way. I thought what a pleasant way of spending the day it must be, driving the train up and down this wild place watching the changing seasons hour by hour, but Terry said he couldn't think of anything more boring. Funny how people see things differently.

It's hard work for the little engine dragging up the steep four-kilometre ascent, but each winter she goes away into a cosy shelter for a well-deserved rest and refit. Her woodwork is revarnished, her handles polished, her curtains cleaned, and her mechanisms stringently checked for safety, and then she waits for spring, and a new season.

We found a campsite for the night at the unfortunately named Saint-Pée, where we had the place to ourselves, and where the rain dripped from the trees and plipped on to Tinkerbelle's roof all night. Next morning started damply, but by the time we set off the rain had stopped and the cloud had lifted to reveal much more of the landscape, and the large Basque houses with their ox-blood painted timbers. Several notable historical events have taken place in Saint-Pée. The *chistéra*, the wicker-work glove used to play pelota, was invented there in 1856. Pelota being the *raison d'être* of the Basque population, this is probably regarded as Saint-Pée's greatest achievement. The Duke of Wellington had a military base there, and it was in Saint-Pée that Napoléon's elder brother Joseph learned he was no longer King of Spain. The town had the misfortune to be one of those at the centre of the great witch-hunt in the Basque region at the beginning of the seventeenth century, and the château was the scene of the torture and trials of men, women and children accused of witchcraft by judge Pierre de Lancre, an unpleasant individual who sent a great number of people to the stake.

The countryside was made up of curvy hills and buttercup meadows filled with grazing horses and blond Aquitaine cattle. Something had struck me as odd the previous day, and I realized what it was: in this green, mountainous region, amongst forests of coniferous and deciduous trees, were lofty palms and banana plants that looked incongruous. I wondered how they had arrived. Did the Moors bring them? Maybe not. I don't think banana plants were introduced into Europe as early as that. Anyway, however they had travelled, they seemed to be very comfortable there.

Known as one of the most beautiful of the Basque villages, virtually every house in quaint Aïnhoa has its doors, shutters and timbers painted deep red, except for one green radical. During the Second World War Aïnhoa was a major crossing point for people escaping from the Nazis, and villagers risked their lives to shelter and help them flee over the border to Spain or beyond with the help of local mountain guides.

Espelette's red peppers are famous, and strings of dried *piments* hung from almost every building. There were shops selling nothing but red peppers in various forms — fresh, dried, pickled like Peter Piper's peck, and powdered. What we couldn't find in Espelette that day was a decent lunch. At the first restaurant we waited politely, patiently and quite in vain for the lady in charge to stop shuffling little pieces of paper around in a drawer at the bar, and take notice of us. After several minutes of being ignored I interrupted her and asked if there was a table free. She glanced up momentarily and just long enough from her paper pieces to say ungraciously: 'No, we're full.'

Across the road the next restaurant was half full of diners on their first course, but the manageress told us with a rather pleased smile that we were too late (maybe because of the unreasonable time we'd lost in the first restaurant). Rather disillusioned with Espelette's hospitality we ended up sitting at a table on the pavement, munching a toasted cheese *panini* which was very good as toasted cheese sandwiches go, but we'd been hoping for a meal that would match the excellent one we'd had the day before in Ascain. As we were on our way out of Espelette without much regret, we passed the Antton Chocolaterie, outside which a coach was disgorging a group of elderly people into the shop, so we followed them and were invited to join a guided tour. Unfortunately it was in French, and for many weeks Terry would remind me bitterly of the hour he spent not understanding a single word; on the other hand I was completely enraptured by what I was able to understand of the romance, history and cultivation of the chocolate tree.

Our guide Virginie was passionately enthusiastic about her subject, and told us how the Spanish, led by Cortés in his excursions into Mexico, were the first Europeans to taste chocolate, when the Aztec king offered them the cup of friendship. Cortés and his merry men repaid this kindly gesture by slaughtering their hosts wholesale.

The Spanish took cocoa trees (whose Latin name means 'food of the gods') back to Spain, but they wouldn't grow there, because the trees can develop only in humid equatorial regions where the temperature doesn't fall below 25°C. They're tender creatures, cocoa trees, and need to grow beneath a protector tree, or 'cocoa mother', to shelter them from the sun.

The large cucumber-shaped pods grow directly from the trunks of the trees, and when they turn brown they're harvested by hand to avoid damage to their delicate producer. From the hard outer casing the precious cocoa beans and surrounding mucilage are scraped out and fermented and then dried, before being packed and shipped to destinations around the world for transformation into temptation. South American chocolate is used with delicate fillings, because it's sweeter than chocolate from Africa which marries better with stronger flavours.

It was the chocolate-trading Jews, fleeing the Spanish Inquisition, who crossed the Pyrénées and established themselves in

Bayonne, which became the chocolate trading centre of Europe.

Virginie had a captivated audience.

'Who eats white chocolate?' she asked.

Several hands shot up.

'Do you know how it's made?'

Several heads shook.

'Well, during the processing of the beans, the contents are separated into two products: cocoa powder, and cocoa butter. The cocoa butter is all the grease from the bean. White chocolate is simply cocoa butter mixed with milk products, and isn't chocolate at all. It's very bad for you!'

The hand-shooting head-shakers gasped and moaned in dismay.

Considerably wiser about chocolate than we had been before (except for poor Terry), we followed Virginie down a mouth-wateringly fragrant corridor to a small laboratory where new flavours are developed and tested, and watched as shreds of crystallized oranges were smothered in thick black chocolate. A girl dressed all in white, like a nurse in an operating theatre, produced a tray of their most exotic chocolates — *ganache de piment d'espelette* — hot chilli pepper ganache. Some of the spectators were sceptical about this unusual idea, but most were eager to experience a new taste. What we mustn't do, emphasized Virginie, was bite into the chocolate. No, no. Instead, place the chocolate in the mouth, and *wait*! Let it melt slowly, and we'd enjoy successive waves of changing flavours and textures. She was quite right. Beneath alternating layers of sweetness and bitterness, the chilli filling is subtle, just sufficiently fiery without being overpowering, and an exquisite gastronomic experience. We bought a box of these exciting delicacies, and then continued on our travels through Cambo-les-Bains, an elegant spa town of large graceful buildings and palm trees, and once home to the creator of big-nosed Cyrano de Bergerac, Edmond Rostand, and from there to Itxassou where we followed a sign for Ardi Gasna, which means, in Basque, ewe's-milk cheese and is traditionally eaten with cherry jam. Although we had heard of it, we hadn't ever managed to find this cheese, and were excited at the prospect of finally tracking it down.

Tinkerbelle bounced and shuddered down a stony track until we arrived at the farm of Nicolas and Mirestxu. On the counter of a cool room was a sign which read Ardi Gasna, and I said that we would like to buy one kilogram. Nicolas smiled, nodded, disappeared and returned with a very large wheel of cheese, laid it lovingly on the counter and said: 'Ossau Iraty.' This Pyrenean-ewe's-milk cheese is my personal favourite, but it was Ardi Gasna that we had come for. Each time I said Ardi Gasna, Nicolas smilingly shook his head and tapped the Ossau Iraty, and so we bought a kilogram of that instead. Nicolas, who told us that his group of 200 Manech sheep is one of the smaller flocks, has dark skin and hair, and sharp bright-blue eyes. While he cut and wrapped the cheese, he talked about the bears in the mountains. There were only about four left, he said, and it was virtually impossible to see them as they're very shy and highly intelligent. He told of moonlit nights spent on the heights with his flocks, and how the bears waited for cloud to slip across the moonlight, and then attacked; and how they would circle patiently until they could slide up and strike from behind. Despite the threat they represent to the sheep, Nicolas didn't harbour any malice towards them, but rather an admiration and deep regret that those still left in the mountains will die out quite soon — like us shepherds, he added sadly.

He was scornful of attempts that had been made to introduce bears from Eastern Europe into the area: millions of francs were spent on the project, he said, and it had been a catastrophe. Although they were meant to be similar to Pyrenean bears, the imported bears didn't stay where they were put but wandered all over the place, attacking herds. A total waste of time and effort, said Nicolas.

We'd have liked to buy some cherries, Itxassou's other speciality, from Nicolas, but the crop had been poor, spoiled by a wet and windy spring. They'd only managed to harvest a handful so far, so that was two things we didn't manage to buy from Nicolas.

I asked whether and where we could watch a pelota game, and Nicolas looked surprised that anybody could be so ignorant as not to know that pelota is played only in the summer, and it was still too early in the year. So off we drove with a wave and our kilo of cheese. Shortly afterwards we saw a sign leading to the Pas de Roland, and followed a ridiculously narrow windy lane which led past pretty white farmhouses and meadows with palm trees and bamboo, and a swishy white-water river dashing along in the valley below. The lane wasn't much more than a mule track; the low stone wall might have stopped vehicles toppling down the side into the river, but probably not. It wasn't very substantial. The side of the road not next to the river was lined with boulders that didn't look particularly firmly attached to the mother rock. What would happen if a vehicle came the other way there was no telling, because there simply wasn't room for two vehicles to pass without one of them either bumping into the rocks or tumbling into the river. Without incident we reached a rocky formation where a plaque tells that Charlemagne's army, led by his nephew Roland, found their passage blocked during their retreat across the Pyrénées. Using his fabled sword Durandal, Roland walloped the rock and opened a breach which allowed his soldiers to pass. From there he'd go on to be betrayed by Ganelon, and to die at Roncesvalles just over the Spanish border, because he was too proud to blow his horn Oliphant in time to summon help. Roland may have had some satisfaction if he'd known how treacherous Ganelon would pay for this beastly act. It didn't do to mess with Charlemagne's kin, as we'd discover when we reached the Ardennes and learned what happened to the four Aymon brothers.

It's such a scenic area, pink Canterbury bells growing through cushions of moss, legions of digitalis, and every so often a beautiful house like one we saw with a large garden of rhododendrons and Japanese maples set off with clumps of lilies, and another roofed with slabs of granite with a garden full of statues. Along the road, making their way in a leisurely manner and stopping every so often to help themselves to wild flowers from the roadsides, came a herd of soft-eyed cattle, guided by a very little boy with cropped hair and a twig. As we climbed to 375 metres we could see the vistas denied us by the clouds the day before, and the countryside was simply gorgeous. On one hand the mountains, and on the other the sea, and in the fields between herds of grazing cattle and sheep, and occasionally horses. The detour led us back via a series of curvaceous hills to the rose- and honeysuckle-covered village of Itxassou where we'd bought the cheese from Nicolas a couple of hours earlier.

When we reached a small utterly peaceful farming hamlet called Saint-Martin, or Lantabat (it seemed to have two names), an apple-cheeked old boy driving a van and herding a flock of sheep at the same time asked if he could help. When we told him we were looking for somewhere to stay for the night, he indicated a *fronton*, the court where pelota is played, bordering the cemetery at the back of the local church. There, he assured us, we would be '*très tranquille*' and nobody would disturb us. We parked in one corner, and took the dogs for a walk, watching as a steady trickle of villagers casually drove past to have a look at the strange English people. A mournful Basset-hound waddled up and stared at Dobbie and Tally, then turned in disgust at their rude barking and plodded off. Our nearest neighbour was an old lady in a cottage opposite the church, who looked at us rather suspiciously and didn't return my wave.

We discovered what the yellow plastic thing was that we'd found on the floor of the van when we were in le Pin Sec: it had been the security pin for the fire extinguisher. Having removed and half eaten it, Dobbie had empowered himself to activate the extinguisher. There was white powder all over the place.

Night came down, silhouetting the mountains against the darkening blue of the sky; lights from scattered houses sparkled from the hillsides; and the floodlit front of the church with its white-painted flat planes and bell tower looked like a scene from a Western. The bells of the church tolled the hour, and the half-hour, and for the first couple of hours, when they did so Dobbie threw back his head theatrically and howled like a wolf.

Through the night the church bells rang half-hourly; owls hooted, crickets chirruped and sheep bells tinkled a delicate, ethereal symphony. We felt very far from the beaten track.

Next morning we were up early, wanting to be dressed before the population stirred. You feel rather exposed sleeping in a tin box in the main square of a village. There was a lady watering flowers in the cemetery, and I went across to talk to her and to say how grateful we were for being allowed to stay in such a beautiful place. Yes, she agreed, there's probably nowhere else in the world more lovely than Saint-Martin, where she was born and will die. But the problem was that there was no work there, so people must travel to faraway towns, which meant that a driving licence and car were essential, and not a luxury.

I mentioned the church bells, and she said they were rung electrically, and that she never noticed them because they'd been there since she was born.

'But,' she laughed, 'if ever something goes wrong and they don't ring the hour, then I notice their absence.'

She was surprised when I said that they struck on the half-hour as well as the hour.

'I never realized that!'

She pointed to some headstones.

'Those are Basque steles,' she said. 'There are no bodies beneath them. They've been found over the years and brought here. But if you go over there a little way,' she pointed to the west, 'you can see the Basque cemetery, where there are bodies beneath the stones.'

While I was talking to her, Tally and Dobbie had escaped and were running about the square. Terry and I chased after them to round them up, and the old lady came out of her door and shouted at me: '*Où allez avec les chiens?*' I wondered if French was her second language, as it wasn't very grammatical, and I said apologetically that we were trying to catch the dogs, but that she shouldn't be afraid because they were quite friendly and harmless. She stared at me with hard green eyes, and said nothing. I noticed that when the lady who'd been watering the flowers in the churchyard passed, the two women didn't acknowledge or speak to each other. Once we'd recaptured the dogs we set off to see the Basque cemetery. I waved to the old lady as we drove away, but she just stared back.

The cemetery was a dismal place. To reach it we drove through a small farming hamlet to a dead end (no pun intended) and a little church that was locked up and falling down in places, with a notice on the door asking for donations for repairs. The ground was dry and cracked, covered in pieces of broken tiles, and there wasn't a single plant growing there, not even a weed. There were about twenty-five Basque headstones engraved on both sides with the date of death and the person's name, although the centuries had effaced most of them, except for one or two sheltered by the church. The oldest legible date was 1627, and on most stones we could just about make out the curly Basque swastika, the *lauburu*, or sometimes the Star of David. It seemed sad that there was nobody to remember these long-dead people, no relatives to place even a single flower upon the neglected graves here in the middle of nowhere, and I wondered whether the inhabitants of the cemetery ever felt resentful, and also what it was like for the active residents of the hamlet to have this rather spooky place in their midst.

Smoke was curling from chimneys, but out in the fields the hay was being harvested. Although it was a bright June day, it was still rather chilly. We drove through oak forests fringed with bracken laced with dog roses, where high in the trees were rustic wooden platforms reached by metal ladders and covered with old fir branches, from where hunters spot and slaughter pigeons, hence the name of the place: '*l'enfer des palombes*' — the wood pigeons' hell. It was very rustic: a herd of cattle here, a small vineyard there; isolated houses, narrow wiggling roads. All

141

the houses seemed huge. In a field of hay a black-bereted old boy was scything by hand; it was a large field, and we wondered how long it would take him to cut it all, and whether by the time he reached the end it would be time to start again at the beginning.

We parked in a village for our morning refreshment, and watched as somebody drew up and parked on Tinkerbelle's bumpers. We pointed out that we'd be trapped, and the driver said we were parked illegally, and if the gendarmes came they'd give us a ticket. So we moved off a little way down the road. When we passed on our way out of the village, we saw his car and another local one cosily parked exactly where we'd been.

The delectable Ossau Iraty cheese we'd bought from Nicolas hadn't lasted long, and we were suffering from withdrawal symptoms, so when we saw a sign for Ardi Gasna 'two minutes away' we set off on a trail which really did lead into the wilderness, becoming narrower and steeper by the centimetre, over a switchback of humps and bumps, round sharp blind bends, along a track that a goat might have had difficulty negotiating. The enticing signs led us on and further on for very much longer than two minutes, through a rural idyll, up the side of a mountain, until we finally reached the end of the road and drove into the immaculate neat and tidy farmyard of Maison Etxepareborda, at Béhorléguy, Unhassorbiscay. If you need convincing of the exuberance of the Basque language, there's a fine example.

The views from the farm were breathtaking and wild: mountains and valleys and a clear blue sky in which several kites circled, singing their joy at living there. Once again we asked for Ardi Gasna, and once again we were met with smiles and headshakes and an enormous wheel of Ossau Iraty. We bought a very much larger piece than previously, now that we knew how much of it we could eat. The lady who sold it to us said that if we wrapped it in a dry tea cloth and kept it in the warmest part of the fridge, it would last for several months. This didn't turn out to be true: it didn't last very long at all. On the return journey down the impossible path we measured the distance: we'd writhed and wriggled a round trip of seven kilometres over almost impassable terrain to buy that cheese. And worth every millimetre. With the precious cargo lovingly swaddled in the dry tea towel in the warmest part of the fridge, we continued our drive through spectacular mountain landscape; the road wound and twisted beside precipices where only the white line on the edge of the tarmac saved the vehicle from toppling down to the valley below. It continued over the unpronounceable Burdin- curutcheta pass, 1,300 metres above sea level. We passed a grey-haired cyclist pedalling casually as we reached the summit of the Bagargui pass and broke through the cloud into sunshine. Like the Pointe du Van, this is a place where the grandeur of nature makes speech superfluous. There's nothing to say.

Notices all around warned that up there in the high pastures dogs must be kept on leads: bad news for our passengers. Dobbie had by now eaten both their Haltis, which help to restrain tugs somewhat so that you don't get pulled flat on your face. Without them, putting either of the dogs on a lead was an invitation to take up cross-country skiing without skis. This was very unfortunate because it meant that they weren't going to be able to have much exercise whilst we were in the mountains. The freedom that they'd enjoyed on the coast was gone. We started the descent from the plateau at les Châlets d'Iraty, down a road as convoluted as intestines, hoping that Tinkerbelle's brakes were in failsafe mode as we twisted and turned round one hairpin bend after another. There was an interesting moment when we met a herd of cattle plodding solemnly up the steep road, their giant neck bells tolling from wide leather collars painted with their names. As if familiar with the procedure, they stepped politely to the side of the road (the side where the high banks were, not the long drops), and stood watching us creep past with a whisker between them on the one side, and the abyss on the other.

Frequently the French road signs had been effaced with black paint in a peaceful display of French Basque nationalism, unlike the more forceful expressions of their Spanish brothers. The scenery was changing to more rugged mountains as we came to the border between the Basque and Béarn regions. At the Gorges d'Holzarté we stopped at an *auberge* for an omelette with onions and potatoes, so good for the waistline. There were assorted fowl strutting about on the patio, and a grey pigeon with a glittering iridescent purple neck who was carefully choosing twigs for its nest, methodically inspecting and rejecting them until it found one that passed its strict quality control criteria. A bantam hen strolled amongst the diners on the terrace, and jumped over the low fence into an adjoining garden. Shortly afterwards she returned leading a whole battalion of colleagues over the gate and into our midst, the cockerels growling and offering morsels of food to the hens, until they were chased away by a waitress with a tray. Unperturbed, sparrows bounced from chair to chair hoovering up crumbs.

If you wanted to, you could walk some distance to cross a precarious bridge that looked like a thin narrow plank spanning a deep gorge. We didn't want to do that, and instead drove along following the course of the river Saison towards Oloron-Sainte-Marie, where we wanted to buy a Basque beret. Climbing again we passed through a string of pretty villages including Aramits, from where Alexandre Dumas took the name for one of his three musketeers, Aramis, who kept a secret mistress and couldn't decide whether he wanted to be a priest or a musketeer (why were they known as musketeers when they're almost always depicted as swordsmen?). We weren't able to find anywhere selling Basque berets in Oloron-Sainte-Marie, but there was a breakers' yard, and unusually it was actually open. Unfortunately the gentlemen standing about in it were utterly uninterested in Tinkerbelle's unfortunate plight or in suggesting anywhere else that might be, so still farting and spluttering we continued on our way into the Béarn district.

After a cool drive through the shadowy gorge of Lourdios in the Aspe valley, brilliant

146

with blue aquilegias and golden buttercups cooled by spray from the river's green pools and white cascades, we came out into alpine meadows grazed by flocks of sheep; ahead the mountains were covered with snow. Farmhouses and stone cottages with steep slate roofs perched on the hillsides among deciduous forests. The only human being we saw was one gentleman relieving himself on to some buttercups. We passed through a tunnel about fifty metres long hewn from the rocks, arriving in Lourdios-Ichère, the sort of sleepy, unspoilt village that you dream of, tucked in a valley protected by beautiful mountains, with a restaurant festooned with geraniums, petunias and impatiens which set off perfectly its pastel-green shutters.

At the village school we asked a young woman if there was anywhere we could camp for the night. She pointed a short way up the hill, saying with a smile that up there was the nearest thing they had to a flat parking area, but that it wasn't very flat. In fact it suited us nicely, on a patch of grass beneath a willow tree, alongside a clump of yellow irises growing cheerfully on the banks of the river.

Whilst we sat half reading and half dozing and soaking up the alpine air and listening to the water chuckling to itself, Dobbie amused himself and us by hunting and digging up

147

small rocks from the floor of the shallow river, plunging his head under the water. With bubbles billowing from his submerged nose and his tail wagging furiously he continued emerging triumphantly until he'd built up a collection of rocks each weighing about half a kilo, in a pile next to Tinkerbelle.

Tally had made his second social gaffe on the journey by mistaking Terry's leg for a lamp post; this meant that Terry had to wash his trainers which he laid out to dry in the sun on the concrete beam forming a crude bridge over the river. Comfortably trapped in our folding canvas chairs, we were unable to reach them before Dobbie had carefully picked them up, one by one, and dropped them into the water, watching in fascination as they bobbed downstream like little boats. Terry just managed to catch them before they were washed out of reach.

When the heat had dissipated itself, we went for a walk through the one street in the village, past the school where the children had set up a 'station biosurveillance' to check ozone levels by means of a row of aubergine plants with pieces of red wool tied to them, although there was no explanation as to how this worked, nor could we find anybody to ask. Strolling down the hill we passed the oldest lady I'd ever seen, who looked at least a hundred and ten and was bent over at ninety degrees from the waist, progressing so slowly that we had to watch her against a fixed object to confirm that she was actually moving.

Towards the lower end of the village we leaned over a stone bridge and watched the waters tumbling over the rocks. A quite large adder with distinctive V markings down its head and back was sunbathing on one of the rocks, but as I moved and my shadow fell on it it shot off the rock and into the water. On our way back to Tinkerbelle we stopped at the *auberge* for a glass of wine, and I mentioned to the *patronne* that we'd seen an adder in the river.

'Ah yes.' She nodded. 'Adders. They bring them here in helicopters.'

I stared at her, looking for some sign of the meaning of this odd statement. Perhaps I'd misheard.

'No,' I said, 'I meant a *snake*, a *viper*.'

'Yes,' she replied, 'I know. They deliver them by helicopter.'

'What did she say about helicopters?' Terry asked.

'She says they deliver adders in them,' I explained.

'She must be barmy,' Terry replied.

Through the doorway into the kitchen we

saw the slow old lady. Astonishingly, she was preparing a mountain of vegetables, leaning over the table and propping herself on her ancient elbows, methodically peeling potatoes and carrots. There was a simply enormous pile waiting to be done, and I couldn't help thinking she was being exceedingly optimistic.

Lourdios-Ichère was utterly peaceful. Back at Tinkerbelle we sat watching the sun fade. A melodic, clinking, drumlike noise signalled the approach from round the corner of a small, important little boy of about six marching with his chest thrust out. Behind him, with large wooden-clappered copper bells swinging from their necks, came a herd of a dozen Béarnaise cattle with their calves, tails swishing, big limpid eyes turning to examine us, followed by a couple of men with sticks, talking to each other. The cattle plodded quietly behind the small boy in a scene of rural life that must have been repeated through the centuries. With the mountains outlined against the deep blue of the night sky, and the faint tinkling sound of distant animals' bells, we went to bed that night feeling we'd found a small paradise. Dobbie sang when the church bells tolled, and he woke us early, groaning indignantly because a fat bay horse with feathery fetlocks was standing in and drinking from the shallow river.

Lourdios-Ichère was no longer peaceful. Cars and trucks appeared from both ends of the village and parked on the roadsides. There was an air of excitement — shouts, laughter, music blaring from loudspeakers. We went down to the *auberge* to enquire what was going on.

La patronne was dashing about setting tables, and in the kitchen the old lady was still peeling vegetables.

Was it possible to have coffee, and a cup of hot chocolate, we asked.

'*Oui, oui,*' said the landlady, but although we waited at the bar for ten minutes the drinks didn't arrive, because she was leaping around with piles of plates and cutlery, darting outside to speak to van drivers delivering sacks and boxes, or peering into the kitchen at the peeling lady. A couple of old boys stood next to us at the bar, sipping red wine.

'What's happening?' I asked as she rushed past.

'*Mais, c'est la transhumance aujourd'hui!*' she exclaimed, as if she couldn't believe that anybody didn't know.

The transhumance is a centuries-old event, when the flocks and herds are driven from

151

their winter grazing in the valleys up to the summer pastures on the mountain-sides. This gives the valleys time to grow the fodder that will be needed to sustain the animals through the following winter, and it gives the animals an opportunity to fatten up on the flowery alpine grass. Abandoning any expectations of sustenance, we joined the chattering crowds making their way down past the church and the niche opposite from where Our Lady of the Shepherds watches over the village. A collection of donkeys and ponies was tethered beneath a tree, and two small self-important boys with sticks marched about on some unknown mission. Fifty metres behind came a little girl wearing a neat red headscarf and waving another stick (absolutely everybody round here seemed to carry a stick), driving a flock of sixty of the distinctive horned, Roman-nosed Basco-Béarnaise sheep over a small stone bridge, bells clanging. Behind the flock came a dog and two bereted men. Berets were the other thing that everybody seemed to have in Lourdios-Ichère. Sticks, berets, sheep.

We followed the growing multitude to the main square, which had been transformed from the previous day's lazy emptiness into a bustle of men setting up barriers, women carrying paper tablecloths and stacks of plastic cups and glasses, children selling drinks and packets of very sweet little cakes from a hastily erected tent, and a few dogs grubbing around. Somebody was testing a sound system, and a dozen self-conscious hand-holding infants were being led around in a circle by a teacher in some sort of Béarnaise folk dance, shuffling a few steps to the left, and a few steps back again to the right. The little boys were particularly unenthusiastic except when they had to jump up and down, which they did with gusto. A couple of men appeared carrying a long pole hung with cow bells of varying sizes from big to enormous, attached to wide leather collars and beautifully painted with flowers, pastoral scenes and wildlife. Even at 10.00 a.m. the sun was blazing, and it was absolutely roasting. Everybody except us seemed to be wearing berets; even a very young baby in a pram had one pulled down to where its eyebrows would have been if it had any.

Armed with the regulation sticks and berets (one black and one purple) two urchins ran down the hill followed by a flock of woolly sheep, some marked blue on their backs, and some marked mossy green. The flocks trotted down the road snatching mouthfuls of ivy and other plants overhanging garden walls, and as they reached the square-bereted men in checked shirts and jeans corralled them into tight enclosures with portable barriers. The noise of the men shouting, the wooden clappers clanging the bells, the sheep bleating, the dance music thumping and the traffic hooting as it impatiently tried to circum-navigate the animals was quite chaotic. To direct the sheep the shepherds tapped their backs gently with their sticks, crying, 'Ay ha!' Ever more sheep teemed into the square, big woolly things with large horns curling round their ears, their backs daubed in vivid colours. Tightly wedged into their pens they looked like a sea of multi-coloured fleece with faces sticking up out of it.

There were two breeds — the Basco-Béarnaise and the black-faced Manech. They all looked uncomfortably hot, and I asked one of the shepherds why they weren't shorn. He replied that sheep in the valleys are shorn in the autumn, when they return from the high pastures. They need thick coats up there to protect them from the sun, and from the cold night air in the mountains. By now there were several hundred creatures bleating and bellowing, and our commentator said we shouldn't mistake this noise for distress: the sheep had been bleating in excitement for several days because they knew the time had come to go up the mountains.

We saw how the animals are marked in the traditional way to identify them: with the aid of a saucepan full of some sort of dye and two stripped maize cobs. Somebody held the sheep by the horns, which made useful handles, and somebody else dipped the cobs into the saucepan and then smeared the dye on the shoulders, back or backside of the animals. Our shepherd explained that the main function of the sheep is to produce the rich sweet milk used in the manufacture of our favourite Ossau Iraty cheese; their wool is of an inferior quality, but experiments are being conducted to find ways of using it as an insulation material.

Once the flocks and herds are up in the mountains, their shepherds remain there too for the summer months, and are provisioned courtesy of donkeys like Nanette, a patient brown-haired girl with enormous ears, dozy eyes and a soft muzzle. Nanette is a very experienced lady who finds her own way up and down the mountain. We watched a demonstration of the meticulous loading of her burden. First a wooden frame was strapped to her back, then various components were attached to it, including two things like gutters used to carry the cheeses down from the mountain. It's essential for the donkey's comfort and the safety of the cargo that the load is attached in a specific way. The donkeys take up the cheese-making equipment, salt, food for the shepherds and occasionally newspapers, and return with the prepared cheeses. Nanette stood happily being patted and stroked by a circle of admirers as more and more paraphernalia was piled on her back.

Next to arrive was a small herd of light golden Béarnaise cattle with their lyre-shaped horns, their calves trotting along beside them. This is a breed, we were told, valued more for its beauty than its meagre milk yield, although it makes an excellent cheese either alone or mixed with sheep's milk. By then the square was absolutely jammed solid with livestock, but that didn't stop the arrival of another herd of 200 sheep. The animals were crammed even more tightly in their pens to make room for the new arrivals. A momentary hiatus was followed by an announcement that the mares were coming, and spectators should keep out of their way, because they had their foals at foot and were big powerful animals running loose. They clattered into the village at a spanking pace, big, muscled, glossy chestnut animals, heads high, snorting as they made their way up the road, and their foals were proud beside them. Some impatient fool in a car tried to push past them, spooking one of the mares so she careered wildly across the bridge; one of the shepherds ran to head her off before she knocked anyone over. Unlike the sheep and cattle the horses were not penned, but made their way straight to a field of belly-high buttercups.

Two hours after the first animals had arrived in the square, they took the next step towards their summer holidays. The shepherds removed the barriers and started encouraging the animals up the hill towards the square outside the church, escorted by a group of people playing bagpipes. The faces of the local folk all had the same contented, weathered, gentle, kindly expressions, as if they were totally happy with their life, and why shouldn't they be in this perfectly idyllic location of mountain and valley, where the air was clean and traffic rare?

In the churchyard a group of shepherds chanted in soft, high voices while the priest roamed around in his white robes stopping for a word here and there. The deputy mayor was there too, marshalling arriving animals into new pens, where they stood panting in their thick fleeces. The cattle went straight past and up a small path and out of sight, but the sheep still had a long while to wait as the deputy mayor, a handsome man, slim and tall in a purple shirt and black beret, began talking. A good orator, he spoke at length. At very great length. He talked of the time when life in the Aspe valley had been hard, and how it had been difficult for men to attract wives because life was so difficult and some people had given up and moved away. But a few people had persevered, and thanks to them and their hard work, and improved communications and technology, today life was good and people were happy once more, and he praised those people who'd had the tenacity to stay. He talked also of the need for communication, how the Internet made it possible to contact people thousands of miles away, but how often people forgot to say hello to their neighbours. He really did go on for a long time as we sweltered along with the sheep, whose sides heaved and heads hung down. A choir of shepherds sang hymns and blessings, and the priest prayed for the flocks and their custodians. Local ladies and children circulated with baskets of wonderful bread, glasses of wine, and the incomparable Ossau Iraty cheese, and still the deputy mayor talked on. The crowd was restless. Even the sheepdogs abandoned their posts and went to lie in the river, where small children sat keeping cool. Behind the square in a barn was a herd of shaggy, horned goats. I asked a nearby shepherd whether they'd be joining the sheep in the climb up the mountain, but he said no, not the goats. They'd be taken up by tractor and trailer because if they were let loose in the village they'd devastate everything in their path.

At very long last the sheep were mercifully released to follow the cattle up to the high meadows. Several hundred bells chimed as they jostled and barged each other in their haste, bleating as they ran. They streamed across a small stone bridge, their painted backs forming a moving abstract canvas, followed by those people energetic enough to undertake the hike to the top of the mountain.

The mares and foals brought up the rear, and I asked another shepherd with vivid blue eyes and a gentle smile what the horses were used for. He grimaced slightly, and said: 'They're bred for meat. The foals go to the butcher.' Seeing the look on my face, he went on: 'Ah yes, it's a shame. I don't like it myself, but if they weren't bred for meat the race would die out.' I've always found that a strange argument. I could no longer look at the carefree, frisky foals bucking and prancing so merrily beside their mothers.

That afternoon we sat by the river in the welcome shade of the willow tree. Tally slept quietly on the grass, but Dobbie, active as ever, kept walking backwards and forwards over the concrete bridge, until he managed to fall in, landing hard on his side on a flat rock. Twice.

We watched a toad scrabbling around in the water, its elbows bent like a fishwife with hands on hips, and the bay horse came back to drink again. Dobbie was indignant, but the horse didn't care. We were almost asleep when Dobbie's high-pitched, still-young bark roused us and down the hillside opposite came a lady in carpet slippers and a flowery apron. She made her way over the narrow bridge, and called out to ask whether the baker had been. I said I hadn't seen him, but she kept on coming and looked into a box on the wall next to where we were, and triumphantly extracted two *baguettes*.

Then she started talking at me. She talked, without comma, let alone full stop, for over a quarter of an hour. She talked about the terrible floods of 1992. How she'd been visiting her daughter when the floods came, and how she couldn't get back to her house. She'd tried to phone her husband, but the phone line was down. He'd been dreadfully worried. She'd never seen rain like it before. The terror of seeing the valley turned into a lake was indescribable. The mayor's car was washed away. How frightening it was that a small stream could grow so fast into a rushing torrent. Of course, it was because people didn't look after the land as the old-timers had done. They didn't clean out the ditches, or dig channels for the water to run away. In the olden days people understood the importance of husbanding the land, but they don't bother any more. No wonder all these dreadful things happened. She'd heard Dobbie singing the previous night — just like the poodle she used to have; how they used to laugh when it tilted back its head and sang like an opera singer! He was a fine dog, and so was the other one under the tree. She hadn't been to watch the transhumance. She did the first year, about nine years ago, but once you've seen it once, there's no point in watching it again. She didn't think there were as many visitors this year. It goes on too long — there's far too much talking.

If I could have got a word in edgeways, I'd have agreed with her.

With her *baguettes* under her arm, she looked as if she could happily stand and talk for ever. She was a warm and friendly soul and I would have really liked to ask her about her life in the valley, but she was like a dam that had burst its banks, absolutely unstoppable. And what about the heatwave last year, she wanted to know. The temperature of the water in the stream had been measured at 31°C, and the trout had leapt out of the water and died.

My head was starting to spin from all the facts I was trying to digest at the same time as listening to her, and in desperation I yelled: '*Serpents! Vipères!*'

That brought her to a halt for long enough for me to tell her about the adder we'd seen in the river yesterday, and to ask whether there were many in the area.

'No, they're rare. The ecologists used to bring them in helicopters, because they were a disappearing species. But whenever we see them, any snakes, we hit them with a stick,' she raised her arm above her head and brought it down with a swish, 'pif! Or we shoot them. All snakes are bad, so we kill them!' she trilled merrily. I wondered how much it cost to bring the poor adders to this place by helicopter, to be killed by old ladies with sticks.

Finally she excused herself and trotted back over the bridge and up the path to her house. A light breeze came up, and looking up the mountain we could see the miniature figures of the people who'd climbed up earlier making their way back down.

That evening we went for a meal in the *auberge*, which was full without being the bedlam it had been earlier. *La patronne* was still bustling around, but in a controlled panic, delivering bowls of soup here, snatching up empty plates there. There was a lot of laughter going on at a table of six ladies who'd been involved in organizing the day's festivities, and they were joined by a gentleman almost incapable of standing up. He slumped into a chair and mumbled at them, and started stroking one lady's thigh. They chastised him, *la patronne* had words with him, and out he wobbled. Then two couples arrived and installed themselves at a table beside the large fireplace. There was much laughter and banter between tables; one of the couples was from Paris, where he had a business cleaning out tankers, and they were with friends from Marseille who were in the paper business. The wobbly man came in and out, ordering drinks and leaving them half finished on the bar, and each time he appeared the tanker-cleaning man ducked under the table. Then the drunk arrived with a huge piece of steak in a plastic bag and asked *la patronne* to cook it for him, and giving him a big hug she took it off to the kitchen and installed him at a table in an adjoining part of the restaurant where he settled down noisily with another party of diners. Periodically he staggered back into our room and each time the tanker man hid. Throughout the evening this strange behaviour continued; it was pure French farce.

The people sitting at the table behind us came from Biarritz and spoke some English, and so did the man from Paris, and for a couple of hours we were the butt of their friendly humour. Innocently we made some comment to the people behind us about how lucky they were to live in such a lovely part of the world, and they looked quite shocked and replied: 'But no — we're not Béarnaise! We're *Basques*!'

They didn't look any different from the Béarnaise people.

The Parisian gentleman was particularly lively and out-going, when he was not hiding under the table, and insisted on paying for coffee for all the other twenty-two diners. After our meal we walked round the village, stopping to look in at the church which was packed with chandeliers, cherubs, lilies, carved painted statues and an ornate altar, and when we came out we met the Parisian couple who explained the odd goings-on in the *auberge*.

The husband had visited the Paris Agricultural Salon and been very much taken with the charms of one of the beautiful

Béarnaise lyre-horned cattle, named Parouquet. The owner had invited him to come to Lourdios-Ichère to watch the transhumance, and he'd decided to bring his wife and their friends from Marseille. That morning he had met up with the owner of the cattle and invited him to join them for a drink at the *auberge* that evening. However, he had not expected his new friend to turn up legless; the alternative to having their evening ruined was to hide under the table.

Before leaving next day we visited the Ecomusée de Lourdios-Ichère, a presentation of life in the Aspe valley in the days when local government was led by a clan chief who considered himself independent from France. There were video presentations of life through the seasons, and the manufacture of the *sonnailles* — the bells worn by the sheep, and chosen with care to distinguish not only herds from each other, but individual sheep too, so that the notes of each flock harmonize with each other but not with different flocks. We stopped for coffee at the *auberge*, and mentioned the melodrama of the previous evening.

'It's a shame,' said our hostess. 'He's a lovely man, but he has a problem with the drink, and he lost his driving licence and his livelihood as a truck driver. He can't get work, so he has to live with his parents. Now all he has is his cattle, which he loves. *Le pauvre.*'

When we left Lourdios-Ichère I felt I was leaving a little of my heart there. It was so unspoiled, and if somebody had waved a magic wand I think we could have been happy to stay there, although we were seeing it at its best, in summer and during the year's biggest event. I consoled myself with the thought that in the depths of winter it would certainly be freezing cold, bleak and isolated, and that we'd probably never see snakes there twined together or basking innocently in the sunshine.

So we drove off, saying farewell to the stream and the cascades of water coming down from the mountains, and the tunnel cut from the rocks, and the winding roads, the wild-flower meadows, and the small moving dots that were cattle and sheep high up on the side of the mountain. Beside the river by a clump of banana plants we passed a group of racing cyclists in their club colours, and a herd of cattle strolling along unaccompanied like a group of elderly ladies taking a riverside constitutional. It was a perfect Sunday morning, the trees silver in the early sunlight, the sky stretched out like a blue sheet between the mountains, below a thin slice of white cloud.

We headed off to Aste-Béon in the Ossau valley, a lovely area of twisting streets and medieval cottages sheltering between the mountains and rivers, and bought a fine black beret for a ridiculously low price, I think it was something silly like €5.

Following a sign to the Falaise aux Vautours we arrived there just in time to be herded into a group of fifty young school-children in the six to eight age group, who had come to learn about the griffon vultures that populate the limestone cliffs. In 1974 the Ossau Nature Reserve was established to help the dwindling vulture population to multiply. At the time there were just 10 nesting pairs and 7 surviving young. By 2002 their ranks had multiplied to 117 nesting pairs and 70 surviving young. What griffon vultures need, in order to procreate successfully, is a plentiful food supply and undisturbed peace and quiet, which is what they find at the Falaise aux Vautours. Throughout the winter and spring they're supplied with meat, and during the nesting period their realm is out of bounds to hikers and airborne traffic. To be able to see the creatures without disturbing them, live webcams have been set up discreetly, projecting into a theatre at the centre where a guide talks about the birds and points out what they are getting up to on the cliffs.

Our small companions were so excited and interested that they were a delight to see. However, for the poor girl trying to give her talk, their fervour was a handicap as she tried to make herself overheard over fifty shrill young voices simultaneously blurting out questions like 'What sex is it?' or 'How can you tell?' Many times she threatened that unless *les enfants* kept quiet and saved their questions until later, she would stop telling them any more about the birds. This only won her brief reprieves. Until our eyes had adjusted to the screen it was difficult to pick out the cliff's inhabitants, but the girl pointed with a cane at nesting chicks and once we'd focused on them and on the large white splashes of the vultures' toilet areas, we began to see more and more birds bopping around on the cliff's edges. Each time one of them moved, it was like a Punch and Judy show, with children shouting out excitedly, 'It moved, miss! Look, it's moving!' They were wildly enthusiastic, jumping up constantly to point at the screen, and we were delighted to see how such young children were being taught the importance and wonder of their heritage.

In ideal conditions griffon vultures can live

for forty years. Carrion feeders weighing about seven kilos, with a wingspan of two and a half metres which can carry them up to fifty kilometres in their search for food, can hold over six kilos of meat in their crop and gizzard. They're fastidious birds, bathing in pools of water to wash off the sticky remains of their food, and then standing with outstretched wings to dry themselves. Their naked necks prevent food remains from being trapped in feathers and causing disease. Because their beaks are not particularly strong, they rely on other birds or animals to break open carcasses before they can eat them.

The Falaise aux Vautours is proud that each year the white-feathered, yellow-headed Egyptian vultures (so named because they were worshipped by the ancient Egyptians) return there, as do bearded vultures and lammergeyers, both of whom eat almost exclusively bones, which they break by dropping on to rocks. A lammergeyer is said to have killed a bald man by dropping a bone on his head, mistaking it for a rock. To keep cool, because they cannot sweat, some vultures pant like dogs. Others urinate on their legs. They must be skilled contortionists.

We spent that night at a pretty campsite just outside Louvie-Juzon, where we were intrigued by the arrival of a Dutch camping car whose driver, a short, moustached gentleman wearing a headband, collared the gnome-like campsite owner and marched him about, all the time swinging a small hand-held machine and pointing it wildly in every direction. Round and round they strode, directing the machine at trees and mountains, conferring, until I simply had to ask the Dutchman's wife what he was doing. Her explanation was disappointingly mundane: the machine was a compass, and her husband had to locate a position where their television could receive the satellite signal without hindrance. Looking at the mountains encircling us, and the trees all over the place, I thought it unlikely that he'd succeed, and that it was strange in a place of such extraordinary natural beauty and with so many wonders to explore that anybody could place that much importance on watching television. But *chacun à son goût*.

The campsite was regulated by a mob of bantam cockerels who acted as alarm clocks, surrounding Tinkerbelle the next morning and roaring until we got up and chased them off towards the Dutch people. In colourful, geranium-decked Louvie-Juzon somebody had been experimenting, not entirely successfully, with topiary, leaving their hedge looking like a collection of decapitated heads. There were beehives in a field, and a sign for goat's cheese — a renegade, apparently, in this almost entirely sheepy area. It was a gloriously hot, sunny afternoon hovering in a blue smoky heat haze. We drove around through forests and fields just enjoying the lovely Béarnaise landscape, on snake-like roads that constantly wound back upon themselves. Each time we rounded a corner it was like *déjà vu*, because the view was always the same. When we broke out of the forest and into golden wheat fields, people were raking up hay with wooden forks, and in one field there was the familiar sight of an old man holding a scythe, as if not knowing quite where to begin.

The outskirts of Lourdes were industrial and devoid of charm but teeming with traffic. We drove onwards and into a wall of onion-scented air. Almost everywhere we visited, with the exception of Lourdios-Ichère, there'd either been the day before, or would be the day after we left, some event of note, but in Trébons, south of Tarbes, we had arrived at precisely the right time to enjoy the last of the three days of their onion celebrations. We needed to know what was so special about the onions from Trébons that three whole days could be devoted to their worship, so we parked and wandered into the town centre, through the square of 19 March 1962, commemorating the ceasefire in the war in Algeria, and over a rustic bridge towards a large marquee filled with several dozen eating people, who were being blasted with music by a lively jazz band fetchingly dressed in white trousers and turquoise shirts topped with jaunty boaters. The Trébons onions, of which we bought two bunches, were like very large spring onions with a fiery taste and an overwhelming aroma that flooded Tinkerbelle and made the dogs sneeze. We were trapped within Trébons's thin streets for a good half-hour as streams of vehicles hunted parking places. Once we'd freed ourselves we proceeded to the graceful town of Bagnères-de-Bigorre, where we enjoyed cake and coffee at a pavement table on a wide avenue, lined by elegant two-and three-storey buildings with arched windows and pretty balconies, against a backdrop of snowy mountains.

It was Sunday afternoon, and apart from Trébons every village we passed was dormant, with shutters closed against the heat, everything asleep except the sunbathing roses, and one suicidal red squirrel that dashed in front of us quite unnecessarily, bringing us to a violent halt and nearly putting us through the windscreen. Naughty Tufty.

We'd heard about a restaurant in Valcabrère serving 'authentic Roman meals', and so headed there, stopping along the way at the twelfth-century cathedral of Saint-Bertrand-de-Comminges, perched upon a small mountain and surrounded by a few narrow streets cluttered with restaurants and gifte shoppes. It was cold and dank inside, and smelt of damp and suffering. As a building it was impressive, a mighty church supported by buttresses, and we wondered how and where the funds were found to construct these huge edifices, and whether the money and effort that went into them could have been put to better and more practical use for the benefit of their congregations.

Valcabrère was a particularly attractive village but the restaurant, although it offered an enticing menu, was out of our price range.

Crossing the milky, silky green waters of the river Garonne into Haute-Garonne, *département* 31, brought us into rather wild countryside of hills and trees, few houses and few animals apart from one herd of silvery-grey cattle. The *forêt domaniale de la vallée du Gers* was a fairyland of young trees, mosses, ferns and fallen bronze leaves.

Tinkerbelle struggled to climb the 1069 metres to the Col de Portet d'Aspet, the needle of her temperature gauge in the red and climbing dangerously high, and there we were almost in the middle of nowhere. But brave old lady that she was, she kept on crawling upward, because there wasn't really any choice, and just when we most needed it we reached the top and a welcome sign to a campsite.

On a scale of one to ten, the location of this site scored eleven. It stood on a plateau surrounded by peaks, with nothing higher except a couple of white-headed mountain tops and the birds circling above. We walked in the cool of the beech trees with the dogs, letting them run off their pent-up energy of the last few days, and later sat silently gazing around us. It was 10.30 p.m., and where two mountains met on the valley floor the sky faded from aquamarine to baby blue below an inverted triangle of golden orange sky where the sun was going down. Utterly gorgeous.

We slept the sleep of the righteous and exhausted, and woke to an early-morning chorus unequalled by anything we'd ever heard before. It sounded as if all the songbirds in the world had gathered in the trees around us and were singing their very best solely for our pleasure. Even the low-battery-warning bleep on Terry's computer joined in. Our hosts had disappeared, so we left the campsite fees with a young German couple in a tent who were our only neighbours and set off again, through the Hansel and Gretel village of Portet-d'Aspet with its curved roof slates and what is probably the most sinuous high street in France, a long series of bends. After our very brief stay in the Haute-Garonne, we arrived in the Ariège and pointed Tinkerbelle to the village of Bethmale, passing a string of mountain villages that were no more than clusters of houses with slate roofs; each commune displayed fluorescent posters advertising transhumances, *vides greniers* or cheese festivals.

Audressein is a picture-postcard village of cottages cloaked in climbing roses, a lichen-covered stone bridge, and a flower-smothered old wooden carriage with wooden wheels. We stopped in green and leafy Castillonen-Couserans to buy their speciality *croustade*, a crispy, sugary tart filled with pears, and then continued until the hamlet of Aret, just outside Bethmale, where we were on the trail of some clogs and a splendid legend.

A series of the spindly lanes characteristic of this part of the world led to an exquisite row of cottages, bordered by pink snapdragons and hollyhocks just on the point of opening, roses clambering down the railings and past a trough whose pump handle had a frog sitting on it. Tinkerbelle was fractions of a centimetre from scraping the overhanging roofs as we pulled up outside a stone cottage almost suffocated with hanging baskets, flower boxes, roses, Californian poppies, and lilies. A beaming lady emerged from this flowery address and said that yes, the *sabotier*'s premises were right next door, but today being Monday he'd be at his workshop in Audressein, where we'd been half an hour previously, so we rewended our way through the obstacle course. Tinkerbelle was still overheating alarmingly and struggling with the hills.

I was particularly looking forward to meeting the *sabotier*, not only because of the legend of the clogs, but because I'd never met a *sabotier* before and hoped to learn how he became one in the first place. Was his father one before him? How many other *sabotiers* made similar clogs? How many pairs of the famed long-toed clogs did he make, and how long did it take? Could we perhaps buy a pair from him? His workshop was down a side street, where we stepped into a room crammed with clogs in various stages of evolution from crude blocks of wood to almost finished footwear. There was a man wearing earphones working at a screeching bandsaw, slicing corners off the blocks of wood. He glanced at us uninterestedly and returned to his task, but an elderly man at the back of the workshop smiled encouragingly, so we asked if he was the famous *sabotier*. No, he laughed, that's the boss there, indicating the bandsaw man.

As the latter was completely immersed in his noisy task, we stood politely for a rather long time, waiting for a convenient moment for him to stop. We moved from one foot to another, looked around the room, and smiled encouragingly at him, and he went on ignoring us and slicing at the bits of wood. I took out a card with my name on it and offered it to him. He took it without looking at it, put it on a bench, and continued with his task. Rarely had I met anybody so totally devoid of charm. I asked the older gentleman whether it was possible to see some long-toed clogs, and he said we were welcome to look round a room at the back of the workshop. This place was stacked from floor to ceiling with racks of half-made clogs, all with disappointingly short toes, apart from one small model that was the sort of clog we'd come to see, long-toed and decorated with copper studs.

When the Saracens were invading the south of France and the Pyrénées in the ninth century, during their occupation of the village of Bethmale the son of the invaders' chief fell in love with a local maiden named Esclarlys, which means luminous white lily. The girl, despite being engaged to a boy named Darnert, welcomed his attentions. The young men of the village took to the mountains plotting revenge on the invaders, and Darnert, fiancé of the faithless luminous white lily, occupied himself with carving clogs with long thin spiky toes, while the other men mocked him because they were fashioning weapons. But Darnert just kept on whittling away at the spiky-toed clogs.

One night while the Saracens slept, the villagers swooped down and attacked them. The next morning Darnert was seen walking around in his strange spiked footwear, each spike topped with something red, shiny and wet. On his left clog dripped the heart of his fickle fiancée, and on the right the heart of the chief's son. It's been a custom ever since for Bethmale's young men to give their lady loves at Christmas a pair of spiky-toed clogs decorated with a heart made from golden nailheads, as well as a spindle and a red distaff; in return the girls give their men an embroidered wool cardigan and a decorated pouch. I found something rather sinister about a custom that seemed to contain a veiled threat to the fiancée to be damned careful what she got up to, or else.

I would have loved to talk to the *sabotier* about the legend, but in the face of his masterly rudeness we lost interest and left him there still bent over his bandsaw, his personality as wooden as his clogs. He's what our neighbour M. Meneteau would call a *drôle de coco*. All was not lost, however, because stopping for our mid-morning hot drink we chose the Auberge d'Audressein, where the extremely friendly staff made up for the horrible *sabotier*. The hot chocolate arrived in a large jug, with a plate of delicate little cakes, and was very nearly as excellent as the chocolate at Biriatou. It was delivered by a gentleman wearing a striped waistcoat and an Hercule Poirot moustache, who said the forecast was for rain on Wednesday, Thursday and Friday, although he wasn't certain if that was just for the Ariège, or everywhere. Under the table was a huge ginger-biscuit-coloured dog called Princesse, a *dogue de Naples*, who looked like an overgrown boxer and quite intimidating, but when I sneezed she ran and hid behind the bar.

Between Saint-Girons and Foix the countryside flattened out into wider, more open spaces and gentle hills, and fields high with hay that scented the air, some cut and lying in ridges waiting to be baled, some already wound into giant rolls. A little grey-haired old lady in a straw hat and checked apron drove a flock of sheep through the village of Rimont, a pretty place perched upon a hillside. We hoped the farmers would manage to get their hay under cover before the threatened rain on Wednesday. There were already puffy clouds building over the mountains.

Our first sight of the Château de Foix, stronghold of the Counts of Foix, was startling because of the sheer size and might of the castle that looked down protectively on to the town snuggled against the mountainside. This was the realm of the powerful fourteenth-century Count of Foix, Gaston 'Phoebus', named for his golden hair after the Greek god Apollo. One of the most dazzling, cultured and clever men of his time, he was also politically skilful, and successfully trod the thin line of divided allegiance to both France and England. Awarding himself the title of Prince of Béarn, he asserted his power as a ruler and warrior under the swashbuckling motto 'Touch if you dare'. A lover of and authority on music and literature, he was also a passionate huntsman, and wrote the classic *Livre de la Chasse*. Fittingly, he died returning from a bear hunt. He left no legitimate heir, having accidentally killed his only son in a fit of rage, an incident graphically described in the *Chronicles of Jean Froissart*, which give such a brilliantly vivid picture of life in Europe during the fourteenth century, and the events of the Hundred Years War. Gaston Phoebus would probably have been delighted to see Foix's wide streets looking so prosperous, filled with busy market stalls and people seated at tables the length of the main street.

The Béarn wasn't incorporated into the kingdom of France until 1620. Almost two centuries after Phoebus' death, a son was born to the Queen of Navarre at the Château of Pau. When his mummy died, eighteen-year-old Henri became King Henri III of Navarre, and was quickly married off to Marguerite de Valois, the daughter of Catherine de Medici and Henri II of France. Henri II had earlier met a rather unfortunate end (we'll come to that much later). A week after the wedding in Paris, the St Bartholomew's Day massacre of Protestants took place under the auspices of Catherine de Medici and her son, conveniently named François to distinguish him from the Henris.

The new bridegroom Henri only escaped death by rapidly converting to Catholicism. As soon as he returned to Navarre, he reverted to Protestantism.

François died of a brain abscess after a paltry year on the throne, but not before managing to marry Mary Queen of Scots and lay the foundations for a claim to the throne of Scotland. His brother Charles took up the reins as Charles IX until he died of tuberculosis and was succeeded by his brother, who liked dressing up in ladies' frocks and became the new King of France, Henri III.

Yet another Henri appeared on stage in the shape of Henri of Guise, and the three Henris engaged amongst themselves in a long war of power and religion. Henri of Guise was eliminated from the game by being murdered on the orders of Henri III of France, who formed an alliance with Henri III of Navarre. The French Henri was fatally wounded by a mad monk and, having run out of brothers, named Navarre Henri as his successor. And so Henri III of Navarre became Henri IV of France. It's perfectly straightforward.

But because the new French Henri was a Protestant, he wasn't accepted by the Catholic League supported by the Spanish, so he converted again to Catholicism in order to finally get the French crown on his head in Chartres, in 1594. As he said, 'Paris is well worth a Mass.' Henri's see-saw religious convictions upset the Protestants, but he consoled them by the creation of the Edict of Nantes which gave them the freedom to worship in their own way.

The new French king wasn't entirely satisfied with his existing wife Marguerite, so he got rid of her and took on a new one, Marie de Medici, his ex-mother-in-law's cousin. Marie is credited with introducing into France the recipe for puff pastry, which would lead to the birth of the croissant, and Henri is remembered for having said there should be 'a chicken in every peasant's pot on Sundays'.

Because he was often absent from France, Henri had Marie crowned Queen on 13 May, 1610. Maybe it wasn't an auspicious date, as the next day he was stabbed to death by a religious maniac called François Ravaillac, not unlike the previous Henri. Marie de Medici became Regent of France for her eight-year-old son who would become Louis XIII and would unite France and the Béarn. Ravaillac was tortured and pulled to pieces by four horses (like sneaky Ganelon centuries earlier). His parents were exiled and the family forbidden to ever again use the name Ravaillac.

★ ★ ★

We stopped for a cold drink, and learned that old Ronnie Reagan had died on Saturday, and that German Chancellor Gerhard Schroeder had stood shoulder against shoulder with Jacques Chirac on 6 June at the D-Day commemorations, a symbol of the new European understanding.

Trundling along quite contentedly through Tarasconsur-Ariège and Ax-les-Thermes, past rocky crags capped by small churches with conical roofs, I made a horrible discovery. Ahead of us on the N20, which was the only road, was the Puymorens pass, 1920 metres high, leading up to the Porte Puymorens. It would be madness to ask Tinkerbelle to haul herself and us up the pass, as she was still overheating and it was certain she wouldn't make it. That left us only one option — the five-and-a-half-kilometre tunnel cut through the mountain. Anybody else who's claustrophobic will know how that felt. Five and a half kilometres. At 60 kph it would take five and a half minutes, an interminable time to be in a tunnel. Speed restrictions made the journey twice as long, and although Terry tried heroically to take my mind off where we were, by the time we emerged into fresh air at Porta I was clinging to the remnants of my limited sanity, struggling for breath, and clammy with sweat.

Now we were in the Languedoc-Roussillon, hugging the Spanish frontier down to Bourg-Madame, and then just for the fun of it driving into the town of Llivia, a Spanish enclave entirely surrounded by French territory, which was the result of a clerical oversight during the Treaty of the Pyrénées in 1659. Under the treaty, thirty-three villages of the Cerdagne area were to belong to France, but somebody omitted Llivia from the list because it was a town, not a village, and so it remained, and still remains, a Spanish territory, just the one town, solemnly maintaining its Spanish identity, language, food and police force. Before the introduction of the euro, the peseta had been the local currency. There's a small museum there housing Europe's oldest pharmacy, established in 1416, which had survived until 1926. It was closed when we arrived.

An earlier treaty of 1375 between the French and the Spanish concerned grazing rights in the Baretous (French) and Roncal (Spanish) valleys. The two sides spent so much time stealing herds and killing each other that the Prince of Navarre and good old Gaston Phoebus met to find a peaceful solution while there were still some sheep and shepherds left. They agreed that each year the French shepherds would ceremoniously present to the Spanish three of their best heifers, two years old, and without spots. That treaty still endures, and every 13 July local dignitaries from both valleys meet for the exchange in a great ceremony which culminates in eating and drinking and general merry-making.

It took twenty-two seconds to drive into and out of Llivia, which was the scene of much building work, and continue on our way past the enormous solar furnace at Font-Romeu-Odeillo-Via, taller than the Eiffel tower, and producing solar energy up to 3,000°C from 9,600 mirrors, and on to Mont-Louis, France's highest fortified town (Vauban again), and headquarters of the French commandos.

The road started to become impossibly wiggly, wigglier than any other road we'd met so far, and it took all Terry's concentration and cool to negotiate Tinkerbelle round the endless hairpin bends perched on the rim of bottomless drops. I found my right foot pressing on to the floor in a pointless attempt to provide a secondary braking system. It was a nerve-racking drive through most dramatic scenery and a string of not particularly exciting villages, catching frequent glimpses of the little yellow toy-like train that runs from Latour-de-Carol a few kilometres west of Llivia to Villefranche-de-Conflent. As cute as it looks, the yellow train is more than a tourist attraction; it provides an important means of transport for the isolated villages along its 63-kilometre track. The station at Bolquère at 1,593 metres is the highest in France. We lost sight of the train often as it ducked into one of the nineteen tunnels along its route, making me supremely grateful that we in Tinkerbelle were merely dicing with death on the edges of precipices, rather than choking to death in the tunnels.

By the time we'd almost reached Villefranche-de-Conflent we were ready to stop, and followed signs to a campsite along a track several centimetres deep in what looked like dry snow, but was actually pollen fallen from the poplar trees. Terry had lost his usual good humour and felt the camping fees were unreasonably high. He rather rudely said to the proprietor that he wasn't prepared to pay the advertised rate, and would only pay €10 for the night.

'Goodbye,' said the proprietor, turning his

back and walking away from us, leaving us in something of a quandary because we were extremely tired and had no idea where or when we might next find somewhere to stay.

We drove on until Villefranche-de-Conflent hit us square between the eyes. Who else but Vauban could have been responsible for such thumping fortifications, and the guardian angel Fort Libéria defending the town from the surrounding heights, the two linked by subterranean passageways? The first thing that strikes you is the great fortified wall, and then the noise of the hurried waters of the river Têt racing around it. Tired as we were it was too good a sight to miss, so we went to explore the town, taking the dogs with us because they'd been in Tinkerbelle for hours.

We entered through the Port de France, past the giant mechanism that operated the drawbridge, through a colossal wooden door pierced with studs and hung with bolts. After the very plain little villages we'd been passing for the past few hours, it was strange to come upon this immensely exotic and very touristy place, with water running down the sides of the narrow alleys and geraniums bursting from window boxes, like finding Miss World amidst the ugly sisters.

Historically Villefranche-de-Conflent was like a bone fought over by packs of dogs, owned in its time successively by the Counts of Barcelona, the kingdoms of Majorca, Aragon, France, Castille and back to France. Under French ownership it hosted an internal rebellion when some inhabitants conspired to bring the town back into the Spanish fold. While an early version of Mata Hari attempted to seduce the military commander, the garrison was massacred. The French regained control and the rebels were put to death, their bodies chopped up and displayed in iron cages on the walls of the town. It was retaken by the Spanish at the end of the eighteenth century, and retaken by the French soon after. They've managed to hang on to it ever since, and in 1890 it ceased to be a garrison town for the French army. The last French soldiers marched away from the Fort in 1918.

Unimpressed with history, Dobbie was occupied in looking in shop windows and yelling indignantly at the large black dog which stared back at him. We roamed around for an hour absorbing the flavour of the place, and then stood outside the walls watching the golden pink colour of the sunset on the rock behind the town. Strategic it might be, but it isn't the prettiest part of the world. Night was approaching and we were really very tired and still looking for somewhere to stay. Ria was full of signs supporting José Bové, the French farmers' and ecologists' moustachioed and pipe-smoking militant little hero leading the fight against globalization and *malbouffe*, who keeps getting put in prison for setting fire to McDonald's. Despite its many elegant buildings, the horde of characters hanging around in the town centre of Prades made us change our minds about staying there overnight.

At dusk the lights were coming on in the hillside town of Eus, and the road was lined with orchards of peaches and cherries and fields of melons. West of Ille-sur-Têt the water lay still in the great dam at Rodès, and a few kilometres further along the final rays of the sun picked out the strange conical rock formations of les Orgues. We still hadn't found anywhere to sleep.

On and on we drove, through a whole load of nothingness — a fine road surface lined with broom in bloom, and nothing else but trees and a slow river. There were no houses, and absolutely nowhere to camp. We drove into Perpignan and became rather lost in some seedy side streets populated with dubious-looking people, and it took a seeming age to escape into the vivid pink-striped sunset, until we eventually reached the Mediterranean coast at Saint-Cyprien. In a scruffy car park beside a large harbour where several hundred yachts were rubbing fenders, half a dozen camper vans were parked up. It was after 11.00 p.m. when we crept in amongst them and fell asleep in no time.

4

THE MEDITERRANEAN — PITCH-FORKS GROWING ON TREES

When we woke at 8.00 a.m. Saint-Cyprien was mostly still asleep apart from a few joggers, some dog walkers, and a camel belonging to the circus standing in a field looking at the sea. After the restrictions to their freedom during our trans-Pyrenean interlude the dogs raced madly around the beach, watched disapprovingly by the camel. We stood in the sunshine, on the sand, beside the sea, looking at the snowy mountains of Spain, while Dobbie plunged into the Mediterranean and Tally in his demure way preferred to trot about on the sands. The harbour was a jungle of jingling masts overlooked by low-rise apartment blocks glowing warmly pink and terracotta in the rising sunshine, enhanced by oleander bushes and palm trees.

We turned Tinkerbelle northwards, and began our voyage up the Mediterranean coast: past the Etang de Canet and the fishermen's huts of twigs and thatch; through

Canet-en-Roussillon whose skyline was laddered with cranes; in and out of the thick sea-mist enveloping Sainte-Marie, and into relatively undeveloped Saint-Laurent-de-la-Salanque. Tinkerbelle's engine-cooling fan was working again, as if she was relieved to be at sea level. We didn't have the heart to tell her the Alps lay ahead.

At le Barcarès we sat on the beach looking out to a sea that was very deep blue, eating peaches, apricots, cherries and grapes, thinking what a very enjoyable time we were having. Back once more on the beach, the dogs agreed.

We made our way to the municipal campsite at Leucate-Plage, where the *gardien* invited us to install ourselves wherever we liked, and then return to the office with our passports, to check in. Having found a mutually acceptable parking area in a grove of tamarisk trees, I walked 300 metres to find the loo. I couldn't get in because I didn't have the requisite 'badge' that was issued to campers. However, I found a ginger-haired campsite worker who obliged and let me in. Then I walked the 300 metres back to Tinkerbelle to get our passports that I'd forgotten, and back 400 metres to the office where the *gardien* needed to know the number of our plot, which I hadn't noted. So

I trudged 400 metres back to Tinkerbelle, made a note of the number and returned the 400 metres to the office. Having successfully registered us, I bought a token for the washing machine, walked 400 metres back to Tinkerbelle, collected our mountain of dirty laundry, walked 300 metres back to the laundry room, loaded the machines, walked the 300 metres back to Tinkerbelle and sat down to wait for the machines to finish their cycles so I could undertake the 600-metre round trip to unload them.

'You've been gone a long time,' said Terry. 'Where have you been?'

*　*　*

The large campsite was just a few metres from a perfect beach and populated by brigades of sparrows that bounced along the sandy paths like clockwork toys. The weather was entirely to my taste, pleasantly warm without being uncomfortably hot. The strong wind that blows on the coast for about three hundred days a year keeps the clouds and rain away, and the surfers and sailboarders flying. With rows of washing flapping in the trees all around us, we sat enjoying the sea air for a few hours, having digested the warnings issued at the campsite office regarding earthquakes, which we were heartened to discover were prevalent in the area. There were three things to remember when a quake struck: not to panic, to evacuate buildings, and to return to our tent or van. We settled down to read while waiting to see whether we'd be caught by an earthquake.

Under the tamarisk trees the dogs were relaxed and happy lying in the sand; above in the very bright blue sky the gulls circled, crying like young babies. An elderly gentleman walked by laden with shopping; he nodded to us and stopped to talk. His name was André and he lived in Quebec, but was currently touring around Europe visiting members of his family and having medical treatment in France for cancer. His shopping bags were full of cat food, because while he was staying on the campsite he was trying to rescue as many of the stray cats there as possible. Those that he could catch he took to the local vet, who was able to find homes for them. There were several cat baskets, beds and bowls, and boxes and tins of cat food stacked up neatly in and around his camper, and he was worried what would happen to the cats when he had to move on.

André was a most charming man, well into his eighties and still fit and handsome. He talked about his life in France during the war when he'd been a young man working for a French company building airfields for the Germans. He said refugees from Paris and the provinces had been refused any help from the French living in the countryside, even a glass of water. And despite the stories of how the Germans were going to cut the hands off French children to prevent their being able to fight, when the Germans entered Paris it was they who fed the starving Parisians.

We also met an English couple and spent an entertaining evening drinking too much wine with them. They regaled us with tales of their life in Papua New Guinea where his job was setting up cattle ranches, and he described how he was able to find suitable land by using the services of a CIA satellite in return for supplying them with information. He also told us the frightful tale of an English lady 'pack-raped' — a strange term that we'd never heard before — by a gang of Papuans, and how they'd been arrested and imprisoned; they'd taken revenge on their victim by getting their friends to go and pack-rape her, too. We thought we wouldn't bother visiting Papua New Guinea.

Nudity was forbidden at the Leucate municipal campsite, which was just as well because I was beginning to look like a porpoise. We took the dogs on to the beach,

196

and although the sand wasn't as fine and powdery as in Brittany, there were dunes for galloping through and a horizon of three stripes — the yellow of the sand, the aquamarine of the sea, and the powder blue of the sky. From the hillside a cluster of pretty peach-coloured houses overlooked the Golfe du Lion. A bicycle went past towing a small trailer flying the skull and crossbones, with a very superior Labrador sitting in it. Tally and Dobbie were outraged by this blatant display of one-upmanship, and bawled at the other dog, who sailed serenely past them with his nose in the air.

Before we left Leucate next morning, past the Fitou vineyards shrouded in morning mist, I asked the *gardien* at the campsite where we'd be most likely to see flamingos, and he said at the African Zoo in Sigean, and that it was unlikely we'd see any in the wild. One of several things we didn't want to do in the south of France was visit an African zoo. In the marshlands between la Palme and Port-la-Nouvelle we saw many kinds of waterbirds, including egrets and herons. Port-la-Nouvelle is a delightfully pretty town whose bright pink, wide pavements give it a splendidly cheerful appearance, and there was a particularly striking house in Sigean painted mustard yellow with bright-blue shutters.

Strange how such colours can look absolutely right in one place, when in another part of the world they'd look simply ghastly. It must be something to do with the light and the indigenous vegetation.

Dawdling along the coastline beside the Etang de Bages et de Sigean, we glanced at a lake on our left and in it, with their long necks curled up just like the croquet mallets from *Alice's Adventures in Wonderland*, was an aurora of maybe three hundred flamingos, on one leg (each — not between them), talking to each other in goose-like croaks. A few of them took off and flew directly overhead, showing us the vivid dark pink and black undersides of their wings. We stood watching them for half an hour while munching chunks of cheese and peaches, before continuing through the tropically attractive village of Bages with its houses painted in vibrant colours and gardens bursting with fig trees, palms, bamboos, roses and ivy, and the traffic-calming technique of troughs across the road. A fleet of fishing boats bobbed quietly in a lake tinted blue and green, in the shade of some rocks with houses perched precariously on top of them.

Just outside Grand Mandirac on the river, the last of the Canal du Midi barges was being brought back to life. Built of oak in

Toulouse in 1855 to transport wine barrels the length of the canal, the 26-metre-long *Marie-Thérèse* had suffered the terrible humiliation of being turned into a nightclub in Sète and later a truck-drivers' restaurant until 1992. In 1994 le Conservatoire Maritime et Fluvial des Pays Narbonnais rescued what was left of her, and they've spent ten long years of hard work to turn her into a floating museum of the Canal du Midi.

'*Cimetière marin*' said a sign in Gruissan, so off we went along the bumpiest, dustiest little road we'd ever been on for what seemed like miles and miles, until we arrived in a peaceful grove of trees and vines, where there were gravestones dotted around telling poignant stories. Gruissan's sailors used to pray at the tiny church of Our Lady of Eternal Hope that they'd return safely from their voyages and they left offerings to encourage Our Lady to keep a watchful eye over them. The collection of gifts, known as *ex-votos*, was stolen in 1968 — how mean can a person be? They've been replaced by *trompe l'œil* paintings. There are no bodies up there in the sunny grove looking down to the sea — the headstones are simply memorials to those lost at sea. Somewhat bizarrely in this remote and barely accessible place, there was a large piece of cardboard propped up against a tree displaying the telephone number of somebody who was interested in buying violins.

We bumped our way down from the marine cemetery to Narbonne-Plage, where near the port a group of men were playing pétanque on the side of the road, in the shade; one of them looked as if he had stepped off the set of *The Godfather*, with his black homburg hat and the thick gold chain round his neck. The high-density housing was tasteful and beautifully landscaped, although even here the roads were corrugated and bone-shaking. We gave Narbonne the bumpy-road award. Without any particular idea of where we were going we ended up in a time-warped little village called les Cabanes de Fleury, where progress seemed to have stopped a century ago. There were several camper vans parked in the village car park, so we joined them and bought an inflatable football from the shop nearby to amuse the dogs. It lasted for 1 minute 42 seconds before Tally succeeded in puncturing it, but they enjoyed playing with it in its deflated state anyway.

I went to the campsite and asked if I could have some of their brochures, and came away with a handful, including one issued by the local council describing the hazards we might encounter while staying there: not earthquakes as at Leucate, but floods from high tides on the Aude; forest fires due to the vegetation, *garrigues*, and resinous trees; and poisoning caused by the transportation of dangerous materials on the A9. There were thorough recommendations as to what to do in any of these events. In case of flood we must get to high ground, close doors and windows, disconnect gas and electricity, not collect our children from school — the schools would take care of them — and listen to the radio for information. Similarly for fires, where we should close the shutters and water the walls, open our gates and lock ourselves in a building; if attacked by dangerous chemicals, do all these things, but don't smoke or light a flame. We shouldn't use the telephone, but leave the lines free for the emergency services.

The roads in Fleury were lined with fruiting mulberry trees, and the beaches were not of the sunbathing/swimming kind, being submerged under layers of dried flotsam and jetsam, driftwood and detritus; they were therefore a paradise for Dobbie who is a natural scavenger and who kept galloping up to us with unspeakable things hanging from his grinning jaws. Shoals of fishermen sat along the banks of the inlet fishing with rod and line, and stretched across the river was what we were told was the very last globe fishing net in France. Like an enormous trampoline which spanned the inlet, the net was raised and lowered by electric winch every five minutes, when any catch was removed by the operator from a small boat and despatched straight to a teeny little shop on the quayside. You couldn't find fresher fish anywhere. The couple who do the fishing and selling are M. and Mme Affre. Mme Affre's greatgrandfather had fished there in 1902, at a time when several dozen fishermen took turns to have the fishing rights for one week at a time. Mme Affre showed us the brick oven where before the days of nylon the old-fashioned cotton fishing nets had to be cured, then rinsed and draped outside to dry in the sun to make them last. She was a friendly lady with very green eyes, and told us that one of her relatives had a headstone marker at the marine cemetery. Looking around at les Cabanes de Fleury, we couldn't imagine that it had changed much over the last hundred years. It was a really unspoilt little backwater, forgotten by time and only used by the local fishermen: some neat houses, a small shop, a bakery and a couple of restaurants. We had a particularly fine dinner at the Globe: fish soup, mussels in garlic cream, and *rascasse en papillote*. The owner told us that the house across from the restaurant on the opposite bank of the estuary had featured in the Louis de Funes film *Le Petit Baignard*.

Early the next morning we headed for the beach, expecting to have it to ourselves at 7.00 a.m., but already local fishermen were arriving on scooters and bicycles. It was an intensively fishy place: everywhere you looked there were fishing lines, fishing nets, fishing men, and a smell, that was not at all unpleasant, of fish. It was the kind of place we could imagine any fisherman would be happy to retire to. From sleepy Fleury we drove to the busy centre of Valras-Plage with its casino, and apartment blocks called Hollywood and Kansas City, with carved Red Indians and totem poles all over the place, and quickly on to Sérignan to buy the most excellent *turron noire*, a sort of nougat made with dark honey, pistachios and almonds, which we ate for breakfast. It had been several weeks since we'd had any contact with the outside world, apart from phone calls to Vivien, and we thought we'd venture into Béziers to find a cybercafé. However, encountering a traffic jam stretching far into the distance we felt that whatever our e-mail inbox held it was unlikely to be sufficiently important to warrant sitting in a roasting camper van in a traffic jam for an indefinite period, and Terry did a nifty U-turn and took us on to the Bassin de Thau.

The cybercafé search was similarly unfruitful in hectic Sète, where helpful people directed us in myriad opposing directions all several kilometres from each other, separated by many hundreds of cars nose to tail. At each of our destinations there was no cybercafé. We began wondering whether locals amused themselves by sending foreigners on wild goose chases just for fun, but decided that it was merely a divine message that there was nothing of any note requiring our attention, and headed off for lunch. I can't remember why we weren't talking to each other at this particular point, but we weren't; probably I'd been held responsible for the state of the traffic. When we found another large flock of flamingos in the marshes between Sète and Frontignan, we stopped to admire them in silence for a while. Over lunch at a restaurant called l'Imprévu on the N112 we thawed out over a *pot au feu au poisson* and a Greek salad. There were times when we were irritable with each other, probably because we were sometimes tired and frequently lost. Terry would drive for up to seven hours a day over what could be very difficult roads, in temperamental Tinkerbelle with her attention-attracting exhaust and unpredictable gearbox, while I was responsible for the navigation which is not my strong point, and occasionally we found ourselves driving backwards and forwards over the same difficult roads. Added to that was the fact that we were living in close quarters for twenty-four hours a day, something neither of us was used to. But on the whole we got on very well and were thoroughly enjoying our adventure.

Montpellier, pretty city, wasn't being spared by the developers who seemed to be swarming all over the Mediterranean coast. Every town we passed was playing host to crowds of bulldozers and cranes, dumper trucks and road rollers. Outside Castries we came across the unusual sight of a small vineyard that was completely dead: every vine was brown and withered, as if it had been deliberately destroyed. Usually we followed the roads round the edge of the country but from time to time we wandered into the interior, which is what we did after leaving Montpellier, driving through rough scrubby countryside of grass and woodlands, the ground very bright and white, glaring in the sun. In the quiet and peaceful town of Sommières, where Lawrence Durrell lived for many years until his death, we came unexpectedly across a cybercafé in the local tourist office, and after half an hour of struggling with a French keyboard confirmed what we had expected — during the several weeks we'd been travelling nothing of note had arrived by e-mail. So we went merrily on until we reached the picturesque medieval town of Sauve in the Cévennes area of the Gard, where the pitchforks grow on trees.

The Conservatoire des Fourches is housed in the old cobble-floored barracks in Sauve. Dominique Sevajol, the lady in charge, most obligingly stopped what she was doing to give us a personal conducted tour. She's passionate about the pitchforks and their fascinating history.

The micocoulier tree, a member of the elm family also known as the hackberry tree, naturally grows very straight. In Sauve these trees are grown and lovingly transformed by hand into three-pronged pitchforks by a technique used for twelve centuries, and probably invented by the Saracens, or the Chinese. When it's just a young fellow the tree is pruned to encourage it to grow in the shape of a trident. Once it's attained the right height it's cut, placed on a rack in the left-hand side of a deep brick oven, and smoked at a temperature of 100°C. The tree 'whistles' to indicate when it's ready to come out, still supple enough to go through the metal rollers which bend and shape the tines into their classic curves. The bark is stripped off, and a narrow strip is wound round the neck of the pitchfork, which goes back into the oven, but this time on the right-hand side, over embers made from the otherwise redundant bark. The oven door is sealed with a mixture of ash and water, and the fork is smoked again for eighteen hours during which time the wood will harden and turn a deep golden brown, resistant to pests. When it comes out, it's a perfect wooden pitchfork, and once the bark is peeled from the neck it leaves the exclusive Sauve 'necktie' design.

'*Très snob!*' Dominique laughed.

Once it's been polished, except for a length at the end, and the tines trimmed, the new pitchfork matures for a year. The unpolished end of the haft makes it non-slip for sweaty hands. The originators of this labour-intensive technique had thought of everything. Dominique's grandfather used the same pitchfork for forty years. But who buys the finished article these days, we asked Dominique.

'Well, they're very good for working with feathers, because they're antistatic. People working with livestock in close proximity like them because they can't hurt the animals. And lots of people buy them simply as decoration.'

If you're near Sauve, do visit the Conservatoire. At €30 each the pitchforks aren't being made for money, but for the sake of keeping the ancient art alive. Unfortunately we couldn't think of any way at all we could keep one in Tinkerbelle and out of Dobbie's jaws until we got back home.

★   ★   ★

Making our way back towards the coast we followed the D1 towards Clarensac, from where there was the most stunning view down over the plains, an amazing panorama in the misty blue heat. We passed a string of peaceful medieval villages where old men played boules in the shade of the plane trees, and water spurted from fountains guarded by life-sized stone lions. People stared as we negotiated the narrow lanes, as if they'd never before seen a foreign-registered camper van with two large dogs looking out of the windows, or heard one making quite such a noise. We met that rarity, a rude French person, in the shape of a young woman driving a car not very competently the wrong way down a one-way street. Arriving nose to nose with Tinkerbelle she flicked one imperious hand at us indicating her command that we should reverse. Terry switched off Tinkerbelle's engine for a while, as the woman became more and more irate, but as she was plainly not going to be able to reverse her vehicle we were obliged to back ours. Because I've always found French people to be almost excessively courteous, it still comes as a surprise to meet one who isn't.

Our next destination was the town of Vauvert where we were looking for the unusual chocolate produced by the Pâtisserie Jouval. They'd recently moved premises and we had great difficulty in finding this wonderland of sugary goodies, where M. Robert Jouval follows in his father's footsteps, producing exquisite cakes and sweets for the discriminating palate. Mme Jouval is a handsome lady with a large smile, and she explained the origin of their novel chocolates, which are flavoured with Camarguais *fleurs de sel*. The local salt producers from the Salins du Midi wanted something special to offer their customers as a gift, and asked M. Jouval what he could create. What he came up with were flat, very dark triangular chocolates stamped with the word *Salins* and filled with a delicate ganache containing a few crystals of *fleurs de sel*. It's a new, sophisticated and rather refreshing taste; not, to my mind, quite such a revelation as the pimento chocolate from Espelette, but still very edible. We bought a box of them and some cakes, which Mme Jouval wrapped so lovingly it felt sacrilegious to open them.

Letting out my waistband another notch to make room for a few hundred grams of salty chocolate, we continued our drive down to le Grau-du-Roi and the sprawling busy campsite there, past white Camargue horses tethered in their dozens along the roadsides, saddled, bored and perfuming the air with the delicious fragrance of sweating horseflesh. Getting into the campsite wasn't a simple matter because a fearsome security guard blocked the entrance, staring at us suspiciously, asking if our dogs were pit bull terriers and whether we had full documentation for them (we did), and barking so many questions that he made me feel guilty about nothing. When we'd overcome that hurdle, the next one was finding somewhere to park amongst the disorganized and chaotic assembly. Although our initial opinion of the site was less than enthusiastic because it was so seemingly shambolic, and our parking space very small, the beach was superb. A Colditz-type fence round the site prevented intruders from finding their way in, and a bodyguard waited at the gate to bash them if they tried; after that was a 500-metre band of dark-brown, coarse sandy salt, followed by some small sandy dunes, and then the beach itself, delicious hot sands caressed by warm Mediterranean waters. It was so far from the campsite entrance to the sea that a string of tractor-towed wooden carriages ferried campers backwards and forwards. With Tally and Dobbie in tow we declined the transport, and enjoyed their delight in charging around after a couple of days when they hadn't really had an opportunity to let rip. A couple of elderly French people were foraging amongst the webbed footprints in the damp sand for *tellines*, chucking them into two yellow plastic pails. Terry was quite successful when he copied them, coming up with handfuls of the tiny shellfish and a small crab, too, all of which he threw back. The last time we'd been in the Camargue was nearly twenty years previously, and it had been a torture of blistering heat and voracious mosquitoes, but this time it was as perfect as you could wish, and I lay plumply and lazily on the sands while Terry gave Dobbie his first swimming lesson. Tally watched with mild interest and wouldn't be tempted out of his depth, but Dobbie didn't

211

need any encouragement and was prepared to swim out to Terry no matter how far it was.

On the way next day we were overflown by another flock of flamingos. They're so ungainly in flight with their large heads stuck out in front of them on outstretched necks, and their legs dangling behind them. Why don't they fold themselves up into neat parcels in flight like herons?

Pyramids of bright-white and murky-grey salt lay heaped outside the Baleine plant at les Salins du Midi in Aigues-Mortes, the perfectly preserved thirteenth-century fortified town originally built as a launching pad for the Crusades. Within the grim five-metre-thick walls of the Constance tower a fifteen-year-old Huguenot girl was imprisoned in the eighteenth century because her brother was a Protestant minister. Marie Durand spent thirty-eight years locked in the tower, caring for and inspiring her fellow women prisoners until her release in 1767. Imagine: to be in the malarial salt marshes, in a prison that was freezing in the winter and roasting in the summer, and to be able to survive. Or even to want to. Now, in the twenty-first century, parents in Aigues-Mortes keep their children in line by telling them that if they misbehave, the magical horse Lou Drape will come by night and take hem away to an unknown fate.

The Listel vineyards dominate the landscape around Aigues-Mortes, where the vines grow from a sandy soil which gives the 'vins des sables' their characteristic flavour. Once the vines have dropped their leaves in early autumn, the ground is planted to cereals, to prevent the light soil's being blown away by the wind. During the winter sheep graze on the resulting crops, which they convert into organic fertilizer. In the mid-nineteenth century some evil little bugs hitched a lift on vine cuttings imported into Bordeaux from the United States (shades of the Trojan horse here, methinks). The vines' deadliest enemy, the devastating phylloxera, had arrived. Within ten years the French wine industry was decimated, except for the sandy-soiled vineyards which are immune to the killer disease. The life cycle of the phylloxera insect is awesomely complex, beginning when a minuscule leaf-eating aphid lays eggs of two sizes — male and female — and progressing, through larvae that kill the roots and ultimately the vine, into pupae which release the egg-laying aphids. They can crawl, fly or blow on the wind to wreak their havoc on neighbouring vineyards.

Although the Listel vineyards can smugly ignore the threat of phylloxera, their existence hasn't been without its difficulties. During the Second World War the German occupation disrupted production and left behind an unwelcome legacy of 35,000 landmines planted to thwart any attempted Allied invasion. These all had to be harvested before the vineyards could be revived.

We travelled through rice fields and a desolate, scrubby landscape where the livestock glowed with good health and seemed to thrive on the sparse vegetation. Signs offered *promenades à cheval* on the tethered white horses, or visits to see the black bulls raised on the *mas*. On the tiddly Bac de Sauvage ferry it took just a few minutes to cross the narrow Petit Rhône lined with boats and fishing platforms. Passing through Saintes-Maries-de-la-Mer, gypsy capital of the Camargue, and up the western edge of the Etang de Vaccarès, past herds of black bulls, white horses, and pink flamingos, we stopped at Mas Neuf to climb a viewing platform and look out over the marshes at horses with their foals, glowing clouds of flamingos, and a coypu with outsize yellow teeth munching its way through a sea of floating weed.

Our arrival in Arles wasn't initially auspicious because we were caught up in the traffic and seemed unable to escape from it; even being rude to each other didn't do any good, and it wasn't until we'd found and established ourselves at a campsite, where it was raining, that we started speaking to each other again.

On the way to Arles we'd seen posters advertising an air show the following day, and we agreed that while Terry, a pilot, went off with Tinkerbelle and the dogs to indulge his passion for aircraft, I could wander freely around Arles for a few hours. Terry just loves supermarkets and would happily spend all day roaming the aisles, and I absolutely hate them, but I do like to meander quietly and at leisure through the streets of strange towns, which Terry doesn't. It seemed like a most equitable arrangement, and on a morning blessed with warm sunshine following an overnight thunderstorm we said our *au revoirs*, and arranged to rendezvous later in the day by mobile phone, one of the rare occasions when we found any use for the things.

My first stop was at the tourist office in the centre of town, where a helpful lady named Isabelle told me where to find a cybercafé, and the most interesting parts of the town, and that I shouldn't miss the *courses camarguaises* taking place that afternoon. She assured me that in that most popular local sport no harm came to the participating cattle, and drew a small map so that we could find our way there.

I started exploring Arles by threading my way through the market, a typically French affair which was at the same time tremendously cosmopolitan. Mingling with chic, tanned and fashionably dressed locals were groups of veiled Middle Eastern and North African ladies in their discreet clothing. Amongst stalls selling cheeses, olives, spit-roasted chickens, dried sausages, breads, rice, garlic and honey, the Catholic Aid Society was selling used clothes. There were colourful ceramics, bunches and sachets of aromatic herbs, glistening fruits and vegetables, gorgeous linens, and in the middle of it all a musical merry-go-round. Racks of jeans hung next to pots of olive trees, bougainvillaeas and other vivid, exotic plants that glowed and smelt wonderful; there were oil paintings, sun glasses, natural, inexpensive cotton clothing, hammocks. At a leatherware stall a colossally fat man was trying to buy a belt. I don't know that I'd ever seen a man with such a vast girth, and it was quite obvious that even the very largest belt on the stall wouldn't go anywhere near round him. A crowd collected and people rummaged through the belts looking for one that might fit. Somebody joined two together, but they still weren't nearly long enough. There was a great deal of laughter and merriment and the stallholder produced a tape measure and proposed to have a belt custom-made for the fat man — but the tape measure was way too short.

There'd been a minor traffic incident and one driver was threatening to punch another. I watched them hopefully for a couple of minutes, but after a loud exchange of words they both drove off. A truck was trying to tow another by means of a rather thin piece of string, which broke repeatedly. It reminded me of something. I walked on through stalls selling straw hats and espadrilles, lawn mowers, saddlery and cages of livestock, dried flowers and incense, and soap in a hundred different perfumes from a stall playing a tape of chirping crickets. I got completely lost in the back streets before emerging into the square in front of the *hôtel de ville* where four men with violins, a cello and an accordion were playing 'Hava Nagila'. I went to look at the monument to the Resistance, a striking sculpture of a group of naked men. A bicycle went past towing a luxurious trailer flying a flag that said 'Dog Taxi'. I like looking at roofs and chimneys and shutters, and Arles is a great place to do that. There were wrought-iron balconies housing pots of bright flowers, and a fine collection of shutters that weren't new or pretty but picturesque and intriguing. In a rather seamy little side street flaking grey wooden shutters framed a second-floor window sill decorated with golden suns and hanging plants, and a family of grinning ceramic cats. The houses were colourful: pink and green, cream and blue, yellow and pink. No wonder poor tortured Van Gogh chose to live in this town of 'blue tones and gay colours', until he cut off his ear because of a quarrel with his friend Gauguin, and was encouraged by the Arlesians to go and live somewhere else.

I'd no desire to visit the Roman theatre. I've always disliked these arenas with their history of death and suffering, the atmosphere of centuries of cruelty clinging to them, the sound of voices baying for blood and screams of pain still echoing round the old stones.

On one corner of a street lined with restaurants and bars a grey-bearded man sat on the pavement playing a tom-tom, while his dog, who looked very much like a pit bull terrier, lay on her back with her legs in the air offering admirers the opportunity of tickling her voluptuous belly; another man stood nearby playing a violin. There appeared to be two sorts of drivers in Arles: the first were males and polite, stopping to wave pedestrians across in front of them through the chaotic traffic. The second were female and all rude, impatient and not terribly competent.

I enjoyed Arles enormously: the knowledge that Caesar's legions had stamped around here, and the vestiges of buildings they'd left behind; the noise and smell of the place, the Provençal colours. If I was going to live in a town, Arles would be a contender high up on my list if it wasn't for the city's unfortunate passion for bullfighting. Stamp collecting, cricket, trainspotting, macramé or Morris dancing I could live with if I had to. Bullfighting, no. I'd been happily roaming for less than two hours when my phone rang, and Terry asked how I was enjoying myself.

'Fabulous. I love it here. What about the air show?' I asked. 'How is it? Are you having a great time?'

'Not really,' he said. 'It's model aeroplanes, I don't want to see them and I've been sitting in a car park for the last hour.'

I couldn't expect him to sit all day in a car park in Tinkerbelle with the dogs, so we arranged to meet in twenty minutes. In the meantime I was in urgent need of a tiddle, but the public toilets were those nasty steel windowless cylinders and I was terrified of getting into one and not being able to escape from it. I approached a woman and asked if she'd be kind enough to stand outside for a couple of minutes and help me if the thing wouldn't open, but she looked at me very strangely and quickly ran away, so I went into a bar and bought a Coke so I could use their loo.

One of the market stalls was selling bread in a range of shapes, sizes and colours, and I'd asked the owner to cut me half of a gigantic rustic cottage loaf when I realized I didn't have any money with me, having spent the few pennies I was carrying on the Coke. I rummaged about in my bag and pockets, and found just a few worthless little coins. I apologized to the man, but he laughed, took my purse and shook it, kept the coins that amounted to almost nothing plus an English sixpence, and insisted I take the great hunk of bread.

Terry somehow managed to get to where we'd agreed to meet, negotiating the manic traffic which grew even worse as the market started packing up for the day. We went to find a quiet spot for a lunchtime picnic, before going to watch the *courses camarguaises*. We could see where we wanted to go, a quiet residential road beside the river, and drove down an exceptionally narrow little lane to reach it, discovering halfway that we were going the wrong way down a one-way street, and having to back up while oncoming drivers hooted and shouted and pulled faces. Eventually we reached our destination and tied the dogs to the iron railings in the wall at the side of the Rhône, so we could all watch the barges going up and down the river while we ate our lunch. While we were in Tinkerbelle assembling our meal a loud panic-stricken yelp signalled that all was not well. Dobbie had gone over the wall and was dangling from his collar over a six-metre near-perpendicular drop, his paws desperately scrabbling on the stone until Terry hauled him carefully back up so that he didn't slip out of his collar. He arrived back on the pavement with a toothy smile, wagging his tail and not seeming at all disturbed by his misadventure.

After lunch we set off to an out-of-town arena for our first experience of *courses camarguaises*. Two of the organizers, slim and tanned, charming, sophisticated and courtly men with red bandannas above their open-necked check shirts, directed us into a shaded area where we could leave Tinkerbelle. Both spoke English and said they'd keep an eye on the dogs to make sure that they were all right.

One of them asked if we were fans of the *corrida*.

'No,' I said quite vehemently. 'We're absolutely against it.'

He shrugged. 'It's a pity. We have one tomorrow.'

'This afternoon, you aren't going to kill the bulls, are you? Because if so, we can't stay.'

'But no! This afternoon we just play with them. It's a game — you'll see that they enjoy it as much as we do.'

'You don't hurt them at all?'

'No. Absolutely not. Not today. But tomorrow,' his eyes lit up, 'we'll kill them.'

I could not reconcile these pleasant, couth men with the abhorrent and degrading activity of bullfighting. Don't misunderstand me. I could thoroughly enjoy it as a spectator just as long as both sides were on equal terms: one to one, and each armed only with a pair of horns.

An arrangement of two concentric circles of maroon-painted wooden boards propped up by robust scaffolding formed the arena. The inner circle was where the action took place, and the outer circle a place for the players to take refuge if they needed to. A man with a hose was watering the sandy ground to dampen the dust, while another man played a guitar and sang lustily. A dozen young teenage lads — *raseteurs* — dressed in white trousers and shirts, with red belts, leapt over the boards, bouncing from the ground to the scaffolding with the skill and zest of a bunch of monkeys, sprayed by the hosing man from time to time. As fast as he dampened the sand it dried out under the blistering afternoon heat.

A truck parked near the arena kept rocking and rolling and emitting bangs and crashes. On its roof two men prodded a pole into the back of the vehicle, trying to attach rosettes to the heads of cattle who, judging by the commotion issuing from inside, were putting up a spirited defence, or maybe they were just trying to smash the truck to bits. We sat melting while preparations took place: the crashing cattle, the leaping boys, the music, and the hosepiping man. Eventually the white-clad young *raseteurs* together with several adults positioned themselves round the arena, and with a great crash a young heifer was expelled from the truck into the alleyway leading into the ring, where she stood looking very small and utterly bewildered, before turning tail and scrambling clumsily over the boards into the outer circle. One of the officials chased her back into the ring, and she showed absolutely no pleasure at all in being there. All she wanted was to get back to the relatively secure truck. The second little heifer was much the same, and trotted half-heartedly towards the lads who raced in front of her raking at the rosette tied between her horns, until one waved it triumphantly aloft.

The third heifer didn't enjoy herself either, continually clambering over the boards and at one point falling and hurting herself. Blood stained her flank and foamed from the side of her mouth. Terry and I were finding it difficult to enjoy the afternoon, too. Although admiring the speed and acrobatic skills of the humans we couldn't see what the animals were getting out of it. Number four into the arena was a not-very-large black bull, who trotted proudly into the centre of the ring and stood pawing the ground, swinging his head around before selecting whom to charge. The boys easily leapt to safety, and the bull's attempts to reach them were very indifferent. As soon as one target ran he turned his attention to another. One of the adult *raseteurs* racing close to the bull's horns missed his footing as he leapt for the scaffolding and fell, landing heavily. Officials gathered round him and the activity in the arena stopped for five minutes until he limped away; his injuries weren't serious, and the men and boys resumed their game with the bull. It wasn't a very exciting spectacle, nor one that convinced us that the cattle were enthusiastic participants. It certainly has to be a better alternative to bullfighting, though, and maybe we weren't seeing the game at its best.

Unconvinced by the *courses camarguaises*, we continued our journey to Saint-Martin-de-Crau, and set about trying to find a particular campsite featured in our little bible of camping grounds, which said it was easy to find. We drove round and round, up and down, backwards and forwards, following miniature hand-painted signs that suddenly stopped at critical junctions; we asked local drivers who shook their heads, cyclists who shook their heads, pedestrians who shook their heads and a lady in a garden picking flowers who shook her head. None of them had ever heard of the address of the place, although one lady whom we stopped exclaimed, 'Ah, you're *campingcaristes*! So are we!'

Terry is never one to give up, and at very long last, after bumping down a track through some vineyards, we emerged into a ghastly scene of desolation and neglect, decaying vehicles and a large barking Rottweiler. It was a cul-de-sac and I asked Terry to turn round and get us out of there, because I wasn't staying the night in what looked like a scene from *The Texas Chainsaw Massacre à la provençal*. As Terry reversed in the narrow lane a pleasant-looking young woman came to the gate, smiling, and asked if she could help us.

'No, thank you,' I replied, 'we just came down here to turn round.'

How idiotic that must have sounded. How many people would drive two kilometres just to turn round? She looked a little disappointed and I felt quite embarrassed, but consoled myself by imagining that she was probably a decoy for a bunch of murderous French rednecks playing banjos on the back patio. I should imagine it was a reaction she was used to. It was such a sinister and untidy place.

We managed to find another campsite in the village, where a violent wind bashing into the plane trees sounded like a storm at sea and crashing waves on a beach, and the constant moving of the leaf shadows was hypnotic.

In the morning we were woken up by a loud shouting noise coming from next to the campsite; it sounded like the Pope holding Sunday Mass through a megaphone while on speed. It went on for so long that we had to investigate, and found that a local sports event was taking place. We strolled around the streets which were surprisingly lively for a Sunday morning, stopping at an excellent cake shop where I couldn't resist a little something to bolster the waistline. The campsite where we'd stayed belonged to a local hotel/restaurant, and we went for our morning drink and to pay our fees. The staff were hopping about like ants from a disturbed nest, but we managed to impale the attention of one girl long enough to order the drinks from her, although it took her a long time and a great deal of lip-biting concentration, and a little help from the manageress, to provide one cup of coffee and one of hot chocolate. When I asked if we could pay the camping fees she stared at me in panic, and turned round in a complete circle muttering to herself. The manageress, probably as intrigued as we were by this strange demonstration, came to ask if she could help, and I repeated that we wanted to pay what we owed. The look in her eyes plainly said she wished we'd just go quietly away and leave them to cope with the floods of customers pouring into the place, mostly gendarmes with side arms, but we stood our ground, and after two more people had come from the kitchen to ask what the problem was we managed to hand over the few euros required and were on our way.

Beautifully situated against a backcloth of rugged wooded hills and with its toes in the deep blue sea, Marseille claims to be France's oldest town, dating back to the arrival of Greek sailors 600 years before Christ. It was love at first sight for the sailors' leader and the local king's daughter, and they married the same day. With Greek expertise the town became a major Mediterranean trading post, and underwent a turbulent history of invasion and disease, punctuated by interludes of prosperity.

When we arrived, they seemed to have everything under control: Marseille's streets were busy without being chaotic, but that was probably because it was Sunday; the freight port was deserted except for a mountain of orange fishing floats. There were cranes all over the place, and raucous arm-waving men playing boules in small parks. Quite why boules players wave their arms so much I don't know, but they do. The harbour front heaved with pedestrians and diners lunching at seafood restaurants and pizza parlours, or sitting outside the Irish pub. Roads lined with slightly grimy but intriguing buildings ran uphill from the harbour into a giant buzzing honeycomb. Signs on the side of the road invited drivers to 'se garer au cheval' — park norse-style — a French way of saying cars may park on the pavement.

This might be a fitting place to discuss for a moment the guillotine, because it was in Marseille in 1977 that the last execution in France took place. Dr Guillotin was not the inventor of the machine, but he it was who proposed that capital punishment administered by decapitation would be a more humane method of execution than those previously practised, which were an extraordinary testament to man's inventiveness, but not to his humanity. The design took some time to perfect, and was helped along by a German harpsichord manufacturer. The first person to enjoy the fruits of Dr Guillotin's compassion was a highwayman called Jacques Nicolas Pelletier in 1792; we will never know, of course, his verdict on the guillotine as a tool of execution, but the French public didn't embrace it at all, because it despatched its customers with indecent haste, without providing any proper public spectacle. A serial killer named Eugene Weidmann was the last person *publicly* executed in France in 1939, and in 1977 a murderer named Hamida Djandoubi earned the distinction of being the last person in France to lose his head to the guillotine, here in Marseille, although he came close to losing the title in

1981, when Philippe Maurice was sentenced to death for killing a policeman. It was M. Maurice's great good fortune that the French Left snatched a surprise victory in the elections that year. President François Mitterrand reprieved M. Maurice, who subsequently served twenty-three years in prison, and is now a respected historian and campaigner against the death penalty throughout the world.

We went to visit Allauch, a pretty Provençal village and a favourite setting for Pagnol's stories. Allauch sits on Marseille's shoulder, perched on a hillside coloured by the flowers of prickly pears, and looking down over rooftops and a colourful extravaganza of green and gold tiles on the church spire on to the waters of the Mediterranean. In trying to reach the summit of the village to view the panorama stretching from Aix-en-Provence to Aubagne, we became trapped in the narrowest imaginable hairpin bend in the village where it seemed impossible that Terry could negotiate Tinkerbelle round and out of the place. Interested and amused pedestrians stood watching, and to their astonishment (and mine) he cleared the walls all round with nothing more than a coat of paint between them and Tinkerbelle's bodywork. I don't know who was more surprised.

Somebody applauded. Our dignified exit was slowed by a Pagnolesque character in the form of a bristly-faced, belligerent fat man in a string vest and braces, who waddled across the road in front of us, glaring sideways as he went.

As we climbed towards Sainte-Baume from Gémenos, the lush green landscape transformed into stunted little trees, and nets pinned to the sides of the hills to keep them in place. The road was wiggly and the visibility fading into almost nothing, so we admitted defeat and turned round, back through the Parc de St Pons and past the remains of the Cistercian abbey, where legend says virtuous nun Blanche de Simiane hurled herself to her death on the rocks, as an alternative to participating in an orgy proposed by some horsemen sheltering in the abbey from a storm. Five centuries later the rocks are still stained with Blanche's blood. The red marks could be due to red algae, of course, but that wouldn't make a good Provençal story.

The great clouds that had been encircling us opened up and emptied themselves with one huge sigh, so that Tinkerbelle's wipers could hardly move, but in Cugesles-Pins people strolled nonchalantly about in the rain in T-shirts and white cotton trousers or mini-skirts. Following the road back down towards the coast, we passed the Ranch Buffalo, *les amis de* Buffalo Bill, totem poles, wigwams, Wild West reconstructions and helter-skelters at the OK Corral theme park. Truly.

Leaving behind the Wild West, we were soon into a very pleasant forest populated by merry, rather short little pine trees, smelling delicious in the soggy wet air. There were no houses and no traffic, just large open spaces, woods and rocks. Thunder cracked and lightning flashed as we headed round sharp bends to the palm trees and pretty apartment blocks and houses of la Ciotat, where the skies were clear and the town was busy with kids on bikes weaving through impatient hooting traffic and ice-cream lickers, and the sea faded outwards from turquoise to dark, deep blue. La Ciotat may not be a very large town, but it has at least two claims to fame. First, it was the birthplace somewhere between 1907 and 1910 of pétanque, one of the many variations of games played with *boules*. A player named Jules le Noir, who was no longer able to participate in the more strenuous version of the game due to advancing decrepitude, created a new set of rules whereupon the game would be played with '*pieds tanqués*' — both feet planted on the ground. A plaque commemorates this event at the boulodrome named in M. le Noir's honour. Second, some years earlier, in 1895 the Lumières brothers had pioneered the moving picture industry, showing a film called *The Arrival of a Train in la Ciotat*.

We couldn't find a municipal campsite in la Ciotat, so we stayed at an extraordinarily expensive place boasting luxurious offices with leather sofas and potted palms, but where the camper vans and tents were jammed together like a refugee camp. To access what was described as the beach, we were given a code to tap into a heavy metal gate, which gave on to a barren narrow strip of uneven and lumpy rock growing out of a bad-tempered sea. We took the dogs for a walk along this place, and naturally Dobbie managed to fall off the rocks and into the sea where he bobbed around looking confused, and had to be fished out with considerable difficulty by Terry. We escaped from the refugee camp early the following morning into a grey curtain of drizzle. The sea was flat calm. Terry had ingeniously made a temporary repair to Tinkerbelle's gearbox by using a baked-bean tin, and also finally discovered how to adjust the driver's seat so that he could reach the clutch without having to extend his leg to its full length. After a month of struggling, with the gearbox and clutch now adjusted, driving had become less of an ordeal.

Mist floated halfway up the hills of the Var. It was warm and humid, the vegetation was tropical, and at 8.45 a.m. there was little traffic. Bandol was overrun with cement mixers and cranes, and decorated with palm trees and wild chicory growing at the roadsides. Crossing a small bridge we came round a bend to the sight of the sea on our left, and the bend went so far back upon itself that the sea then popped up on the right. Despite a beach that was just a narrow strip of pebbles, we voted Sanary-sur-Mer the prettiest village we'd seen so far, elegant, genteel and flowery. By mid-morning we hadn't yet found anywhere for our regular hot drinks, nor had we had anything to eat. Every *boulangerie* we passed was either closed or impossible to park near. We found a roadside stall selling fruit and agreed that we really should make a serious effort to control the expanding waistline and eat fruit as a healthier alternative to a croissant or a sticky bun. I joined the end of the modest queue of two old ladies, and waited patiently for a long time, my tummy rumbling loudly while old lady No. 1 talked and talked to the stallholder, who talked back to her. While talking No. 1 picked up dozens of pieces of fruit, turned them round, stroked or prodded them, sniffed them, and put them back on the pile. After ten minutes she was still talking, and hadn't selected a single piece of fruit. Old lady No. 2 had her arm in a splint, and I foresaw standing in the queue while these dear old ladies chatted and poked pieces of fruit until I died of starvation, so we abandoned the fruit-buying effort. Now sick with hunger we continued on our quest, skirting north of Toulon, following a rubble-laden municipal vehicle at snail's pace up a long, winding, wooded road leading to Mont Faron, until we eventually came upon a bakery that was not only open and near a parking place, but next door to a large shop selling all types of fresh and dried fruits and vegetables, spices and herbs. In a frenzy of hunger we filled a trolley with crystallized ginger and halva, sun-dried tomatoes, apricots, melons, nuts, strawberries and grapes; from the bakery we bought a fragrant baguette and half a dozen florentines, and sat munching madly for ten minutes before setting off again in search of coffee in Hyères, whose flowery delights we were able to enjoy at leisure while sitting for half an hour in one of their traffic jams.

It had been raining since Toulon and it was

still doing so when we reached le Lavandou, where the inhabitants walked around in clinging nylon raincoats and jackets. Le Lavandou was busy, trafficky and pretty with bougainvillaea, acacias, eucalyptus and coniferous trees, boats bobbing cheerfully at anchor in the harbour, and the sea on our right dented by occasional small coves.

Just as we reached Cavalaire the sun emerged rather timidly; the sea looked like a slightly creased sheet of aluminium, flat and silvery-grey in the weak sunshine. The US 3rd Infantry and First Division of the Free French landed in the bay of Cavalaire on 15 August 1944 in an operation code-named Dragoon. Their landings, which met with less ferocious resistance than those of their comrades in Normandy, are commemorated by several large memorials in the bay.

The view on to the Corniche des Maures was beautiful, the hilltops smothered in trees in this pleasantly wild stretch of coastline along which we wiggled over green little hills and through pine forests to Saint-Tropez, where it was once again raining. We lunched overlooking the gulf of St Tropez and watching yachts racing in the rain. The Riviera is, in relentless drizzle, as uninviting as anywhere else, in two-tone grey: the light grey of the sky and deeper grey of the sea.

Colour came from bobbing umbrellas reflected from puddles on the pavement; the gutters ran with grey water, and irritable women tugged soggy little children about. In modest Tinkerbelle we were smugly warm, dry and cosy.

After lunch we drove round the gulf to Sainte-Maxime, and the les Eléphants beach. This is where elephants come from all over the world for their annual holidays to frolic on the sands and splash around in the shallows. No it isn't really, I'm afraid. It's named after the Belgian author Jean de Brunhoff, who created the Babar books and lived in the area for many years.

Even in the rain it was a pretty drive along the coast to Fréjus, where we were delayed by a group of grim gendarmes taking measurements around a mangled motorbike at a road junction. To avoid the tumultuous traffic in Fréjus we bypassed the Corniche d'Or and took the N7, past the memorial to the dead of the Indo-China war, through the Forêt de l'Esterel, past Mont Vinaigre and the village of les Adrets, where Gaspard de Besse, the legendary eighteenth-century French Robin Hood, used to meet one of his lady-loves. The rain had fizzled out and the air was fresh and clean, filtered by the trees in this leafy place amongst the pink rocks, as we made our way into the Alpes-Maritimes and down to la Napoule and the Côte d'Azur. By the time we reached Cannes the sun had come out. In the harbour hundreds of yacht masts rattled between the motor cruisers, and amongst the bleak and dreary metal-shuttered apartments lining the promenade the only building with class was the Carlton. At one end of the narrow empty strand, neatly brushed and combed like a small boy's hair, a giant earth-moving machine was scooping up the dirty beach and replacing it with clean imported sand. Some kind of eatery on the seedy stretch between Cannes and Antibes was advertising the 'new 100 per cent vegetable chicken', whatever on earth that was.

At least Cannes had been blessed with sunshine. By the time we reached Antibes it was raining again, and we headed for a campsite located on the other side of a bridge whose height limit was five centimetres less than Tinkerbelle's declared height but which she somehow managed to squeeze under unscathed. At the campsite a charming Charles Aznavour lookalike met us at the gate and escorted us to an *emplacement*, after peering at the dogs and saying jokingly, 'Ah, what handsome pit bulls!' He was a friendly man with a bad heart, who rode around the site on an electric Trotinette. We took the dogs for a walk in the rain, which they didn't really appreciate, then sat reading for a few hours waiting for the deluge to abate, which it didn't, so we settled down for the night to the sound of raindrops beating on the roof, aeroplanes growling overhead, and cars, trucks and trains rumbling and rattling along nearby. The campsite's showers scored top marks. Endless floods of lovely hot water.

Next morning the weather had cleared when we went to explore the old town of Antibes, and admire some of the gleaming white and silver boats like small ocean-going liners moored in the harbour. I made it clear to Terry that if one day we had to have a boat, it would have to be one like that, or not at all.

We followed the Baie des Anges towards Nice, along the stony beach north of Antibes which was dotted with scruffy vans selling fast food. The sea there was a particularly pretty colour, a milky greeny-blue. Looming ahead of us in Villeneuve-Loubet a new apartment block was a most peculiar design: it looked rather like a coliseum that something had started eating at the edges. Nice was really very pretty, with wide palm-lined avenues and a space-age airport building, although the omnipresent cranes were active, putting up large new buildings wherever there was an empty space. Overlooking the stony beach were long rows of five-to six-storey rather soulless apartment blocks, with wonderful sea views, and tucked between them odd, ancient, flaking buildings where we imagined old people living, who'd lived there for decades and had no intention of moving aside for property developers: little old ladies who wouldn't go away. These old buildings, and a fantastic, wildly decorated little house with a cupola and a statue of a nude in the courtyard, lent much-needed charm where it was otherwise rather lacking. On the Promenade des Anglais flags of the world's nations flapped slowly; there were few people about, and little traffic, so it was a good time to be there to view the flamboyant Negresco. On the other hand, we found the art nouveau Palais de la Méditerranée disappointingly dull. The most attractive area was round the harbour, which was lined with old Provençal buildings in ochres and yellows, reds and creams, and old green shutters, one of a very few unspoilt oases on a coastline I found overdeveloped and rather pointless except as somewhere to pose; so anaesthetized that it had lost its charm. We were shocked to see how urbanized the French Riviera had become, and how it was being buried beneath tasteless developments.

240

It may epitomize glamour, but it made me quite sad. There was so little natural beauty left and the beaches were generally poor, too. It was as if exquisite Brigitte Bardot had been transformed into a plastic Barbie doll.

Tinkerbelle chugged out of Nice, past the aristocratic houses that live up the hill, and into pretty, tropical Villefranche with its glorious views down into the harbour, and ever-so-slightly downmarket Beaulieu-sur-Mer, set off by craggy hills and cliffs leaning out threateningly, menacingly, as if they were straining to get to the sea. On past Eze's hillside houses and cliffs sprouting flowers, scruffy Cap d'Ail, and into the toy-town kingdom of Monaco, a garish Legoland simply teeming with people, vehicles and policemen; everybody scurried around laden with shopping parcels and talking into mobile phones. There was a pervasive sort of 'Eat, drink and be merry for tomorrow we die' atmosphere. The traffic was a chaotic frenzy of prestige cars and nippy little scooters. Incredibly, the cranes were busy there too, elbowing aside existing modern and rococo buildings already jammed tightly against each other to cram in still more. It hardly seemed possible. I was transfixed by the weirdness of Monaco, and the fact that people actually wanted to live here. Then I remembered the tax benefits. But even so . . . Tinkerbelle farted her way through the bedlam, attracting looks of appalled disbelief from Monaco's *glitterati*. For fun we drove around until we found the starting grid for the Formula 1 Grand Prix, lined Tinkerbelle up in pole position, and made vrrrmming sounds to match her roaring exhaust, which made more noise than an entire field of F1 cars.

We roared off the grid through Monte Carlo and Roquebrune, where the roads were being dug up, and arrived in Menton, genteel, beautiful and not trying nearly as hard as its neighbours to be 'in'. We drove right up to and over the Italian border, just for the fun of it, then back to Menton where we had a postcard view of the houses clustered round the church on the hill. On our way back there was a sharp bend to negotiate, partially blocked by a coach coming from the opposite direction. The driver was a lookalike of that great character Mohammed Al Fayed (or maybe it was him — doesn't he live somewhere around that part of the world?). He obligingly reversed and signalled us past with his familiar ear-to-ear gold-toothed grin.

5

ALPS — ABOVE THE SNOW AND BENEATH THE CLOUDS (JUST)

With the Riviera behind us, what lay ahead was the Alps. Off we set, along the D2566, otherwise known as the Route des Grandes Alpes, 700 kilometres of daunting mountain passes and breathtaking alpine scenery. In the little hamlet of Monti, stuck on the hillside looking down on to Menton, was a huge boat outside a house on a narrow corner on the edge of an abyss. There were several more large boats parked around the place, and we couldn't see how they'd been navigated up there along the weeny, wiggly little road, or indeed why. In fact we began to wonder exactly why anybody would want to live up there in the first place, because apart from spectacular scenery there was little to recommend it; there were no gardens, the houses were all but inaccessible, and precarious in the extreme, stuck on the edge of mountains that were constantly shedding parts of themselves, as witnessed by boulders and scars of shale that had escaped from the

243

rather flimsy-looking chicken wire meant to secure them. But the landscape was magnificent, sharp-peaked mountains smothered in trees and wild flowers. In Sospel the old stone bridge was lined with geraniums, and houses perched right on the river's edge. One house there had even managed to find some relatively level land where two fine horses grazed.

Through the Gorges de Piaon, 406 metres above Menton, where small rocks had jumped down on to a road that was a tribute to the skill of the builders, who'd managed to drive it through the strata of rocks twisted, contorted and sandwiched together by millennia. The road and the scenery were equally awe-inspiring and hair-raising: sharp bends a single car's width; to our left boulders threatening to roll down and squash us, and to the right a drop plunging into nothingness. There was no way of knowing whether another vehicle might appear round the corner at any minute, and I found myself holding my breath and digging my fingernails into the palm of my hand. Terry was rather quiet, too.

When we reached Moulinet at 762 metres we found clean green mountain air, and more open, dramatically wild and craggy scenery. Terry did a simply fantastic job of driving the awkward vehicle round the difficult roads. It wasn't a drive for the faint-hearted or lily-livered. There was no turning back and absolutely no room for manoeuvre or error. One patch of road had completely collapsed, leaving a gaping hole surrounded by a few scaffolding poles and a strip of red-and-white plastic tape strung across them in a half-hearted attempt to prevent the unwary from dropping into it. When we weren't looking uneasily at the precipices beside us we could appreciate beautiful alpine flowers like campanula and saponaria sprouting from the rocks. Ahead the mountains were wrapped in cloud; the air was cool, and the road surface wet. The pine trees growing in the valleys needed to be very tall to reach the light. In between Moulinet and la Bollène-Vésubie we crossed the Turini pass, one of the most exciting and demanding stages of the Monte Carlo rally. Coiling back upon itself like a five-kilometre snake, it was a challenge for Tinkerbelle even at a very sedate pace; hurtling around this serpentine road at anything more than a snail's speed was almost unthinkable.

We stopped for the night at the medieval village of Saint-Martin-Vésubie, a truly idyllic Provençal collection of intriguing courtyards and ancient doorways saturated in atmosphere, in a setting of mountains and valleys, clean fresh air and alpine flowers, and the first French village to be electrified, in 1893. From the pleasant farm campsite it took just a few minutes to walk up into the village and amble around alleyways so narrow that the multitude of overhead wooden balconies almost touched. One of the only two remaining open streams called *gargouilles* in France burbles down the street. Running through the village centre they enabled the inhabitants to deal with any fires that broke out. Such a contrast with the Riviera we'd left that afternoon, yet only seventy kilometres away. We allowed ourselves to be lured into a bar for a *petit apéritif* before walking back to Tinkerbelle at sunset, when we met a chic lady shaking a bowl of cat biscuits and calling to summon cats from all directions. She told us she cared for all the feline strays in the village.

A plaque on the wall of the Hôtel des Alpes commemorates a visit by the French President Félix Faure in 1899, just a few months before his sudden demise at the Elysée in the company of his mistress. There's a very French account of this event, which relates that a chambermaid found him and cried: '*Il a perdu sa connaissance!*' meaning 'He's passed out!' but which can also translate as

'He's lost his lady friend!' Somebody replied: *'Elle est partie par l'escalier de service'* — 'She left by the back stairs.'

Looking back on all the places we visited on our journey, Saint-Martin-Vésubie rated as one of our favourites.

★ ★ ★

Sick of Tinkerbelle's rude noises, which were desecrating the beauty of the mountains and slowly coating her interior with a layer of black dust, and with no apparent prospect of finding a replacement unit, Terry had decided he'd fix the exhaust himself. He walked to a local supermarket and came back with a repair kit, then started burrowing about in our rubbish bin from which he dug out an empty tuna tin, and cleaned it out.

Using the repair kit he patched up the broken exhaust joint, and reinforced it with the tuna tin clamped on with two jubilee clips. When we left the next morning the only sound from Tinkerbelle was the contented purr of her engine. Off we drove with dignity, over the St Martin pass and the Colmiane summit, noticing in the distance scatterings of snow on the peaks. A sign warned we were approaching six consecutive hairpin bends; it was fortunate we didn't meet any daredevil drivers whilst negotiating the turns, but in the short distances between each bend we encountered a steady stream of suicidal drivers driving at breakneck speed regardless of the precipices and unforgiving rock face. One lunatic who sped past, his wheels dangling in space, was even talking on a mobile phone.

There was frequent evidence of rockslides and warnings that more were probably on the way, but no advice as to what to do in the event. Presumably if you get caught, there's not a lot you can do about it. With boulders of varying sizes on the road indicating recent minor avalanches we were quite looking forward to being somewhere else. A sign said we were driving on the Route de la Bonette, which advertised itself as the highest road in Europe, at 2,800 metres, in the wild and vast Mercantour National Park. Quite how or why we were on it we didn't know, because the last sign had said it was the Route des Grandes Alpes. Tinkerbelle took it all in her stride.

We followed the course of the river Tinée through the Gorges de Valabres, stopping to allow a solemn herd of cattle with bulging udders and clunking bells to squeeze past. We were very close to the Italian border; the mountain scenery was spectacular and at the same time menacing. Huddles of deserted, derelict cottages looked as if they'd simply become too tired of the struggle to exist. It was a relief not to be roaring as we drove along, not least because noise can trigger an avalanche.

Terry pointed out how the sides of the road were crumbling away, like the rocks all around. This was a particularly crumbly sort of place. Ahead the mountainside was bare of any vegetation, and the devastated and deserted little village of le Pra with its caved-in rusty tin roofs was surrounded by wide sweeps of fallen rocks and shale. A sad and ugly place, desolate and without hope, a victim of floods and the perpetual threat of avalanche. It was a powerful illustration of the supremacy of nature, and the fact that when a mountain has something in its heart that it wants to do, there's nothing that man can do to stop it.

A great ditch beside the road was filled with fallen rocks, and a series of vigorous waterfalls pounced unexpectedly from the side of the mountain on to the tarmac. In this bleak place clumps of alpine flowers sprouted from the stony surface, fragile and beautiful works of nature surviving where the man-made buildings couldn't. On the very edge of one of the endless hairpin bends was a road sign consisting of a blue circle with a white arrow pointing over the edge, as if indicating that cars should jump off there. Either the road had collapsed, or it was being dug up, because most of it was composed of a large hole. Tinkerbelle throbbed her way happily upward, past lovely alpine flower meadows and tussocky fields punctuated with bleak areas of loose rocks and scree. Across the valley the snow was below us. Impossible to believe, but the road was even more hair-raising than it had been the day before, narrower still, barely the width of the vehicle, with no edges, although at least the terrain was momentarily level and we weren't in imminent danger of toppling into an abyss. Around us patches of snow, brown and grimy where dust had blown over it, were still frozen and clinging tenaciously to life. It was here that we saw our first marmot, a funny fat little brown animal that popped up from behind a rock, stared at us and disappeared, to be followed by a very similar one, or maybe even the same one, that chose, pointlessly and unreasonably, and very stupidly, to dash in front of Tinkerbelle's wheels. With vast open space all around it, and 360 compass degrees from which to select a direction, it chose that which could have led to its death, leaving us to suspect that a marmot is not blessed with a particularly awesome intellect. As Terry jammed on the brakes the dogs flew off their bed, their water slopped over the floor, and all the food and crockery in the lockers crashed and rattled. The jay-walking brown creature bounced safely to the other side of the road and into the snow.

The higher we climbed, the worse the road, if it could even qualify for such a title, became. It was almost impassable. There was snow all around, either side of a few centimetres of ragged tarmac. National Forest Office engineers abseiled on the rock face, chopping down trees and fixing safety netting to hold the rocks in place. With a final bump, we reached the Bonette pass, altitude 2,500 metres, where the dusty brown snow had been blown into waves and ripples by the wind. Since we'd left the Camargue the dogs hadn't been having much exercise. If let off the lead they disappeared into the great blue yonder regardless of traffic, sheep and any other hazards, and completely immune to our calls and whistles. At home Tally was a well-trained dog who came when called; on the loose with Dobbie, he did just what he wanted. This worked to their disadvantage now we'd reached the Alps, because with animals in the pastures and the danger of traffic there was little opportunity for them to run freely, so they were spending a lot of time wrestling on their bed while we drove. Occasionally we let them off where we thought they'd be safe, and each time we regretted it, because they always got themselves into trouble of some sort. However, they didn't show any signs of suffering from their lack of exercise, and when we stopped each evening they played happily on their chains, chasing a football or digging holes.

Now that we'd reached the snowline proper, the marmots, or Marmites as Terry insisted on calling them, were popping up everywhere, and Tally was beside himself with excitement, yelping and trying to climb out of the window every time he saw one, or saw what he thought might be one. Often it was no more than a small boulder, but he was enraged at these impudent things and howled and wailed at them until he was hoarse. Dobbie was quite puzzled by the whole affair and kept looking at Tally as if seeking some sort of understanding. On the summit the road surface was perfect, and beneath the brilliant sun the snow melted in streams across the tarmac. Terry stopped to scoop up handfuls of snow for the dogs: Tally wasn't impressed, but Dobbie enjoyed holding it in his mouth and letting it leak out of the side of his lips.

Where the snow was plentiful it was patterned with Marmites' footprints, but until they moved you could never be certain whether or not you were staring at a rock. They seemed to be in mid-moult, with ragged and patchy coats, and are probably by nature suicidal creatures because a second one hurled itself in front of us, almost putting us all through the windscreen for a second time. Having succeeded in not being killed under the wheels, it began trying desperately to scramble up a perpendicular snowy bank about two metres high. It continually slithered back down, clutching vainly at the snow as it went, and although it could have very easily crossed back to the other side of the road and jumped into the snow there it continued in its frantic and futile struggle to climb the steep bank.

We chugged upwards over the Restefond pass, where we stopped to stand and gaze at a clear mountain lake, whose surface was broken by the merest ripple of wind, filled with icy meltwaters from a snow-topped mountain gazing at its own reflection.

We drove on through the high valleys of the Ubaye, past the fortifications of the Fort de Tournoux occupying a whole mountain, a strange-looking place with grilled windows peering out of the rocks.

The Redoute de Berwick owes its name to James Fitzpatrick, the Marshal Duke of Berwick, an illegitimate son of James II and his mistress Arabella Stuart. He followed a very busy military career and joined the French army in 1691, later becoming a naturalized Frenchman and a Marshal of France. Already holder of probably more titles than any other person before or since because of his military exploits and his relationship to the English king, he continued adding to the list by his services to the French crown, until a cannon ball knocked his head off in 1733 during a battle between France and Austria.

It wasn't unusual during those turbulent times for people of one nationality to fight on the side of another, and to change their allegiances quite frequently. During the Spanish War of Succession, English-born Berwick commanded the French army, and German-born General Schomberg, who'd taken French nationality, led the English army. In the course of his military career General Schomberg served Sweden, Holland and France. Because of his Protestant convictions he was eventually forced to leave France, and died heroically at the Battle of the Boyne, at the age of eighty, fighting for William of Orange against the Jacobites.

The wind had cranked itself up to gale force at the Vars pass which was just about the coldest place I'd ever been. Terry braved the elements to stand and photograph the scenery, whilst I rummaged about in a wardrobe for a jumper before making a cup of tea. I'd forgotten to turn off the gas bottle that morning and a strange smell alerted me to the fact that Dobbie had learned a new talent, turning on the cooker and two rings. Thank you to whichever god it was who warned me before I struck the match to boil the kettle.

Once Terry's photographic instincts had been satisfied we set off again, and once over the Vars pass the scenery became gentler. Sheep and cattle grazed shallow slopes in a weak sunshine, and by the time we arrived at Guillestre campsite, surrounded by misty blue mountains and overlooked by Mont Dauphin, another piece of Vauban handi-work, the blue of the sky was only marked by the distant con-trail of an aircraft. We shared the campsite with uncountable millions of winged insects.

Had we known, before we set off, the size of task we'd be expecting of her, we probably wouldn't have attempted the trip in Tinker-belle. But because we'd deliberately not researched our route, because this was meant to be an adventure, and they're no good at all unless there's plenty of unexpectedness, we had asked a great deal of her and she'd risen splendidly to the challenge. She maybe had a few aches and pains here and there, but her heart was stout. Beside the younger generation of camper vans with all their mod cons and high-tech fittings she looked small and humble, and also rather homely with her pastel-blue curtains neatly held in place with Velcro. The fabulous experience we were having, seeing the most beautiful scenery that France can offer, we owed to Tinkerbelle's gallant efforts.

From Guillestre we went to Réotier to see the petrifying fountain, a natural phenomenon created by the incessant trickling of mineral-laden water from a spring, forming a rocky outcrop that has shaped itself into a long nose which drips constantly from its end into a clear turquoise lake below. For the dogs it was an opportunity to really stretch their legs. Tally shot away like an arrow from a bow, and long before we reached the fountain we could see him standing at the very tip of the 'nose', looking down on to the opalescent waters of the lake. Dobbie, heavier, less athletic and by nature more cautious than Tally, stayed close to us, apart from a brief excursion on to a railway line just a few yards away, and then puffed and panted his way up the steps to the viewpoint above the fountain.

Chopin's ancestors came from a small hamlet near Saint-Crépin where we went in search of coffee, but both the bar and the restaurant were closed (not physically closed: they were open, and the staff inside were friendly enough, but apparently not open for business). However, we admired a couple of pretty pink marble fountains and a fine *cadran solaire* (sundial) painted on the beautifully restored Maison d'Étape, where in days of yore no less than five kings and three popes had stayed during their passage from Turin to the Rhône valley along the old Roman road, the Via Cottia.

There seemed to be two categories of communities in this mountainous region: alpine villages of great charm and character, or rather dull little places that looked as if the heart had gone out of them. The rocks beside the winding mountain road in the Queyras Regional Natural Park looked as if they were tired of clinging to the mountainside and would like to let go and tumble down to the bottom. Fort Queyras was sturdily perched on the vantage of a great rock where Vauban had sited it, and a little further on one of the strange columns known as a *demoiselle coiffée* poked up from the ground. They're an odd sight, tall pillars carved from the rock by wind and erosion, tapering up to a point on which is balanced, as if by a giant hand, a heavy rock, the entire structure held up by its own compressed weight.

Just over two kilometres above sea level, Saint-Véran claims to be the highest village in Europe. So do several other places. But it's the highest in France, and beautifully set in spacious meadows, unlike many mountain villages that are hemmed in on all sides. You need a strong pair of legs and lungs to visit it, because you must park and walk up a never-ending hill, past quaint and ancient houses built on two storeys, a stone ground floor topped by higgledy-piggledy sagging wooden floors that look ramshackle, precarious and ready to fall down, but we learned that this is how they're built. Whole families live in them, and during the winter their animals come in too for shelter, in exchange providing 'central heating'. A sign outside one old house announced that it was 'a rough but happy life', and so it must have been, with no traffic or mod cons and no stress or pollution. The village is divided into five separate quarters, so that if fire should break out, it could be contained in one part. It was busy when we arrived, with hikers, cyclists and motorbikers. Although the Mediterranean seemed far away and long ago, we were still in Provence, but surrounded by mountains topped with snow rather than the more usual scenes of lavender fields and olive trees. Dobbie hadn't been idle while we were exploring. He'd dug out the printer from its storage box beneath the bed, and begun eating his way through my typed notes, as well as disconnecting a wire from the car alarm, rendering it useless — all this despite the fact that his range of toys currently included four different-sized plastic bottles, three tennis balls, a wooden log, a rubber bone and a football.

The status-conscious hamlets of the Upper and Lower Prats are both at 1,500 metres altitude, so even the Lower Prats are fairly elevated. Abriès, where we went to find a cash machine, is a smart little village of just 400 inhabitants, which had been rebuilt after it was destroyed during the Second World War. In 1728 its cemetery had been swept away by the river Guil. Not far away, in a hamlet called le Roux, we found a shop called la Plantiflore selling the most delicious artisan-made plant and fruit syrups and liqueurs, where we bought a large bottle of a very wonderful raspberry liqueur called Amour de Framboise.

There were several pairs of cyclists

struggling up the horrible climb to the top of the Col d'Izoard. I thought what a weird thing it was to do from choice. It looks so exhausting. We lunched at the pass, where coloured jumpers painted on the road surface — a yellow one, a green one and a red and white one — were a reminder that the Tour de France had celebrated its centenary in 2003. There were words of encouragement, too: Go Bruno, Yannik, Laurent, Udo, Yann, Kim, Guy, and Nobby. Not forgetting, of course, Lance. And a few women's names, as well, although women are banned from competing in the great race, which is regarded as too gruelling for the weaker sex. Snow two metres high lined the side of the road at La Casse Déserte, where baby trees and clumps of tiny purple flowers grew among long sweeps of fallen shale. The barren rocks flushed a soft golden beige, almost apricot, in the afternoon sunlight, and handsome long-horned goats, a deep russet colour, grazed the meagre vegetation among the snow patches. Glistening ice-melt ran down the rocks in little waterfalls, and the road narrowed even further between crumbly edges and sheer sides. We gaped in delighted disbelief into a field of wild flowers where a couple were sitting stark naked in the warm sunshine just a few metres from the road, as if it was the most natural thing in the world.

The busy sprawl of Briançon, Europe's highest town, didn't detain us as we trundled on towards the Col du Lautaret, past swathes of pink and purple flowers and an unsuccessfully acrobatic juggernaut that had overturned and completely demolished itself just outside le Monêtiers-les-Bains. Around us were mountain tops, and behind them more mountain tops, and beyond them yet more mountain tops into the distance as far as we could see. From the Col du Galibier a brief tunnel led into the Rhône-Alpes region and the *département* of Savoie where the thick snow was a popular playground for the comical frolicking Marmites bouncing about amongst the rocks.

At Valloire the campsite nestled in a meadow crowned by a small chapel. The *gardienne* told us that the town was positively heaving with restaurants and we'd be quite spoilt for choice. This was absolutely true: there were *auberges*, pizza parlours, *brasseries, crêperies*, restaurants and hotels all over the place, but they all appeared to be closed in the in-between-winter-and-summer season. After we'd tramped hungrily around for half an hour we managed to get into the dining room of a hotel with a peculiar atmosphere. As we walked in, I had the impression that everybody in there felt guilty about something. I can't explain why, but our fellow diners were muted and slithery-eyed, ate quickly and exited stealthily. Very odd. The *maître d'* was a tall, angular and quite handsome woman, a Martina Navratilova look-alike, wearing a strange, ill-fitting outfit that rustled, in a fabric that I think used to be called bombazine in Queen Victoria's day. It really did look very strange. The food was welcome and not unpleasant, if unspectacular, but like the other diners we ate swiftly and escaped back to Tinkerbelle through night air that was suddenly cold.

A glorious morning was waiting next day, the sun stroking the battalions of wild flowers that jostled each other for space in the meadows around us, although in the shade the air was crisply invigorating. Terry found a tiny black butterfly whose wings were heavy and soggy with moisture, which he put on a sheet of paper to dry out, and then on to a leaf in the sun until it flew away. A small golden beetle was careless enough to plunge into the washing-up bowl, and we had to dry that out too and see it safely off on its daily business before setting off to the Télégraphe pass. The *relais* at the Col du Télégraphe is planted in a bower of blue and pink lupins and looks out over a great panorama of white-haired mountains. We sat in the garden there, amongst a coven of black-leathered bikers, sipping our coffee and chocolate, and drowning in the beauty of the place for an hour, before writhing our way down to Saint-Martin-d'Arc where we gave Tinker-belle a rest by taking the N6 for a few kilometres, through Modane and the historic terraced forts at Aussois. There were some quite unpleasant areas between here and Bramans in the Val d'Ambin, where hotel-sized chunks of rock had detached themselves from their mother and slid down to the road which is called the Chemin de Baroque, and at the same time the Route des Grandes Alpes again. In Lanslebourg many buildings had roofs made of large flat slabs of stone that reflected the sunlight, and there's a fine example of a Baroque church with its distinctive 'jester's hat'-style spire.

In the eleventh century St Landry, a local curate, was sent to Lanslebourg to whip the locals into Christian shape after years of Saracen occupation. He was a popular priest who sadly died by falling or being deliberately pushed into the river Arc at l'Ecot. Just in case he'd been murdered, the neighbouring hamlet of Fausan was wiped out by an avalanche in an act of Divine vengeance. God personally reported Landry's death to his flock. A processional cross that moved all by itself led them to his body, which they brought and laid in a gilded coffin in the chapel of St Joseph in Lanslevillard until republican soldiers smashed it up in 1794. It was put back together again, and laid in a gilded wooden shrine where it remains, except for his head, right arm and little pinky which are kept down the road in Lanslebourg. St Landry sounds like the decent sort of fellow who'd have approved of sharing his person between the two churches. It's believed in the Haute-Maurienne that he's the person to get in touch with when rain is needed in the area.

The cows in the meadows were fat and glossy, the beehives painted blue and yellow. Waterfalls rushed from beneath sheets of unmelted snow clinging to the mountainsides. A boulder of snow, a huge thing that must have weighed at least a tonne, had rolled down on to the road. This was the rockiest place we'd yet been to, thousands of tons of boulders balanced on and around each other, held only by gravity: if they decided to move, nothing would be able to stop them. I was starting to become obsessed with the dangers of rock-falls.

In blinding white snowdrifts three metres high in places, people had stopped to carve their names. We thought about it, but it was bitterly cold, so we didn't, but drove on to the Iseran pass, 2,762 metres up, where it felt as if we were standing on the very top of the world with the snow-covered mountains all around us. It was a marmot paradise, where gangs of the little creatures bounced and bounded about in the deep snow, and Tally rushed from one side of the van to the other, squealing and yelping. Dobbie still hadn't worked out what it was all about. After we'd driven through some short but nasty little tunnels we arrived at the lac du Chevril, the dam beneath whose waters lies the old village of Tignes. When the farming community in the valley, still recovering from the Second World War, heard in 1946 that the French government planned to submerge their little village to create a dam to generate electricity, they didn't believe it; and they certainly didn't accept it. But despite all their protests, on 10 March 1952 a child wrote on the blackboard of the village school: 'Last class.' A fortnight later the villagers had to remove the bodies of their relatives from the cemetery to be reburied, and two days later it was all over for the Tignards. Although they received generous financial settlements, and the new Tignes became a prosperous resort, it couldn't ever compensate the villagers of old

Tignes for the loss of their heritage. Beside the lake is a beautiful tall bronze figure of a slender girl in a long skirt, erected on the fiftieth anniversary of the flooding of Tignes, and a haunting poem called 'Larmes et Lumieres':

Tears and lights, just two powerful
    words

Tears:
Tears at our last meal in our lost family
    home
Tears on our last day at school — on
    the blackboard the words: 'We won't
    let Tignes die'
Tears during this last Mass as the
    hymns die in our throats.

Lights:
Lights in the windows at 2100 metres
Lights shining bright in happy villages
Lights of projects shared to enrich our
    lives

Yes, after the tears of suffering, the
    lights of hope.

Every ten years the dam is drained so that its integrity can be inspected. When this was done in May 2000, the surviving original villagers returned to the remains of their drowned homes and celebrated Mass in their drowned church.

The hay-making season was in full swing in Bourg-Saint-Maurice where two men, a young woman and a very small child were gathering up cut hay with old-fashioned wooden rakes, followed by an ancient tractor towing a baling machine, and on a hairpin bend a very elderly lady was, single-handedly, forking a massive pile of hay lying in the road into a first-floor loft. I felt we should leap out of Tinkerbelle, snatch the fork from her, sit her down and stack the hay. But we didn't, instead sitting patiently for the little time it took her to unhurriedly clear a passageway round the side of her hay mountain. We followed the valley of Chapieux up to the Cormet de Roselend, one of the loveliest places we'd seen since we started our journey through the Alps. It sits at nearly 2,000 metres on a broad plateau of mountain meadowland, and on that particular day was glowing in bright sunshine. Two women, an older woman with a stick and a younger woman, very slim and tall, with long legs in short shorts and hiking boots, were marshalling a herd of maybe two hundred copper-coloured cattle in and out of a mobile milking parlour towed by a tractor.

★ ★ ★

Except for Tally finding his way into a field full of cattle and being chased by them, our overnight stay in Beaufort was unremarkable. When we left next morning, on a mild overcast day, parascenders were floating down over hills that were alive with the sound of motorbikes. From the start of the alpine leg of our safari we'd met numerous herds of bikers roaring along the hair-raising roads at breakneck speed. As they whooshed past we could feel their exhilaration, but they wouldn't have noticed the wild flowers so tightly packed into the ground that there was no room for grass, nor how the wooden chalets sagged under the weight of geraniums dangling from their balconies.

Haute-Savoie was blanketed by a sky in various shades of grey when we reached the Chamonix valley, and with impeccable timing and a despairing squeal, Tinkerbelle announced that her brakes were worn out. What a heroine! She'd safely carried us over hundreds of kilometres of dangerous roads before finally succumbing.

Our very special friend Peter was waiting

for us in Chamonix with his girlfriend Marianne. Dobbie and Tally sped off to investigate the house, and Dobbie returned in a few moments proudly waving a pair of lady's knickers. We spent the evening dining on a whole bass and *crème brûlée* with strawberries, then slept in a comfy bed, had a bath and proper breakfast, and washed our clothes in a washing machine. Sheer luxury. Thank you, Pete and Marianne, for that very enjoyable and welcome interlude.

After the dogs had enjoyed a long wet walk in a boulder-strewn pine forest we went on a small detour to the sad remains of the village of Montroc. In the first week of February 1999, an unusually high quantity of snow fell on the mountainside just a little north of Argentière — as much snow as would normally fall in a month fell in just two days. The weight of this caused a slab of snow one and a half metres deep and covering an area of thirty hectares to detach itself from the mountain and descend towards the valley, gathering speed until it reached 150 kph. The monster avalanche charged down the mountainside, leaping the river Arve, its impetus carrying it uphill and over the villages of le Tour and Montroc, burying twenty-three houses and their inhabitants five metres beneath 100,000 tonnes of snow. Twelve people died, and all that remains of the demolished houses are the overgrown foundations, and one large three-bedroomed house knocked on its side; across the river the bare mountainside still shows the path of the avalanche. If you would like to see what a mountain can do when it sets its mind to it, have a look here. For failing to protect Montroc's inhabitants by evacuating them when the risk was evident, the mayor of Chamonix was prosecuted and given a suspended prison sentence for manslaughter. (He was also found guilty of manslaughter in connection with the fire in the Mont Blanc tunnel, and was fined 1,500 euros and given a six-month suspended sentence.) Seeing the result of this avalanche underlined my personal feelings towards mountains and their invincibility. Man can climb them, cycle up them or reach their summits in various ways, if the mountains will let him. But how can anybody claim to conquer them? Conquering implies subjugating, and how does something as comparatively insignificant as a man subjugate something as comparatively indestructible as a mountain? I was starting to look forward to leaving the Alps behind us. Beautiful and majestic as they are, I wasn't at ease amongst them; I have a belief that they don't really like people and only allow humans to live amongst them for as long as it suits them. Apart from their scenery and clean air, I don't much like them, nor their aura of melancholy.

Around the Chamonix valley, the glaciers, part of whose function is to hold the mountains together, are beginning to melt as a consequence of global warming. Maybe man will eventually destroy the mountains, but what will the mountains do to man in the process? As the glaciers melt they form lakes and release trapped boulders and rocks and threaten the ecological balance; just like a mountain, a glacier is a very powerful creature, and unless it remains frozen, it's a threat. In the mid-seventeenth century the Sea of Ice glacier on Mont Blanc was creeping towards the valley, raising fear in the bosoms of the local inhabitants. It had already swallowed up farms and villages when the residents of one village, le Bois, called upon the bishop of Geneva to exorcize the evil from the satanic thing. It took several years for the bishop's magic to work and the glacier to stop its advance. For now.

We drove on to the dark pink azalea-covered hills of Vallorcine, which had given shelter to the nineteenth-century outlaw and counterfeiter Joseph Farinet. He was born in the French-speaking part of the Aosta valley in Italy, the son of a blacksmith who used his father's techniques to manufacture currency in small denomination coins which he gave to the poor. Farinet is thought to have produced 100,000 counterfeit twenty-cent pieces, which at the time were the most common coins. He spent fifteen years evading the Swiss and Italian forces of law; they sometimes caught and imprisoned him, but he usually managed to escape. He met a mysterious death at the age of thirty-five, shot in the back of the head and thrown into a mountain gorge near Saillon, in the Swiss canton of Valais. There was a large bounty on his head, because it is hard to imagine a crime more likely to outrage the Swiss than producing false money, but the reward was never claimed, and whoever pulled the trigger was never discovered.

In 1980, to mark the hundredth anniversary of his death, a memorial was created at Saillon to the values of love, freedom and understanding embodied by Farinet. Known as the Vine of Peace, the world's tiniest vineyard covers less than four square metres, with just three vines planted in soil brought from all parts of the world, and beyond: fragments of volcanoes and pyramids, the Acropolis and the Matterhorn, and even a sample of soil from Mars. Each year the grapes are pruned and harvested by celebrities and mixed with local wine, and auctioned to raise money for deserving causes. A pathway lined with twenty-one stained-glass windows leads to the vineyard, and a statue of the man himself. Traditionally the people who come to tend the vineyard, who include film stars and sportsmen, fire a gun and shout, 'Long live Freedom!' The Dalai Lama declined to fire the gun, preferring instead to just touch it symbolically.

On our way again we twice crossed the path of the red-and-white Mont Blanc express, the train that links Chamonix with Martigny, where coincidentally Farinet was arrested and sentenced to four years in prison for counterfeiting in 1871. He escaped. Because it was a damp day, mild, with clouds rolling down from the mountain and floating into the valley, the multitudes of hikers were dressed in gnome hats and pixie hats, back-packs and anoraks. We drove up to Passy to view the Route de la Sculpture, which was rather disappointing, because after half an hour of driving backwards and forwards we could only locate two large steel sculptures, which in any case were less striking than Passy's violently pink *mairie*.

The Chamonix valley is densely crammed with Savoyard houses, with elaborately carved timbers and exterior walls decorated with agricultural implements. We went to have a look at the Cascade d'Arpenaz, 270 metres of water plummeting vertically to the ground, where it has carved a basin. Once again we were on the Route des Grandes Alpes, and cyclists' names were painted on the road — Virenque, French hero, and Pantano, the Italian ace who had recently tragically died. Even in the drizzly weather the road between les Gets, world capital of mechanical music — music played by machines like hurdy-gurdies and musical boxes — and host to the 2004 World Mountain Bike championships, and Montriond was very lovely, wooded and green and regularly punctuated by waterfalls. No longer rumbling and farting, Tinkerbelle now drew attention each time Terry had to brake, with a tooth-cracking screeching noise as steel ground against steel. Just after le Biot, at the unbelievably named Urine, there was grim evidence of a recent rockslide, and the poor trees that had been uprooted stood with their heads buried in the ground and their roots pointing to the sky. Nylon-jacketed people were exploring the great cleft at les Gorges du Pont du Diable, where we clocked up the 4,000th mile of our journey. The rock formations were spectacular, cracked and split, and somehow still holding together.

We'd chosen for the night's stop a campsite at Saint-Paul-en-Chablais, beautifully situated on a green almost-plateau overlooking Lake Geneva. The owners were absent when we arrived, but a helpful lady scampered from her camper before we'd stopped rolling, to tell us that we should just install ourselves; the owners would be back within half an hour, and if we needed any information, she had it. We thanked her and started driving around trying to find somewhere that was (a) level, and (b) not a quagmire, because the land had clearly been recently reclaimed and laid to grass, and was very squidgy beneath the wheels, and it had been raining for two days. All the suitably firm places were already occupied. We tried here, there and everywhere, watched complacently by the other *campingcaristes* peering through their steamy windows, and finally gave up, because Terry was certain that if we did put down our roots that night, we'd be stuck in the morning. So driving gingerly across what was quickly becoming marshland, we headed off through the thickening rain down towards banana-shaped Lake Geneva, central Europe's largest freshwater lake. Driving around rather aimlessly, barely able to see through the windscreen, we found a campsite; I've no idea where it was. The office was closed, and interested parties should enquire at the house, which was up a very steep pathway. I banged on the door for several minutes, increasingly loudly, until I succeeded in attracting the attention of a grumpy teenage boy who suggested that we just parked wherever we liked and waited for his parents to come back.

Terry backed Tinkerbelle into a fine level space, and switched off the engine. We unwound the awning, and let the dogs out. Before their paws had touched the grass, a distraught old lady in a nightie (it was 6.00 p.m.) scrambled out of an adjacent camper van and shuffled over to us, babbling and waving her hands, and pointing at the dogs. It wasn't easy to understand her, because she sobbed at the same time as she babbled, but it appeared that she was frightened of dogs, and their noise would keep her awake, and at her age it wasn't right for foreigners to upset her.

We moved to a spot further away. As we set up again, irritated sounds came from the terrace just up from us, where an old couple were sitting in chairs under the awning of their caravan, huddled in rugs, and tutting because we were blocking the view of the lake they would have been looking at if it hadn't been totally obscured by driving rain. The man waved his hand to indicate that we should move elsewhere, so we waved back and stayed where we were. As soon as we'd let the dogs out and attached them to their chains, yet another protester arrived, pointing out that it was possible for the dogs to obstruct the passageway to the sanitary block. I replied pleasantly that as it was pouring with rain and they were lying peacefully beneath the awning, they were not obstructing anything or anybody, and that it was unlikely that they would decide to do so, and that furthermore we would be leaving early the next morning (the earlier the better, I felt). He shuffled away grumbling about foreigners and threatening to complain to the management if the dogs so much as looked at the sanitary block with the intention of blocking the way to it.

When we had stayed with Peter and Marianne we'd washed two loads of clothes — almost all our clothes, in fact — and they'd been festering in bin bags all day. The clothes we were wearing were wet from all the tramping around and setting up of Tinker-belle, and we faced the prospect of having to put on wet clothes the next day. Hanging anything under the awning was no use; even if the rain stopped there was no wind and the air was very moist. All we could do was light the heater and string everything up inside the van. The dogs were unhappy under the awning, and demanded to go to their bed in the cab.

Having laboriously draped all the washing over a network of clothes lines tied to door handles and draped over cupboard doors we had effectively put the cooker out of action, with several pairs of shorts and socks dangling inches from the gas rings. So we contented ourselves with the last morsel of the Ossau Iraty and a couple of croissants we found in one of the cupboards, and attacked the bottle of Amour de Framboise.

Being trapped in a camper van in the rain is a very disagreeable experience; if we stood up we were swiped by wet laundry. The heat from the radiator coupled with the moisture from the clothes transformed Tinkerbelle into a steamy capsule where we sat huddled with our books, having to wipe our glasses every few minutes to be able to read. When we took off our shoes our feet were white and crinkly. The air smelt of wet dogs and damp trainers, and the rain lashed the awning so that Terry had to go outside and wind it back in. When we wiped the streaming condensation from the windows we could just see the grey and choppy waters of Lake Geneva as the rain dwindled to drizzle.

Aided by the raspberry love we slept like proverbial logs, and awoke damp and early to bright sunshine. We strung up our still-wet clothing under the awning to catch the sun, released the dogs from the cab and put them on their chains, watched by the vigilant owner of the next-door caravan, and sat looking at the now perfectly calm waters of the lake, and the city of Lausanne on the far side. On the terrace above us the gentleman was pointedly moving his chair about to underline the fact that we were interfering with his view, and outside the sanitary block a cheerful lady was doing her washing, using a thing like a stiff yard broom to scrub her clothes so forcefully that I wondered if there would be anything left of them.

By 10.00 a.m. our clothes were nearly dry and the dogs still hadn't crossed the sanitary block line, so we thought it a good time to leave, and made our way to the town of Saint-Gingolph, at the eastern end of the lake. There were plenty of empty parking spaces in the town, and we found a shaded area behind an apartment block where we could leave the dogs in comfort, and there was unlikely to be anything happening to disturb them and set them off barking. Terry carefully parked the van, we drew the curtains to keep the dogs sheltered, and had walked about two paces when a voice shouted from a balcony above.

'You can't park there; it's only for residents!'

'But it's empty — there's nobody else here, and we're only going to be an hour,' I called back.

'No, no, you have to move. It's only for residents.'

Another balcony-woman rapped on her window and waved us away.

There was room for at least a dozen cars, and we were the only vehicle in sight.

'I'll phone the *gendarmes*,' threatened woman No. 1, so back in we got and moved across the road, watched by the two harpies. A man fishing on the lake glared at us, as if he was trying to think of a reason why we shouldn't be there. I began to wonder whether there were xenophobic pathogens in the water, or the air, in this part of France which is inches from Switzerland. In the main street, slap bang in the middle of Saint-Gingolph, a Customs post divides the town in half. The post office, railway station and sports stadium are in Switzerland, the church and cemetery in France, and each half-town has had its own school and town hall since the sixteenth century, when Saint-Gingolph was divided by treaty between France and

Switzerland. There was once a shipyard here where the old sailing boats known as 'barques du Léman' were built to transport materials to the towns and villages on the lake, and a few are on show in the local museum (Swiss). We posted a letter in the French post office, and crossed the frontier. Sitting next to the harbour where boats rolled gently on the slapping waters of the lake, in the company of a pair of sparrows that jumped around the table and the backs of our chairs, it was pleasant to do nothing for a while. On such a peaceful day it was difficult to imagine anything disagreeable happening in Saint-Gingolph, but during the Second World War a foolhardy attack was made by the Resistance on the German-manned Customs post, and in the inevitable reprisals the French part of the town was burned, and several people, including the local priest, were executed. The luckier French inhabitants escaped into the neutral Swiss zone, where they were sheltered and safe.[1]

Having satisfied the sparrows and a flotilla of ducks who paddled up to demand their share of our croissants, we walked back into France and back to Tinkerbelle, where we were given a frosty glance by the fisherman,

---

[1] Ivan Sache, 2 April 2000.

who didn't respond to our '*bonjour*', and we set off westwards to circumnavigate the lake.

Meillerie once thrived on its fishing, quarrying and boat-building industries but today is simply a pretty village on the banks of the lake. Shelley nearly drowned there when he was sailing with his friend Lord Byron in 1816. We thought it was the sort of place where it would be pleasant to sit and have perhaps another cup of coffee, or a cold drink, but some unseen guardian angel discouraged us, happily, and we decided to press on a little further before stopping. *Le Matin* would report, a few weeks after our visit, that the tap water in Meillerie had been found to contain '*matière fécale*' or, as we might put it more succinctly, shit. It seems that news of this distasteful fact had been very slow in reaching Meillerie's inhabitants when it was originally discovered, and there were no warnings at all for tourists like us. Accusations were made that the mayor had been aware of the situation long before the nasty news became public, because he had been seen buying unusually large quantities of bottled water.

The southern side of the lake, between Saint-Gingolph and Thonon-les-Bains, was one of those blessed places that seemed to have been bypassed by developers, the only slight disadvantage marring the small towns and villages being the fact that the N5 ran right through them. Instead of drinking the sewage-rich water in Meillerie, we stopped in clean, civilized Evian-les-Bains, where the ceasefire between France and Algeria was signed in 1962, and bought a couple of the four million bottles of pure water they produce each day. Thirsts quenched, we strolled along the promenade, which was crammed with roses and trees, and wandered round the harbour where crested grebes floated between moored boats, and sparrows mopped up the crumbs that fell from the snackers seated on the waterside benches. We were impressed by a sticker on a trimaran declaring that it had been 'proudly made in France by Virusboats, a successful builder of sailing boats'. You have to admire the optimism of a manufacturer who chooses such a name. Maybe there was some obscure link with Meillerie? Amongst the ornate older buildings the ubiquitous cranes were working to squeeze in new structures. We loved Evian's copper-tiled roofs, the fancy wrought-iron balconies of the Savoy Hotel, the flowery roundabouts and air of elegance and unrushed prosperity.

We detoured to the Réserve Naturelle de la Dranse to see if we could spot some of the beavers living there. A notice said that if we were patient and lucky, we might. Although we were quite patient, we weren't at all lucky, and didn't see any beavers, or any signs of them or their dam-building activities. We slid around on muddy jungular paths, our faces scratched by elephant grass, looking as hard as we could, and we did see a grebe with a clutch of fluffy babies, a large flock of screaming gulls with small black heads, and some very pretty ducks — the unfortunate ruddy duck which was introduced from North America, and has become so prolific as a result of its adaptability that it's under threat of eradication. We began discussing why beavers actually build dams, and didn't come to any conclusion on which we could agree. Once we were home, we did some research to find out the reason, and it's one that neither of us had thought of. Beavers build dams, apparently, not because they are hyperactive creatures who need something to do all the time, nor because they have a capacity for engineering and are eager to demonstrate it; they do it because they are irritated by the noise of running water.[1] The effect of increasing water depth is a consequence, not a cause. One scientific

---

[1] Jim Jung, 2003.

study noted beavers building a dam against a wall in a dry room when the sound of running water was played through a loudspeaker in the wall.[1]

Anyway, after patiently and unluckily not having spotted any beavers we climbed back into Tinkerbelle and shrieked our way through the lunchtime streets of Thonon-les-Bains, deciding not to visit almost-unpronounceable Excenevex or medieval Yvoire, for fear that Tinkerbelle's noise might get us arrested. Instead we went to Annemasse to find her a new set of brake pads. I was mesmerized by the head of the first man who served us: he seemed to have two foreheads. The lower forehead was unusually high, and balanced upon it was a further high forehead, all topped with a shiny pink dome of hairless skull. The distance from his eyebrows up was twice the distance from his eyebrows down, and I simply could not take my eyes off him. He was busily talking to a friend at the counter while he attended to us, but he kindly wrote down the number of the part we needed, which he didn't have in stock. Without breaking off his conversation with his friend, he directed us to a shop where he assured us we'd find what we

---

[1] White Oak Society, Inc., 2001.

wanted. At the next shop I thrust the piece of paper with the part number on it over the counter to a helpful youth who sold us a heavy box, and with relief we set off to find somewhere for Terry to change the pads. Skirting the Swiss border to avoid the vigilant attentions of the Swiss police, we followed the road through countryside that had become peacefully agricultural, turning northwards at the Fort de l'Ecluse, a nineteenth-century stronghold fortified by, once again, that busy man Vauban. We chose Gex for our stop, as it was familiar to me, being the final campsite where I'd stayed on my hike across France in 1998.

In Tinkerbelle's living area a small sliver of something glistening blue and metallic lay on the floor, which Terry recognized as the remains of one of the arms of his reading glasses. Dobbie had been busy once again. We found the lenses, intact, but the frame was quite past saving. Dobbie was puzzled by Terry's shouting, and sat with his head tilted sideways, staring at Terry as if he was conducting a psychological study of a raving lunatic.

The miserable grey wet weather returned and formed an impenetrable curtain of heavy rain shrouding the lake, and the Jura mountains behind us. Poor Terry struggled soggily to get Tinkerbelle's wheels off to change the brake pads. I heard him cursing and grunting while I stayed dryly inside cooking; then came a roar of frustration as he discovered that we'd been sold the wrong parts and they didn't fit Tinkerbelle. He replaced the wheels and climbed back inside, dripping from head to foot and very cross indeed.

When the rain stopped we took the dogs with their new football to play on an open space that we thought was securely fenced. But as soon as they were off their leads they vanished from sight, racing away even as we called. Tally reappeared after a few minutes, but there was no sign at all of Dobbie. We hunted everywhere; we whistled and called, and walked round the site and asked if anybody had seen him, to no avail. When we got back to Tinkerbelle to decide what to do next, Dobbie was sprawled out on the bed, happily working his way through a packet of dog biscuits he'd found. He glanced at us briefly and then tried to swallow the whole packet before it was taken from him.

The following morning it was raining again. We had to find the right parts for Tinkerbelle, but without driving all the way back to Annemasse. While Terry started packing up, I went for a shower. Out of the twenty or so empty cubicles, I chose one at random, and as I switched on the water something fell to the floor, making me jump. It was a baby sparrow, which must have been perching on the tap. It hopped under the wall into the adjacent cubicle, so I wrapped my towel around my expanding person and tried to catch it, but I was clumsy and missed, making it panic and fly away. I heard it crash into a window on the other side of the room where I found it on its back in a basin, its tiny claws clenched, its eyes closed and its head flopping on its neck.

I was heartbroken for causing the death of the little bird by my clumsiness, and held it in my hand against my shoulder, sniffing and saying how sorry I was. I felt a faint heartbeat, and kept holding it against me in the warmth of my hand, wandering around in the shower room in the towel as people came and went, looking at me slightly nervously. After ten minutes the heartbeat seemed stronger, but the head was still limp and the eyes closed. As I couldn't very well walk back to Tinkerbelle in the rain dressed only in a towel, and I daren't put the chick down, I struggled into my clothes, which isn't easy clutching a fragile body in one hand. Terry found a small plastic box and a large wad of cotton wool with which we made a sandwich of the little bird.

'It isn't going to recover, you know that, don't you?' said Terry.

I nodded. I knew it didn't stand much of a chance.

We left it in the cotton-wool sandwich for an hour, and then, when we peeled back the top layer, its eyes had partly opened. Encouraging as it was, it posed a problem, because it was time for us to leave, and travelling with a weak baby bird and the dogs wasn't feasible. Nor could we successfully release it into strange territory, so I went to the campsite office to see if anybody there could help.

There was a kindly, professory-looking man in the office. He was doubtful that they could keep the bird there, because they had a cat, but he agreed that they'd keep it somewhere safe for a while and release it if it recovered sufficiently. He obligingly found a yoghurt pot, and as I fed the sparrow into it the little thing began struggling strongly. I took it back to the shower block and placed it on the ground, beneath a thick hedge housing a mob of sparrows. As I released it from my hand, it erupted skywards, like my heart, and disappeared into the branches.

Terry and the professor were as delighted as I was. It gave us something to be cheerful about on the soggy cold day, as Tinkerbelle made her banshee-shrieking way to the nearest Citroën garage, where we managed to find the correct brake pads. Terry was taking no chances this time, and in the garage forecourt jacked Tinkerbelle up in the air, took off the wheels and fitted the pads. At last we could drive around without attracting stares, and we headed for Geneva to visit Terry's good friend Herman, from Mexico.

Herman works at the International Labour Organization, founded in 1919 primarily to protect the rights of workers and to abolish child labour. In an imposing building, decorated with works of art from countries all over the world, people of all nationalities wander around in corridors or pop out of lifts. You see men and women of every colour and creed, in different costumes, speaking different languages, united in their efforts, and it's an inspirational place to visit. We sat drinking coffee with Herman, a charming, quietly spoken law professor who explained one of the problems facing Mexico City — the population explosion. The populace has grown from five million to twenty million over the last two decades, largely due to improved health care and infant vaccination programmes. However, there's no work for all these people, so by the eradication of one problem, another has been created.

On our way out of Geneva we passed the 12-metre-high wooden sculpture of a chair with a broken leg standing on the roundabout in front of the United Nations building. It's the work of Swiss sculptor Daniel Berset, and was erected by Handicap International in 1997 to symbolize the horror of landmines. The sculpture is to remain there until the ratification of the Ottawa Treaty to ban landmines and destroy stockpiles. Called *Broken Chair* (a *double-entendre* here, as 'chair' means 'flesh' in French), it's a simple design conveying a poignant message. Every fifteen minutes somebody is killed or maimed by a landmine in this, the twenty-first century.

6

JURA — MADNESS IN A BOTTLE

We retraced our route to Gex and climbed up to the Col de la Faucille, where we had a fine lunch, before setting off towards Pontarlier. Terry had set his heart on staying the night at the airfield which we'd visited many years before, when he'd owned a Beagle Pup aircraft. The Jura mountains are a gentler, more curvaceous and hospitable crowd than the jagged and unforgiving peaks of the Alps, and didn't make me feel either melancholy or trapped. They're the home of Comté cheese, which is made from the milk of the Montbéliard cows who spend the summer grazing the flowery pastures, and every bit as good as the delicious Ossau Iraty. Tinkerbelle purred along through Morez, home of the national school of *luneterie* and capital of spectacle-frame manufacture in France since 1796, when a gentleman with the glorious name of Pierre-Hyacinthe Cazeaux bent a nail into the shape of a pair of glasses. I suggested solemnly that we try to find a replacement frame for the one which Dobbie had mangled the day before. Terry wasn't amused.

Not far from Morez is the town of Morbier, where the cheese of the same name comes from. It's a cheese I've never particularly enjoyed. In fact, I haven't enjoyed it at all. It's probably most appreciated by those people living in Morbier, rather like sago worms are relished in Papua New Guinea, whale blubber in Iceland, or witchetty grubs in the Outback. This is how Morbier is described by online source Wikipedia:

'Morbier is a semi-soft cows' milk cheese. It is ivory colored, soft and slightly elastic, and is formed in two layers separated by a thin layer of ash. It has a rind that is yellowish, moist, and leathery. The bottom layer consists of the morning milk and the upper layer is made of the evening milk. The aroma of Morbier is somewhat obnoxious, though the flavour is rich and creamy, with a slightly bitter aftertaste. The ash has no flavour. It is added between steps to prevent a rind from forming during the molding process. This cheese dates back to the dark ages, from the monastery of Morbier.'

If you're on the lookout for an obnoxious-smelling, bouncy, elastic medieval cheese in a leathery rind with a slightly bitter aftertaste, in two layers encompassing some tasteless ash, consider Morbier.

We drove quietly along through the Regional Natural Park of the Haut-Jura over gentle hills, along roads splattered with cow dung, and past fishermen standing chest-deep in streams. The unhurried atmosphere was accentuated by the fact that several villages were still flying their Christmas decorations, and it was now mid-June, five weeks since we had left home. Unlike the Alps, the roads were not trembling from the roar of motorbikes. The south-facing walls of the houses are clad mostly in metal, which reflects the afternoon sun. The purpose of this, we were told by someone in a bar, is to protect the wall during the winter months when snow accumulates on the roof and melts beneath the sun. A practical idea, although it doesn't greatly add to the aesthetics of the houses.

Terry was delighted to be back at the aero club in Pontarlier. We'd enjoyed their hospitality many years ago when we'd landed there during a fierce storm, just as the members were going home for lunch. 'Make yourselves at home,' one of them had said, 'you'll be comfortable and dry in here. We'll leave the clubhouse open, so you can help yourself to anything from the bar. We'll see you later.'

The current president of the club, Christian, said we were most welcome to stay on the airfield that night, so we set up Tinkerbelle on the tarmac outside a hangar, cooked a meal, and went in to spend an hour with Christian and Opale, his faultlessly mannered large white poodle, friend Louis — call him Lou-Lou — and Philippe, a pilot with Air France who spoke perfect English. Terry's French was improving daily, but it was a nice change for me not to have to act as interpreter, which I would have found rather exhausting after a couple of hours of conversation which revolved exclusively around aircraft and aviation exploits.

There had been no indication that we should expect a thunderstorm during the night, and accordingly we hadn't rolled down the awning. When flashes of lightning and drum rolls of thunder shook Tinkerbelle, and a deluge rushed in through the open roof vents and on to the bed, Terry had to brave the weather to go out and dismantle the awning to stop it collapsing beneath the weight of water.

By morning it was merely drizzling sullenly. That didn't matter, because we planned to visit the Espera Sbarro concept-car exhibition

295

just a couple of hundred metres from the airfield. But when we wandered over there it was locked up, and wouldn't be open until 2.00 p.m. Four hours of hanging around on the airfield in grey weather didn't appeal, so we started to get organized to move on.

Terry opened the cab to move the dogs into the back. Dobbie gave a loud yelp, something he does quite frequently and rather dramatically if he thinks something frightful is going to happen to him, as, for example, if Tally looks at his bone prior to snatching it away, so we don't take much notice. He bounced cheerfully into the back of the van and up on to his rug, while I put away the washing up, secured the kettle and turned off the gas bottle so Dobbie couldn't gas us all if he decided to turn on the oven again. This took three or four minutes, and when I turned round I was horrified to see blood everywhere I looked: all over the floor, the door, the front of the fridge, the rug. Dobbie was sitting on the rug, licking his foot, with Tally trying to help, and there was a thick red stream flowing from one of his pads. Although he was wagging his tail he simply would not let us examine the wound, and it was impossible to see what damage he'd done. We searched every square inch of the tarmac around Tinkerbelle, but there was no sign of anything that could have injured him. It's remained a mystery to this day.

He was lying peacefully licking up the blood, and we decided we'd wait until the bleeding had stopped, when we'd be able to assess the damage. For as far as we could see, which was quite a long way because Pontarlier is France's second highest town after Briançon, the sky was heavy with dark grey clouds, so we went to explore Pontarlier and see what entertainment it offered to visitors in inclement weather. We found a most excellent *belle epoque*-style bar and café for a breakfast of croissants, coffee and thick, frothy hot chocolate, and after looking at as much of Dobbie's foot as he would allow, which confirmed that the worst of the bleeding was over, we drove through dripping pine trees to the Château de Joux, thinking we'd spend a couple of hours there.

Almost a thousand years old (and updated by the indefatigable Vauban), the château squats menacingly on top of a crag, surrounded by a mournful pine forest, and on that gloomy day it was the personification of desolation. We'd not been able to discover anything merry about this place, not a single story to make you laugh, or even smile. Nothing but misery, beginning with the tale of Berthe de Joux, wife of Amauri III, lord of

Joux, who had galloped off to the Crusades. During his absence, Berthe fell in love with a handsome young knight named Amey de Montfaucon. The inevitable happened — why hadn't Amauri locked her in a chastity belt before he went off gallivanting, I wonder? Anyway, after a long absence Amauri returned unexpectedly from his adventures only to catch Berthe and Amey *in flagrante*. Filled with justifiable Christian indignation, he killed Amey and had his body suspended from a gibbet. He was kinder towards Berthe, and only had her imprisoned in a cell sufficiently high to enable her to kneel, with a little window from where she could enjoy the sight of the swinging and diminishing remains of her lover. After her husband died, Berthe's son released her from her imprisonment, and she retired to spend what was left of her life in a convent, maybe inspired by the years she'd spent on her knees.

Then there's the cheerful tale of Loïse de Joux, whose fiancé Thiébaud also went crusading in the Holy Land. Many years after his departure, a visored knight arrived to let Loïse know that her fiancé was living the life of Riley, surrounded by beautiful women, and that he'd quite forgotten poor Loïse. The dim-witted girl replied that as long as her beloved was alive, that was all that mattered.

The visored knight then revealed himself to be none other than, yes, you've guessed it, mischievous Thiébaud. Overcome with joy, Loïse fell down stone dead.

These tales of love and death are nothing compared with the tragedy of heroic little General Toussaint Louverture, leader of the Haitian slave revolt, who was imprisoned on Napoléon's orders in the awful château. Standing there on that mid-June day, cold and wet and waiting for the guided tour to escort us round, it wasn't difficult to imagine what it had been like for a sixty-year-old man, a child of the sunny Caribbean, to find himself locked in a small bare cell in the coldest region of France, where the temperature has been known to fall as low as $-41°C$. Betrayed by his own people, tricked and kidnapped by the French, the poor man succumbed to cold, misery and apoplexy in 1802, and never lived to see Haiti declared the first black republic in 1804. The age of chivalry seems to have bypassed the Château de Joux.

As if all this wasn't enough, a few weeks before our arrival at its sinister doorstep a large chunk of the château, weighing several tons, had fallen off due to the action of ice in a crack in the rockbed. The château had failed to kill anybody only because the collapse happened at lunchtime, so there was nobody standing beneath the disintegrating walls. There were municipal vehicles and barriers all over the place, and worried-looking people in hard hats walking round measuring. A coachload of French ladies queuing ahead of us were becoming impatient as we stood waiting for the ominous wooden door to be opened. A harassed guide kept appearing and reassuring us that the tour would begin very shortly, and saying she was very sorry for the delay.

As we stood at the doorway into this monumentally depressing place, I began having serious doubts about our visit. Even walking around beneath the weeping pine trees seemed a jollier prospect. I thought of dungeons and cellars, and dark passages, so next time the guide popped up I collared her and asked whether one was free to roam at will around the château. No, she said, unfortunately that was too dangerous following the recent accident, and the visit could be conducted only in the company of a guide. Was it suitable for claustrophobics? I asked. She pulled a face, and said that some people did find the narrow staircases uncomfortable. That decided me. Terry declined to go on the visit without me, and so, feeling we'd imbibed more than enough doom and gloom for one morning, we returned to Pontarlier to look for something to uplift our spirits, and made our way to the Distillerie Guy.

Pontarlier was the birthplace of the first absinthe distillery and is world capital of absinthe production. The original recipe was an adaptation of an eighteenth-century herbal cure-all, based on wormwood, and developed over the years into a notorious liqueur. Cheaper than wine, and with a staggering alcoholic content of 72 per cent, it was favoured by the poor and the bohemian, and notables like Van Gogh, Toulouse-Lautrec and Baudelaire. In 1901, during a fire, a quick-witted workman opened the storage tanks of the Pernod distillery allowing the spirit to flow into the river Doubs, instead of exploding and probably burning Pontarlier to the ground. The locals, *pontissaliens* as they are known, were able to drink to their hearts' content directly from the river, the soldiers using their helmets to scoop up its potent waters.

Absinthe's popularity was a challenge to France's wine producers, and the effect it had upon its consumers didn't find favour with the National League against Alcoholism, or the Croix Bleue as it was otherwise called. They campaigned energetically for it to be banned. Known familiarly as the Green Fairy, the drink was credited with 'making you crazy and criminal, provoking epilepsy and tuberculosis, and killing thousands of French people . . . making a ferocious beast of man, a martyr of woman, and a degenerate of the infant, it disorganizes and ruins the family and menaces the future of the country.'

It was, claimed a leading antagonist, 246 times more likely to cause insanity than wine, and furthermore 'the real characteristic of absinthe is that it leads straight to the madhouse or the courthouse. It is truly 'madness in a bottle' and no habitual drinker can claim that he will not become a criminal.'

The death knell tolled for absinthe production when a Swiss farmer called Jean Lanfray in 1905 shot his pregnant wife and two children before trying to kill himself. His actions were attributed to the two glasses of absinthe that he'd drunk prior to the event. No account was taken of the six glasses of wine, glass of cognac, glass of crème de menthe, brandy-laced cup of coffee, another litre of wine and then a further shot of coffee laced with marc that he'd drunk the same day. It was indisputably obvious that it was the absinthe that had caused his behaviour, and this added the necessary fuel to the campaign to ban the stuff. Shortly thereafter, in Geneva, an absinthe-bingeing man named

Sallaz killed his wife with a hatchet and a revolver. Inexorably the garrotte tightened round the Green Fairy, and it was banned in Switzerland, Belgium, the United States, and, in 1915, in France.

Eighty-six years later absinthe production was legalized again in France, with a reduced alcoholic content of 45 per cent, and in April 2001 the Distillerie Guy planted fifty-five thousand wormwood plants. Harvested by the end of September, and dried during October, on 15 December 2001 the first bottles were sold.

Our tour of the distillery was a most enjoyable interlude. The place buzzed with enthusiasm, laughter and the rattle of glasses. An exuberant employee came and asked whether we'd like to taste any of the products, and yes, we replied, could we have a sip of absinthe? Our new friend delivered us to a young girl who beckoned us to follow her. Absinthe, we learned, isn't something you just glug into a glass, top up with water, and knock back. There's a time-honoured and traditional way to drink it. We had a lesson in absinthe etiquette.

You need first of all an absinthe fountain, a fancy glass container filled with cold water, with a varying number of spigots growing out of it. Then you will need for each person a tall glass, a perforated silver spoon, a sugar lump, and, of course, a bottle of absinthe.

Fill your tall glass with the required level of absinthe; balance across the glass the perforated silver spoon, and place upon it half a sugar lump. Place the glass, the spoon and the sugar lump beneath one of the spigots, and allow the cold water to drip slowly, slowly, drop by drop, through the sugar lump and into the absinthe, which will '*louche*' — turn cloudy.

This ceremonial completed, your absinthe is now ready to drink. '*Et voilà!*' chirped the girl, handing each of us a cloudy glass, and taking one for herself. '*À votre santé!*'

'*À la vôtre!*' we replied, savouring our carefully prepared drink. It was really delicious. The word 'absinthe' comes from the Greek word meaning undrinkable, because wormwood is so bitter. The Greeks may have been clever, but they obviously didn't know about the sugar lump. The Russian word for wormwood is '*chernobyl*'.

As we stood at the table sipping, workers came up and helped themselves to tots, and local people popped in to say hello and have a little drink. The place was heady with fumes from the various concoctions being brewed and bottled. If we'd closed our eyes we could have imagined being seated at a table with

Van Gogh in a decadent Parisian bar.

Our first friend, the gentleman who'd offered us the tasting, came to ask if it had pleased us.

'Very much indeed,' we told him.

He reached for another bottle, and poured a slug of yellow syrup for each of us.

'Try this. It's made from pine. Very good for sore throats.'

It slid down nicely.

'Now you'll like this. It's *anis*, not as strong as absinthe.'

He wasn't pouring the mean little thimblefuls that we'd occasionally managed to squeeze out of other producers at tastings, but generous glassfuls.

A selection of fruit liqueurs followed, and our host became increasingly enthusiastic.

'I only speak very little English,' he confided. 'Except when I have some drink, then I'm fluent!' He roared with laughter and sloshed a pink liquid into our glasses. Terry had to abstain, because he was driving. But I wasn't.

'How many different drinks do you actually produce?' I asked.

'Twenty-two,' he replied happily. 'What would you like to taste next?'

Reluctantly I declined, saying truthfully that I'd had sufficient. I'd tasted six.

'Let's buy some,' said Terry, uncharacteristically, because we had an agreement to keep our extravagances under control on a trip which had already cost a small fortune in fuel and food, not to mention the purchase of Tinkerbelle. Usually we resisted the lure of local souvenirs.

Beaming at our fellow shoppers and the staff, we ordered a large bottle of absinthe, and another of the *sapin* syrup. Would I like any of the fruit liqueurs, Terry asked, or one of the beautiful fancy bottles? Wouldn't I just, I thought, but instead opted for a couple of posters, one a copy of an original showing a large black cat, and the other a delightful painting of the original Distillerie Guy which had barely changed over the decades.

We felt really happy skipping back to Tinkerbelle, where we sat for half an hour laughing, hiccuping and feeling ridiculously pleased with ourselves, despite the fact that it was still pouring with rain. Any lingering depression from the Château de Joux had evaporated, and we continued on our way up to Montbenoît, following the Doubs, a gentle and orderly sort of river on this day. A pair of swans proudly escorted a clutch of grubby cygnets on the still surface; beside it stalked several herons, while a very large bird of prey strutted around in a field looking important.

While we were in the aero club at Pontarlier we'd been urged to visit the republic of the Saugeais; you can ask them to stamp your passports, Christian said. The Saugeais Republic covers an area of 100 square kilometres and encompasses a dozen villages. This little-known democracy originated in the twelfth century when, as a way of atoning for the sins of his ancestors, the lord of Joux gave a parcel of land to the Archbishop of Besançon. The minuscule state seems to have been happy to maintain a low profile until 1947, when a local hotel owner, M. Georges Pourchet, jokingly told a visiting dignitary that he needed a passport to enter the Saugeais. Entering into the spirit of the occasion, the *préfet* pulled some strings and M. Pourchet found himself named as the first president of the republic. When he died, his wife Gabrielle stepped into the presidential shoes. The republic has its own anthem, postage stamps and Customs officer, and is looked on benevolently by the French governmental hierarchy, the president receiving invitations to state functions at the Elysée. When M. Pourchet met the so-very-patrician Valéry Giscard d'Estaing, he said that he looked forward to discussing matters 'as one president to another'. We bowled along with our passports at the ready, but when we reached Montbenoît just before noon, there was a decided air of nothing happening. I asked a pedestrian where we should deliver our passports, and he looked at me as if I was a potentially dangerous maniac. I went to the post office and asked the lady behind the counter, who was startled but wanted to be helpful. She knew nothing about the regulations, but took me into the office of the supreme head of the Saugeais post office, who was very charming and suggested that I tried the tourist office.

Just as I reached the door the incumbent was coming out, and said it wouldn't be possible to entertain any requests until 3.00 p.m., when they would, if I went back, issue us with a *laisser passer*. They didn't stamp passports.

We were a little exasperated by then with trying to fulfil these very lax immigration requirements, and drove off and spent an hour exploring the rustic and unspoilt lands making up the republic, including the rock formations of the Défilé d'Entre-Roches, where two caves have been carved by time and weather in the limestone, so perfectly that they look man-made. One cave is known as the Treasure Grotto, and the other houses the chapel of Our Lady of Remonot, which is a place of pilgrimage. The legend tells that a

308

hermit placed a statue of the Blessed Virgin in the cave, where the local people came to pray. Water trickling from a spring flowed over the Madonna's feet, and subsequently cured eye diseases. When the hermit died, the monks of Montbenoît nabbed the statue for their monastery, which they thought to be a more fitting residence for the lady. The miracles stopped. One night the statue made her escape, walked back to the cave and reinstalled herself. The water regained its magical properties.

Whilst we were on our tour of Saugeais, the sun had come out and shone down on the realm, as we followed the Route Courbet towards Ornans, where Gustave Courbet, the first of the school of realist painters, and something of a revolutionary, was born. It was a rather perilous road coming up to Mouthier-Haute-Pierre, apparently, where a M. Tompierre had fallen over a precipice 'a victim of his own zeal', and only a little further along, on 27 October 1943, a whole busload of travellers had gone over the parapet; eleven of them had perished, and two somehow survived. They must have been made of rubber, because it's a monumental, sheer drop to the valley below.

Ornans, where Lou-Lou, whom we'd met the previous evening at the Pontarlier aero club, had a hotel, is a particularly attractive town, spread along the banks of the Loue and crammed with scarlet geraniums, and a splendid sculpture of a leaping trout twisting over a fountain on a roundabout to illustrate that it's a great fishing area.

It began raining again just after Ornans, really raining, raining so hard we could barely see through the windscreen. It was like driving through a tsunami, and we saw nothing of the countryside at all as we closed on Besançon. It was as much as we could do to see the road in front of us. We found our way to a campsite, and scampering from the van to the office I was up to my ankles in water. Thunder and lightning joined in, and two little dogs in the campsite office were frantic with excitement at every crash and flash. Anybody who set foot outside was drenched to the skin in seconds. It was raining so torrentially it became funny; it was late June, and this was like a monsoon. A whole group of dripping people stood in the office laughing, bordering on hysteria.

Once we'd been allocated an *emplacement*, we sat steaming until the storm had exhausted itself; the sun popped out and within a few moments it was like a warm summer day. We were parked next to a German-registered camping car in a beautiful location beside the river Doubs, which wraps itself around Besançon, and we unwound Tinkerbelle's awning. The moment it was in place, a freak gust of wind swept off the river and lifted it into the air, ripping it backwards over Tinkerbelle's roof, wrenching the metal frame half off its moorings, and breaking a window. Seconds later a blond giant appeared from the German vehicle; he reached effortlessly over Tinkerbelle's roof and lifted the crumpled awning down as if it was a paper napkin. He said something we couldn't understand, and I asked whether he spoke any French or English.

'*Nein, Deutsch,*' he responded, pointing at the number plate on his vehicle.

I only know six words of German — *kleiner, grösser, danke Sie, bitte* and *dungemittelfabrik.*

'*Danke Sie,*' I said, as none of the others seemed appropriate.

After straightening out the twisted metal legs with his bare hands as easily as if they were paperclips, the giant took Terry by the upper arm with a huge paw and started explaining in German how to make repairs, miming unscrewing the rails from Tinkerbelle, taking the thing apart, bending the rails into a straight line, drilling holes and remounting the awning. Although he and

Terry didn't share a single word between them, they seemed to understand each other perfectly well.

His wife came over to join us, and they talked happily away. Every so often we caught a word we recognized, like Alsace, or Hanover, but all we could do was nod and smile, and point at the sky which was changing from clear blue to heavy cloud, and grimace.

Terry walked off to a nearby hardware store to buy some screws to mend the awning, while I persuaded Dobbie to let me see his injured foot. There was no longer any bleeding, but there was a very deep jagged cut right through one of his pads. It didn't seem to be bothering him, but we decided to take him to the vet the following day.

Through the night rain drummed on to the roof, but by morning the day was bright and sunny, and I was excited about our visit to Besançon where we'd come to explore the town aboard Segways: electrically driven, self-balancing pairs of wheels with a handle, steered and driven by body weight. It was solely for the opportunity of playing with one of these things that we'd diverted from our 'outside edge' course to visit Besançon, and I telephoned the tourist office to ask what we needed to do to get our hands and feet on to the Segways.

'There are no Segways in Besançon,' said the first person I spoke to.

I explained we'd come to Besançon specifically because of an article published in the glossy Doubs magazine, summer edition, produced by the Economic and Tourist Development Agency for the Doubs, which clearly featured the delights of exploring the town by Segway, over two pages, complete with photograph.

The tourist office was unmoved, and suggested I telephoned the town hall, who were slightly more apologetic for the absence of Segways in Besançon, for reasons they weren't willing to explain; they suggested that as we were there we might as well have a look at the town, after all, and hoped our visit wouldn't be spoiled, because Besançon was a town crammed with interest and beauty.

Before setting off to find out whether this was true, Terry had to reattach the awning to Tinkerbelle. There was no room for it inside: it had to go back on. So he drilled the holes and fitted the new screws, which entailed quite a lot of messing around, and our blond giant neighbour arrived at precisely the right moment to help lift the thing into place and hold it while Terry screwed it back on. Having spent five or so minutes enjoying a conversation that nobody could understand with these friendly people, we bid them *au revoir* and *bonne route*. He lifted a hefty motorcycle from its bracket on the rear of their camper as easily as if he was picking up a child's bicycle, and clamped on a safety helmet. His wife climbed on behind him, and they purred away.

We examined Dobbie's foot. It definitely needed veterinary attention, and we drove into Besançon city centre to look for a vet. We found one that had closed for lunch two minutes before we arrived, and wouldn't reopen until 2.30, so we took advantage of this space in our day to go and explore the town. Even if we had been lured there under false pretences, the town hall had been quite truthful in saying that it was worth a visit, because it's a most attractive town of beautiful parks and riverside walks, with a lively and friendly atmosphere which reminded us rather of 'our' home town, Poitiers. Besançon is notable for being the birthplace of that great man of French literature, Victor Hugo. The Quai Vauban is a magnificent arcade of seventeenth-century houses, and the Centre for Applied Linguistics draws students from all over the world, giving the town a cosmopolitan air. We explored the historic and colourful Battant *quartier*, and found a simple restaurant with the menu chalked up on a blackboard, the walls decorated with ethnic carvings and hangings. There was no printed menu or wine list; you got what was on the board. I explained to the charming Middle Eastern waiter that we were vegetarians, and *pas de problème!* He indicated the blackboard: cheese tart, tortilla, boiled eggs, tuna-stuffed tomatoes, all served with piles of salad and a cheerful *rosé* wine. Unlike the customary reverent hush of a lunchtime French restaurant, here the conversations were animated and reggae music played at exactly the right volume so that it wasn't intrusive. The clientele was rather bohemian: two guys in black leather jackets with the sleeves pushed up their forearms, with wildly standing-up hair and designer stubble; a woman in mustard-coloured trousers and a plastic lilac raincoat; another with violent pink hair; and an elderly professorish fellow wearing a crumpled linen jacket with the sleeves rolled back accompanied by a sullen girl entirely in black. He kept stroking her leg under the table, and didn't get any response. She stared at the wall behind him and blew smoke down her surly nostrils. It was an agreeable change to eat food not typically French, and to be part of the relaxed lunchtime bustle in the pedestrian street. The meal itself was very reasonably priced; the anonymous wine was shockingly expensive.

We whiled away half an hour roaming round the wide pedestrianized streets, admiring the pretty colours of the local stone — pale blue, beige and pink — and then set off to retrace our steps to the vet, past a fountain where a pigeon was taking its bath, sitting in the water and lifting its wings to wash fastidiously beneath them.

Somebody was ahead of us at the vet, and stood on the step looking at his watch. It was nearly ten minutes past the stated opening time. He was a good-looking young man wearing a friendly smile, and made a great fuss of Dobbie, who reciprocated. By the time a slightly harried man turned up, with a younger woman rattling some keys, it was fifteen minutes later than the time posted on the door. Never mind. We all piled in, the woman installed herself behind a desk, the harried man disappeared, the young man and we stood waiting. The harried man kept coming and going, appearing in a white jacket, disappearing. On one of his appearances he gestured that we should seat ourselves in the waiting room, which we obediently did. He held up a finger that seemed to indicate he would keep us only one minute. While we sat looking at posters of different breeds of cats and dogs, an advertisement for worming products and the lifecycles of fleas and ticks, a conversation between the receptionist and the young man became louder and more excited. We sat for ten minutes, thankful that Dobbie wasn't haemorrhaging, and then the receptionist showed us into a small surgery. She smiled and said the doctor would be with us 'tout de suite'. A moment later in he came, shook our hands, and went out. Shortly he was back again, and started asking what our problem was, only to interrupt himself and disappear out of the door once more. There was a lot of shouting coming from the lobby. I don't know how long we'd waited by the time the vet was ready to turn his full attention to us. The next time he came in he picked up a stethoscope and draped it round his neck, which seemed to signal he was ready to treat us. He pulled a card from his desk and began writing down our details, and then put his pen down and sighed.

'That man hasn't paid his bill,' he explained. 'He owes me money. He brings his animals for treatment, and doesn't pay. The whole family are dishonest,' he said. 'Dreadful. Scandalous.'

We tut-tutted.

'Now, your dog. How old is he?'

'Eight months, approximately.'

He lifted his eyebrows, looking at enormous Dobbie.

I explained about Dobbie's foot, and the vet examined it, squatting on the floor while Dobbie licked the back of his head.

'Yes, it's a bad injury. I can't stitch it, though. The texture of a dog's paw is like cork — it won't hold stitches. What I'll do is clean it and put some staples in; they might hold.'

But amiable, easy-going Dobbie had absolutely no intention of letting his foot be cleaned or stapled, and put up a tremendous, although very good-natured, fight, which he won. He slouched triumphantly against the wall, his long pink tongue dangling, while three of us panted and heaved.

'I'll have to sedate him.'

The receptionist was summoned, and between all of us we managed to hold Dobbie still long enough for the vet to give him a sedative injection.

He slowly subsided from standing to sitting, to slumping, and by the time we'd lifted him on to the table he was unconscious.

The vet worked away cleaning the wound, and punched some staples through it while I looked out of the window. Then he wound a length of bandage round the paw and secured it thoroughly with adhesive tape. Dobbie didn't move through the procedure. In fact he was so deeply asleep he had to be carried out to Tinkerbelle on a little stretcher, and was placed on the bed where Tally sat licking his mouth gently.

Back in the surgery, the vet asked if I could translate a few French words into English for him, as he had several English clients, and although he spoke a little of the language there were some words that failed him, like '*vomir*'. He talked about his son, who worked in Marble Arch as a computer programmer, and told us that once a fortnight he travelled to Paris to meet all his other children, because when they were little he'd spent too much time with animals and not enough with his family, and now he was making up for that lost time. He was a very sweet man.

The bill for Dobbie's treatment was more than twice our worst fears and represented two weeks of our budget.

We'd planned to visit Besançon's famous citadel (and yes, in case you are wondering, Vauban had a hand in it), which houses several museums, but decided instead, because of the heat that had taken over from the rain, to keep driving until we found somewhere cool to stop where Dobbie could recover in peace. Our route led eastwards, to get us back on our track, and there was one heart-stopping experience on a hairpin bend at Laissey where we met an unadvertised and completely unexpected narrow tunnel, immediately followed by another one, which led into gently undulating countryside patched with wheat fields, and the typical large Comtois farmhouses. The hills became smaller and the landscape more open in this peaceful and prosperous part of the Doubs.

At Maîche we stopped to stock up our larder, and to stand at the gates of the privately owned sixteenth-century Château de Montalembert, where in November 1944 General Charles de Gaulle and Winston Churchill met on the eve of the grand offensive towards Belfort and the Rhine. A plaque outside the château marks that meeting of the two titans.

Picking up the Doubs again at Saint-Hippolyte, we followed its course to Epomanduodurum as it was called in Gallo-Roman times or, if you prefer, Mandeure as it's now known. Personally, I just love saying Epomanduodurum. We decided to stop there for the night at the spacious and peaceful campsite, where Tally had a good run and a game with his football while still-dozy Dobbie was happy to lie watching through one half-open eye. Both dogs ate their dinner enthusiastically, but Dobbie seemed to list to starboard every so often, and we thought it would be comforting for him to stay in bed with us that night. The bed wasn't particularly large, in fact it was particularly small, and it was like sharing a bed with a Shetland pony. Although he was quiet and still he took more than half of the small amount of available space, and while he slept soundly, we didn't.

By the time he woke, and we'd drunk several cups of coffee to compensate for all the sleep we hadn't had, Dobbie was as lively as a cartload of monkeys, and doing his best to eat off the expensive wrapping round his paw.

Epomanduodurum has a fantastic main road, wonderfully adorned with the signs of the zodiac, all portrayed in huge floral motifs, topiary and natural materials. The municipal authorities and gardeners who created this outstanding display deserve full marks for its design and execution. We saw many beautifully decorated towns and villages on our journey, but I think Epomanduodurum would take a lot of beating.

You can't help noticing that all around Montbéliard there are a great many Peugeot cars, almost to the exclusion of any other make. Perhaps that's because it's a Peugeot stronghold. The dynasty's roots there go back to the fifteenth century, when the enterprising family was already established in the area as farmers, artisans, military men and builders of windmills round which industrial sites would grow. But the Peugeots didn't simply wake up one morning and think, hey, let's build motor cars! Oh, no. First they started with mills, which developed into steel mills; then they began manufacturing modest tools, coffee grinders, irons and steel armatures for corsetry like bustiers, brassières and crinolines. They progressed to hair clippers, ice skates, sewing machines and bicycles and from there, logically, to automobiles. We went to visit the Peugeot Museum in Sochaux, just east of Montbéliard.

I'd suggested the visit in a spirit of sacrifice, to atone for dragging Terry round the chocolate factory which he kept reminding me about, and I didn't expect to be greatly interested in the history of the Lion, but as it turned out the Peugeot Museum is far more than an exhibition of automobiles. It's a trip into the past, a look back to the age of elegance, and lots more beside. Beautifully laid out, the museum displays examples of Peugeot's earliest designs: there are bicycles, including wooden ones made for children;

penny-farthings and tandems, tricycles and bicycles with wicker sidecars and children's seats. The very bicycle upon which Richard Virenque won his fourth consecutive best hill climb in the 1997 Tour de France is on show. There are displays of marine and aircraft engines, sewing machines and absolutely divine old motor cars, their brass polished to a mirror finish, the leather glowing with elbow grease and good health. These vehicles must have been draughty, cold and quite uncomfortable, but their elegance is unsurpassable.

In a small theatre a realistic Columbo lookalike hologram — shabby mac, cigar, wonky eyes — tells the history of the company, and the development of their cars over the last century; there are glass cases exhibiting all kinds of Peugeot memorabilia and collectable items.

Among the cars displayed are East African Safari winners (I saw those actual cars during the events in the 1960s when I lived in Kenya), and the cars that won Le Mans under the leadership of Jean Todt, current boss of the boringly successful Ferrari F1 team. There are examples of all the Peugeot models over the decades, and the latest outrageously futuristic concept car, and also the Popemobile used during John Paul II's visit to the Alsace and Lorraine in 1988. Ninety-nine per cent of the vehicles are in pristine condition, and there's a private collection of 3,700 die-cast model Peugeot vehicles. The cars are displayed against backgrounds of contemporary photographs, and there are video films of rallying and racing. A really interesting and enjoyable place to visit. The restaurant, which is in the middle of the museum so you can continue to admire the exhibits while eating, was filling up by midday, and we managed to squeeze into the last remaining table for two and had an excellent, very reasonably priced lunch there that wouldn't have been out of place in a superior hotel.

After lunch we were itching to test the rally car simulators. As I settled behind the wheel an endearingly earnest little boy of about ten climbed uninvited into the passenger seat. He pointed out the controls of the car, and advised me which circuit to select. His grandfather tried to extricate him, but my co-driver explained that the lady was going to need somebody like him to help her, so she knew how to drive the car, and I agreed that I'd be grateful for his *savoir faire*. The boy was almost unable to contain himself from snatching the wheel from me in his enthusiasm to demonstrate his driving skills, but we agreed he'd handle gear changes while I steered. It wasn't an entirely successful partnership because apparently I kept doing something wrong, and after a few circuits I handed over the wheel to Terry, who wasn't quite so panicked by the boy's yelled directions, and he acquitted himself rather better than I had. During the three very enjoyable hours we spent in the museum, Dobbie removed most of his expensive bandage.

Despite being intensively industrial, the area around Montbéliard is nevertheless attractive, with plenty of plants and trees to soften it. Hugging the frontier with Switzerland, we found ourselves in a peaceful suburban landscape, with a Peugeot in every driveway. If we hadn't known we were nearing the Alsace, the presence of painted storks or painted storks' nests on houses would have been a clue.

At Joncherey there's a memorial to Corporal Peugeot, who holds the unhappy distinction of being the first French person killed in the so-called Great War on the Western front, even before the formal declaration of hostilities between France and Germany. This is what happened. Although France and Germany were already mobilized, a tenuous hope remained that war might be averted at the very last moment, and the French troops had been ordered to withdraw twelve kilometres from the German frontier. Corporal Jules Peugeot, a nineteen-year-old teacher, was washing his hands when he was alerted by a child that the Prussians were coming. Eight cavalrymen appeared, and responded with gunfire to Corporal Peugeot's order for them to halt. One shot mortally wounded the young corporal who nevertheless, before succumbing, was able to return fire and kill Lieutenant Camille Mayer, a twenty-year-old from just south of Mulhouse (which at that time was part of Germany). The two young men died on 2 August 1914, at a few minutes after 10.00 a.m. The following day, Germany notified France that they were officially at war. Corporal Peugeot was buried with military honours at his home a few kilometres from Joncherey. During the Second World War German troops destroyed the memorial erected to mark the event; the French replaced it with a bigger one in 1959.

Fields of golden wheat and corn, and hectares of baby trees in dense rows, made up the landscape of the Sundgau. Village names became Germanic: there were -*dorfs* and -*lachs*, -*bachs* and -*kirchs*, -*ingens* and -*heims* and -*willers* all over the place. The architecture changed abruptly. Sprawling

Franche-Comtois farmhouses were replaced by more modern, taller buildings, with steeper roofs, painted in absolutely wild colours. We passed intricately timbered houses painted lime green, bright red, pale lilac, deep pink, daffodil yellow, various shades of blue, and ox-blood red. It seemed no colour was too fantastic for the local homeowners, and not content with the colours, many of the houses had paintings on the walls: of storks, milkmaids, birds and plants. What was so surprising was just how beautiful, and how absolutely right, these colours were. Just a few hundred metres away, in the Franche-Comté, they would have looked vile, grotesque, but here in the Alsace they were perfect. Balconies were stuffed with geraniums and petunias in equally vivid colours that managed to blend into their backdrops.

We made a brief stop in Ferrette, because Terry needed a haircut and I needed to get a larger pair of shorts. The first supermarket we stopped at was attached to a hairdresser and there was an immediate vacancy for Terry. He was taken over by a Julian Clary lookalike, lithe in black leather trousers draped with clinking chains, pointy-toed black boots, and a skimpy black top displaying his smooth brown arms and their spiked leather bracelets, the ensemble topped with pink-and-blond spiky hair. He gave Terry a painstaking haircut, snipping a tiny piece here, a little bit there until he had achieved what they both agreed was perfection.

7

ALSACE AND LORRAINE — PINK CASTLES AND RED MULLET

From Folgensbourg, the Swiss city of Basel spread out before us. Cherry-tree branches sagged beneath the weight of fruit, and Europe's busiest waterway, the Rhine, popped up at Rosenau. Once a polluted nightmare used as a dumping ground for waste, the river is gradually being cleaned up. It's a paradoxical stretch of countryside along here: frequent ugly hydroelectric plants are separated by patches of unspoiled bucolic landscape and thick woods.

Neuf-Brisach's star-shaped fortifications have survived centuries of warfare and were designed by Vauban as an ideal city. We enjoy looking at roundabouts on the outskirts of towns, but those at Neuf-Brisach were quite horrid: ill-kempt, rich in ugly weeds and overgrown, so *nul points* here, I'm afraid. We left the Rhine for a while to visit Kaysersberg, Albert Schweitzer's birthplace, and also in the hope of catching sight of some storks. Although the outskirts of Colmar aren't anything you'd want to photograph, and its roundabouts were also unpleasant, the old town centre is a ravishing panorama of technicoloured medieval buildings that managed to escape destruction during the war. It was the birthplace of sculptor Frédéric-Auguste Bartholdi, creator of the Belfort lion and the Statue of Liberty, whose face is said to be modelled on Bartholdi's mother. A twelve-metre-high replica has been erected on a roundabout on the northern edge of Colmar to mark the hundredth anniversary of the sculptor's death.

Each afternoon our thoughts were on finding somewhere pleasant to stay overnight, and I had four different sources of information, books and maps, that I had to balance on my lap and search through at the same time as navigating, translating if necessary, keeping my eyes skinned for any interesting features, and at this time also keeping a watchful eye on Dobbie to prevent his removing the staples from his foot. This was a stressful period each day, when documents slithered and slid all over the place, Terry fired questions and directions at me like gunfire, and we frequently overshot turnings because I hadn't seen them in time. On this particular day we'd selected Kaysersberg as our port of call, and had driven to the north of Colmar, past the endless crosses growing out of the mowed lawns of the national necropolis; then through Holtzwihr where, tucked away inconspicuously, is the Audie Murphy memorial, a stone wall with the silhouette of a tank against it, and a figure on the tank firing a rifle at an invisible enemy. It was erected in 2000 by the people of Holtzwihr to commemorate the heroism of the men of the 3rd Infantry Division, under the command of the 1st French Army. For his epic one-man stand against six Panzers and 250 German infantry, Audie Murphy was chosen to epitomize the bravery and sacrifice of the American soldiers. Rejected by the Marines and paratroopers because of his small stature, if ever a film star lived up to his gung-ho screen image it was this diminutive little man who won his Medal of Honor here, to add to twenty-seven other decorations including two French, *Croix de Guerre* and *Légion d'Honneur*, making him the most decorated American soldier of the Second World War. He died in a plane crash in 1971.

Just a few kilometres away at Sigolsheim, the Stars and Stripes flies permanently from the hilltop known as Blood Hill, or Hill 216 by the Americans, beside a monument to the American troops who fought there beside the French. Sigolsheim was taken and retaken seventeen times in a single month. Lieutenant-Colonel Keith Ware of the 3rd US Infantry won a Medal of Honor there, America's highest award for bravery. Although it's sometimes known as the Congressional Medal because it's presented by the US president in the name of Congress, its correct name is Medal of Honor. Lieutenant-Colonel Ware led a small party in an attack on German machine gun emplacements, killing a number of the enemy and taking the rest prisoner. He reached the rank of General, and died in a helicopter crash during the Vietnam war.

The area is covered in monuments and cemeteries and Sherman tanks parked on roundabouts outside the towns and villages; in its present state of immaculate neatness, peace and prosperity, it's impossible to visualize it as a battleground.

Kaysersberg's campsite was full, and the camper van parking area crammed with vehicles with only inches between them. One of the slithering guide books offered a campsite a little further away, at Fréland, so that's where we went, and found a pretty village perched on a hillside in the foothills of the Vosges, a few kilometres north-west of Kaysersberg. Fréland is one of five villages in the canton of Lapoutroie where the local patois known as Welche is still spoken amongst the older generation. At the campsite the proprietor spoke perfectly normal French, and invited us to install ourselves wherever we wished, as there was only one other vehicle there, which also belonged to English people, who displayed the same lack of interest in us as we did in them, in our insular English way. It was chilly up there, shaded by the Fréland pass, but peaceful. In the morning we had to stop in the village to draw some cash from a machine, and Terry parked rather haphazardly and without any warning, as he quite frequently does, causing an angry hooting from a car behind us. When I climbed down from Tinkerbelle, the driver drew alongside and gave me a fearsome mouthful of abuse, making his feelings about women drivers, especially English women drivers, quite plain. I didn't have an opportunity to point out I was merely a helpless passenger, because having unloaded his spleen he roared loudly away to underline his feelings.

It would be difficult to find a more perfectly picturesque town than Kaysersberg, birthplace of one of the twentieth century's and my greatest heroes, Albert Schweitzer. At the time of his birth in 1875, the Alsace belonged to Germany, and Schweitzer would always regard himself as a German. During the First World War he was brought back from his hospital in French Equatorial Africa and interned by the French as an alien.

Beautiful, ornate old buildings positively buried in geraniums, immaculately clean cobbled streets, cafés wafting the smell of freshly brewed coffee and hot chocolate, and new-baked cakes and pastries: that's Kaysersberg — seriously touristy and unbelievably quaint. In a *pâtisserie* I found an evil thing called *berawecka*, a Kaysersberg speciality. Sold by weight, its ingredients include dried pears and dried apples, figs, dates, candied citrus peel, plums, bananas, spices, hazel nuts, walnuts, almonds and kirsch. You wouldn't want to eat this, it's terribly fattening and horribly expensive, so I'll tell you what it's like: texture-wise, like an uncooked Christmas pudding, but far heavier; taste-wise, a voluptuously ambrosial mixture of sweet and spicy, rich and exotic that satisfies all the senses. For €10 we bought a deceptively small lump, but it lasted for a couple of days, because a little bit goes a very, very long way, even with me. Oh, yes, and also some *kugelhopf*, a couple of *escargots* (*pain raisin*), and a delicious onion tart. The *kugelhopf* was pleasant enough, but not at all in the same league as *berawecka*. It was here I gave up all idea of trying to maintain my current weight. Our trip was a once-in-a-lifetime experience, and for the rest of it I was going to stop worrying and keep on eating all the delicious local specialities I could, provided they didn't contain meat.

Kaysersberg has a shop selling old weaponry, whose windows were filled with all types of guns, daggers, swords, maces, axes, nineteenth-century brass helmets, a splendid gargoyle, and a magnificent original sixteenth-century complete suit of armour that tempted Terry. What we didn't like was the church, which was unnaturally cold and damp and unspeakably gloomy. From the stone bridge we watched four pigeons washing themselves on a boulder in the river. All around the hillsides were exclusively covered with tall vines, in neat rows running in every direction, from the crests of the hills right down to the edges of the roads. They basked fresh and green in their ripening sunshine, and spread for as far as the eye could see, like armies massing for a decisive battle. We followed the Alsace wine route to Mittelwihr and Riquewihr, and in Zellenberg, quite unexpectedly, something large, like the shadow of a pterodactyl, passed over Tinkerbelle's roof.

'Stork!' I bellowed.

We drew up on the side of the road to watch the dangly-legged bird circle and drop on to a heap of branches dumped on somebody's chimney. An adult bird and a juvenile sat on this nest peering down at us with scholarly interest, unperturbed by our presence or Tally's wild yelping. A few metres down the road another nest was stuck on top of a tree stump, with a crowd of sparrows happily cohabiting in the basement area beneath a stork family of parents and one infant. The nests were about two metres across, the branches closely woven, and their inhabitants watched us placidly in between preening themselves delicately with their long beaks.

At the beginning of the twentieth century thousands of storks lived in Alsace, but by the 1980s only two couples remained. We were standing looking at what twenty years previously had represented the entire stork population of the region. There was something very endearing about these large birds choosing to make their homes upon the roofs of human houses, and we spent a happy half-hour watching them and listening to the clapping of their beaks, before continuing on the wine route and reaching the fairytale village of Hunawihr with its Hansel and Gretel gingerbread houses. The glazed orange, green and maroon diamond-patterned tiles gleamed on the bell tower of the Gothic church, which since 1687 has been shared between the Protestants and the Catholics under what is known as the *simultaneum*', each religion being allocated different times for its services. Whilst in life worshippers share the same church, the departed reside in separate parts of the fortified cemetery, so that in the hereafter never the twain shall meet . . .

We saw a sign to 'Parc des Cigognes', and debated whether we actually wanted to see storks in captivity, having so recently delighted in seeing them living on people's chimneys, but decided to have a look. What a good decision that was! A self-important stork was striding round the car park like an attendant checking that cars were parked correctly, parading up and down in front of a cluster of laughing children and obviously relishing the attention he was attracting. Their size is impressive — they're about a metre tall, and they're very handsome birds with their long red bills, kohl-lined eyes and sleek white-and-black plumage. The Parc des Cigognes opened in 1976, its purpose being to halt the decline in numbers of the white stork, which was on the very brink of extinction. During migration the storks are at greatest risk, and an estimated 90 per cent of them will die, either by electrocution when they land tiredly on an electric cable, or in Africa, where they fall victim to hunters, droughts that deplete their food stocks, and poisoning as a result of the toxic chemicals used to combat locusts. So all in all, it would be far better for the storks if they stayed where they were, nesting on rooftops as a symbol of prosperity and happiness, which is what the Parc des Cigognes is trying to achieve, by breeding out their migratory instinct. It isn't the cold weather that makes them migrate in winter, but the scarcity of food. What the park does is to collect some eggs from the nests each year, incubate them and raise the babies by hand. The baby storks spend the first three years of their life in a large, natural enclosure covered with netting, before being released into the wild; by then the migrating instinct has withered. The birds will mate either with other captive-raised storks, or with the wild ones. When the time comes the wild ones will still migrate, but the captive-raised birds will remain, fed abundantly at the park. The young of these birds will still be born with the migratory instinct, and will in their turn be brought up in captivity for their future safety. Each generation undergoes the same treatment — the basic instinct remains but the migratory habit is erased. Thanks to this very successful programme, by 2001 more than 250 pairs of storks were nesting in Alsace.

Other birds live in the park, too: Magellan geese, buff-backed herons, cormorants, black swans and many varieties of duck. The sound of dozens of stork bills clacking out messages to each other was almost deafening. They were everywhere around us, in the aviary, up in the trees, and flying overhead. The Parc des Cigognes is also a centre for the breeding and reintroduction of otters, and from an observation point you are able to watch these shy creatures playing and feeding in their holts. A pond is home to several coypus and terrapins, and each afternoon cormorants, penguins, otters and sea lions give a fishing display. The current year's crop of stork young were in groups of three, on man-made nests, large circular constructions of woven sticks covered with straw on tree stumps about one metre high, where the fuzzy-haired youngsters sat sunbathing and watching the world go by, their beaks still black, but their distinctive eye markings already evident. This was one of the most enjoyable places we visited on the whole trip, and it was heart-warming to see what the park has achieved in its efforts to save the baby-delivering birds from extinction.

Another creature under threat is the giant Alsace hamster, and there was a large display by an association set up to protect it, showing photographs of the animal. Given all the jokes about giant hamsters, I was very undecided as to whether this was serious, so I contacted an Alsatian wildlife association and asked them whether the creature really existed. They were quite upset that I thought there was anything amusing about the giant hamster, because it's a very real animal, unique to Alsace, about twenty centimetres in length, rather like a guinea pig, and almost extinct. Its dilemma is caused by the fact that its remaining habitat is almost exclusively planted to maize, so that when the hamster emerges from hibernation in late spring there is no cover for it, because the maize is not yet growing. Another threat comes from the irrigation of the maize, which can flood the hamsters' homes and drown them, and finally rapid urbanization is swallowing up land where the hamsters normally live. And according to the gentleman who was kind enough to give me this information, Stéphane Giraud of GEPMA — Groupe d'Étude et de Protection des Mammifères d'Alsace — the general public doesn't really care. Next time you hear a hamster joke, please think about these threatened animals.

★ ★ ★

With dozens of châteaux littering the hills around us, we wanted to see at least one, and it was to Haut-Koenigsbourg that we headed. On the way we passed through Ribeauvillé where several storks had made themselves at home: the thoughtful Ribeauvillagers had actually built a platform round the church spire where the birds could, and did, nest, and three more storks were stalking (no pun intended, for that is what storks do) round a fine stone fountain in the middle of town. Just north of Ribeauvillé is Bergheim's German military cemetery amid the vineyards, where over 5,000 victims of the Second World War are buried, their graves orientated to face their homeland. German military cemeteries in France are maintained by an association funded by the German government.

Driving through Thannenkirch we passed two small urchins on a fishing expedition, with very basic equipment of rods made out of sticks with pieces of attached string carried nonchalantly over their shoulders. What you notice around here is that the earth and the stone of the buildings are a very deep pink colour, and the pink stone confection that is Haut-Koenigsbourg castle is no exception. The castle sits upon a craggy hill 800 metres high, on the departmental boundary between Haut-Rhin and Bas-Rhin, looking out over thousands of hectares of beautiful Alsace landscape, over the plains to the Rhine, and almost as far as Switzerland.

The history of Haut-Koenigsbourg dates back to the twelfth century. It enjoyed a turbulent, ping-pong existence until in the seventeenth century it was besieged and taken from the Austrians by the Swedes. Thereafter it fell into ruins and remained so until 1871, when Alsace became German and Kaiser Wilhelm II, Queen Victoria's grandson, and uncle and cousin to two British kings, acquired ownership of the ruins. Wilhelm undertook the restoration of the castle, and whether the current version bears any resemblance to the original I don't know, but it does make for an enjoyable visit. Despite its great size and robust construction (the walls are over six metres thick in places) there's nothing sinister about the place. You can't take a pink castle too seriously, and this one is seriously pink, built from the red Vosges sandstone. Not timid, pallid, pale maiden's blush pink, but deep-rich-almost-raspberry pink. It looks as though it was put together without any particular forethought, with turrets and towers and windows all over the place in a rather disorganized but very charming fashion; there are no unpleasant dungeons or cramped stairways, and visitors are free to wander at will through the high-ceilinged rooms, up to the top floor where there's a collection of rather splendid cannons, which are almost works of art if you can forget their purpose. Slits and slots are pierced in the walls for shooting things at invaders and dropping scalding liquids upon them. The wooden doors and ironwork are superb, and as for the *salle de fêtes* — wow! Intricately carved wood, wonderfully painted murals, rich hangings — this room is so over the top. A wrought-iron fireguard round the very pink fireplace bears the poignant words, *'Ich habe es nicht gewollt'* — 'I did not wish for this' — presumably referring to the war in which Europe was embroiled. At the end of the First World War Alsace reverted to France; reoccupied by Germany during the Second World War, the castle was liberated by the Americans in 1944. Whatever else the Kaiser might have done, in restoring Haut-Koenigsbourg he did recreate something rather beautiful with this romantic, fairytale castle.

Back on the road, we drove through Sélestat, a cheeky town claiming to be the birthplace of the Christmas tree. So do many other places. What Sélestat also claims is that it was where the continent of America was christened. A geographer called Martin Waldseemuller was collaborating with a teacher named Mathias Ringmann from Sélestat to translate a work of geography. They found documents written by Amerigo Vespucci, the Italian-born naturalized Spanish explorer, containing glowing descriptions of the new land he had 'discovered'. They didn't find anything written by Christopher Columbus, who'd found the continent a while earlier (although several centuries after the Asian and Scandinavian explorers). The two scholars didn't seem to have heard about Columbus's voyages, and decided the New World could and should rightly be named America. And so it was, and the first time the word was seen in print was in the year 1507, when their translation was published.

We crossed the canal that links the swan-covered Rhine to the Rhône, and resumed our drive, through the little town of Rhinau. A treaty signed in 1542 gave this French town almost 1,000 hectares of land on the German side of the Rhine, which serve as a nature reserve. Since 1494 a ferry service has linked the two sides, and it still runs, carrying passengers between the banks every fifteen minutes.

Through a guard of honour formed by pitchforks, wielded by ranks of check-shirted yokels with straw in their hair, a bride and groom laughed their way out of a church in Plobsheim, where we stopped to stock up at a local supermarket.

We arrived in Strasbourg in what we thought was ample time to find and settle ourselves into a campsite. Three hours later we were still driving around searching for any sign that there was such a thing. It was the wifely responsibility to ensure smooth travel arrangements, secure comfortable overnight accommodation, produce pleasant food at regular intervals, maintain a regular supply of clean clothes, and navigate through unfamiliar territory. The husbandly responsibility was driving, vehicle maintenance and livestock management. In Strasbourg I failed quite miserably to find anywhere for us to stay. We considered whether we might park unobtrusively in a quiet street, but decided against it. A swarthy man directed us into a tree-shaded car park and demanded one euro from us in a foreign language. We stayed there for a while and agreed that being surrounded on four sides by hurried traffic didn't augur well for a peaceful night. Round and round we drove, searching for the familiar *camping municipal* sign, or any camping sign: we were prepared to be flexible. Terry became so frustrated at driving in circles that he stopped in the middle of a road in the centre of Strasbourg and commanded me to find the tourist office and make them tell us where the campsite was hidden. I scampered obediently in the direction of an arrow pointing to the tourist office, which led to the square where the magnificent cathedral stands, and managed to squeeze through the doorway just as the office was closing for the weekend. A helpful girl handed me a little folded piece of paper with the name and address of a campsite on it, and a map of the city, and mentioned that it was permitted to park and sleep in the city's streets and car parks if we wished. Clutching my trophy I retraced my steps to where Terry had deposited me, and found he was no longer there. Traffic was busy; we'd made no contingency plans for where to meet, and I wondered how I would survive in Strasbourg with no husband and no money, and nowhere to stay. After I'd stood sadly on the pavement for a few minutes Tinkerbelle's rooftop appeared in the distance over the oncoming cars, and I climbed back in, relieved to have successfully accomplished my mission and to be reunited with my family. As soon as we'd successfully planted Tinkerbelle we planned to spend an evening enjoying the sights and sounds in town. There was a brass band playing in a square, competing with the sound of the cathedral bells; the bars, cafés and restaurants were filling up, and for once we looked forward to spending time in a large town. It seemed there was only one campsite in Strasbourg; we had the address, and four different maps, but on none of them did the address appear. The map given to me by the tourist office girl only showed the tram routes. Up and down, backwards and forwards, round and round and round we went, unable to find any clue as to where the damned Green Mountain site was hidden. We began to know Strasbourg like the back of our hand, and to strongly resent its secretiveness regarding the campsite. By 8.30 p.m. we were angrily hungry and barely speaking to each other, and decided we no longer cared where we slept, as long as we could stop driving. Abandoning the evening out idea we agreed to head out, anywhere, until we could find a camping site. The road westwards led through dozens of villages all called something or other -*heim*, one of which forbade cycling within its precincts, and none of which had any camping facilities, until at 9.00 p.m. we arrived in the small town of Rosheim, about 15 miles south-west of Strasbourg, and were met by the welcome sight of camping facilities on a farm. It was just a simple cherry orchard, but the relief of being able to get out of Tinkerbelle and let the dogs out was really quite overwhelming.

Dobbie had removed the entire bandage from his paw, and also one of the staples. As the vet had warned us, it would take a long time for the wound to heal, and it still gaped horribly. We tried bandaging it again and were defeated by Dobbie; the best we could do was to make sure we kept the wound clean.

By a coincidence, the cheese we'd bought that afternoon, which now seemed so long ago, had been produced in Rosheim. It was a variation of Munster, called Hansi au marc de Gewürtztraminer. The recommendation on the wrapper was to enclose the thing in aluminium foil and bake it until it became all runny. For somebody who didn't feel inclined to any great culinary effort at 9.30 p.m., it sounded like a quick and easy meal. Whether I did it correctly I couldn't say, but after the baking the foil revealed a strong-smelling slab of hot, grey, gluey cheese, which Terry professed to enjoy greatly and I didn't. Our neighbours in the cherry orchard were a French couple who studiously avoided us but watched us through a crack in their curtains, and a friendly German couple on their way to Kaysersberg, who fell in love with the dogs. The farmer and his wife came round to collect the negligible camping fee and spend ten minutes chatting, and invited us to help ourselves to cherries, which were a welcome antidote to the heavy greasiness of our weird dinner.

The next morning we went to give Strasbourg another chance to enchant us, driving through hundreds of hectares of maize fields, and back through the -heim villages growing out of their deep red soil. What we both wanted was to take a ride on one of Strasbourg's sleek trams, if only we could find a place near to one where we could safely leave the dogs in comfort. That wasn't easy, and we drove round the town becoming exasperated all over again. But finally, with the help of the tourist-office map, we found a stop near a quiet parking area where there were sufficient Sunday morning pedestrians to guarantee the dogs and Tinkerbelle would be safe for a couple of hours. We studied the automatic ticket machine on the platform, but we didn't have a coin between us, only a few euro notes, and in any case we didn't know how much a ticket cost. A lady I asked trilled, '*C'est gratuit!*' and so when the next tram glided up to the stop we jumped on and sat watching the outskirts of Strasbourg slide past. We realized we didn't know where to get off: for all the different maps we had, none of them told us what we wanted to know. While we were trying to correlate one of them to the diagrams on the inside of the tram, a gently drawling American voice said: 'If you want to get to the centre, the best place for you to get off would be *here*.' He indicated a diagram. 'Then you just cross the street and you'll find yourselves facing the cathedral. Have a nice visit in Strasbourg.' He touched a panel next to the door, which opened in silent obedience, stepped out and was gone.

Following his suggestion, we found ourselves walking towards the pink lacework stone of the stunning cathedral whose 142-metre-high spire dominates the city. The cathedral took three hundred years to build, which is no surprise because it's simply gigantic, and the intricacy of the carvings is what makes the place so wonderful. We are not cathedral people, but Notre Dame in Strasbourg is something quite exceptional. A Mass was taking place, and the interior was ablaze with candles, and reverberating with music from the grandiose organ. We stood for a few minutes, just long enough to savour the atmosphere, and then went to find out how we could visit the cathedral's famous astronomical clock. In a tiny ticket office, no more than a cubicle, a woman behind a desk talked on the phone to her boyfriend. She glanced up and dismissed us as being of no possible importance, and addressed her attention fully to the other end of the phone. After two minutes of standing listening to her, I decided to match her rudeness with some of our own, and yelled: 'Can we have tickets to visit the clock, please!'

She moved the receiver to her shoulder just long enough to say it was out of action for the day, thus saving us the pointless bother of joining the long queue forming on the pavement outside, unaware their wait would be fruitless. Instead we walked around the clean, smart streets, mingling with the other tourists to watch street entertainers, amongst them a man wearing a dinner jacket and standing on a box pretending to be a statue, and a couple of cheerful gentlemen demonstrating puppets. Mouth-watering smells came from every corner, and we settled at a table outside a restaurant just off the main square. Terry ordered the fried Camembert and fried potatoes, and I had a *tarte flambée*, washed down with a *pichet* of *rosé* which was very dark red, and rather expensive. The day became blazingly hot, and in midmeal we had to ask the waiter to move us under the shade of an awning. A couple who'd been sitting next to us asked to move too, and settled in the shade, fanning themselves and rolling their eyes. We were concerned for the dogs in Tinkerbelle and worried they might be too hot, even though we'd closed the curtains and left all the vents open, so we finished our meal quickly and found our way back to the tram stop. When we reached Tinkerbelle, the dogs were cool, and sleeping peacefully. We spent a couple of hours driving around Strasbourg, through the pretty Petite France area, around the European Union buildings, and I felt it was one of those rare things, a city where I would enjoy spending a few days.

The Alsace is a strange place, in many ways, because it's so unlike anywhere else in France. Of course, its history and geographical situation impart a strong German influence. Under German occupation in 1940, Alsace was incorporated into Germany. A third of the Alsatian population had been evacuated to the Dordogne when war broke out, but 140,000 men of fighting age were forcibly conscripted into the German army and put in the intolerable situation of being forced to fight against their own countrymen.

They were called the 'malgré nous', meaning against their will. Thousands died on the Russian front, or spent long years imprisoned in Siberian labour camps. Those who survived and returned after the war were seen as traitors by the rest of the French, and there's still a great deal of bitterness towards them, particularly those who were part of the German division responsible for the massacre at Oradour-sur-Glane. What a cruel destiny those men were dealt.

It was in this least French region that the French national anthem was born in 1792, the child of Claude-Joseph Rouget de Lisle (a rather strange name — a *rouget* is a red mullet). He was asked to write a stirring piece of marching music for the French army, at the time engaged in war with Austria, and he composed the music and wrote the belligerent lyrics overnight whilst garrisoned in Strasbourg. The first public recital of his work, called 'The Battle Song of the Army of the Rhine', was given at a banquet hosted by the mayor of Strasbourg, M. de Dietrich, and was an instant hit. The bloodthirsty song was adopted by revolutionaries on their march from Marseille to Paris, and became known as 'La Marseillaise'. It's since been banned several times because of its association with the Revolution, and suggestions have been made that its lyrics could benefit from being toned down, but so far it has remained true to Red Mullet's composition, and is the definitive French national anthem. Ironically, Red Mullet was a royalist and only just escaped the guillotine. M. de Dietrich wasn't so lucky.

While Alsace certainly isn't German, it isn't really French, either. It's simply Alsace.

The flat countryside north of Strasbourg was planted to maize. Anywhere not covered by a house or an industrial building was under maize. No carrots; no potatoes; no vines; no cabbages — just maize, maize and maize. I could understand the giant hamster's problem. Nevertheless, it was peaceful and pleasant driving along in the sun beside the Rhine. When we reached Sessenheim there was a traffic hold-up. There were half a dozen stationary cars halted at the barriers of a level crossing, their drivers milling around talking animatedly to each other, and looking left and right. From a queue of a dozen cars coming from the other direction, one of them threaded his way round the barrier and past us with a cheery wave. Another driver followed, and another, and soon everybody was wriggling their way round the barriers. We followed suit, past the one remaining stationary vehicle on the other side, a

German car whose driver was staring in pop-eyed shock at such anarchic behaviour.

From Seltz we snipped a corner off our route and drove through a lot of -*bachs* and -*willers* until we reached Wissembourg, the northernmost town in the Alsace, just in time to have missed some event that had been happening there. The town was heaving with vintage cars, chopped hogs, and Germans, and we were very hot and I was parched and desperate for a sip of water, so we squeezed into an ice-cream parlour-cum-cake shop. It was unadulterated pandemonium, one waitress and one waiter chasing around with trays loaded with outsize sundae glasses piled high with ice cream, topped with mountains of whipped cream, cherries, paper parasols and sparklers, and only because we were very determined and patient did we succeed in making the waitress deliver our drinks. Wissembourg is a pleasant town around which to stroll, the most remarkable building being the Salt House, which has a peculiar roof filled with four rows of attic windows. Historically what makes the town interesting is the fact that it was home for a while to Stanislas I, the on-and-off King of Poland during one of his 'off' periods. His luck changed when in 1725 his 23-year-old daughter Marie Leszczynski was chosen as wife to Louis XV, who was sixteen. She was a fruitful, quiet and dignified lady who, after producing ten children, kept herself to herself when her royal spouse sidelined her to cavort with his mistresses, Mesdames de Pompadour and du Barry. Marie's grandson, Louis XVI, and his wife, of whom more later, would lose their heads one day; Marie wouldn't be around by then, having died in 1768. As father of the Queen of France, old Stanislas did quite well for himself: although he didn't manage to be a king again, he lived in great style in France, entertaining up to 300 people to dinner each night, until he met an unfortunate end in his ninetieth year, when his dressing gown caught fire and he was engulfed in flames. Although he was pulled out by his old housekeeper, with whom he managed a joke about their both being inflamed at their age, he died of his injuries shortly afterwards.

At Wissembourg we turned left to follow the Franco-German frontier westwards, pausing at Lembach to visit one of the remnants of the spectacularly ineffectual and embarrassingly useless Maginot line. While Terry explored an old bunker there, I hunted for somewhere for us to stay that night, and settled on a campsite at Sturzelbronn. We drove through the green beauty of the North

Vosges Regional Park, and a valley peopled by Highland cattle with long fringes, long horns and long, rich-red shaggy coats. We'd crossed the regional boundary into Lorraine, and it was almost a relief, because Alsace is so perfect, so picturesque, that we'd started being overwhelmed by it. That doesn't imply Lorraine isn't a beautiful region too: it certainly is. But like *berawecka*, a little of Alsace goes a very long way.

Sturzelbronn's campsite lies beside a lake in a wooded area. Most of it is occupied by mobile homes, which are not at all mobile because their owners have attached brick-built extensions with tiled roofs, larger than the original building, patios, garden sheds and ponds. It was an ideal place for a quiet weekend, with children playing on sandy beaches and people swimming in the lake. To get in, though, took some time. New arrivals had to park behind a barrier, and walk to the office up a long steep slope. Off I went, and found an old lady pushing a mop around. She pointed me to a stern woman sitting behind a desk. This person agreed that we could stay for the night, and asked how we would pay, bearing in mind that they didn't accept credit cards. We had no cash, and the nearest cash machine was goodness knows how many miles away. So I said we'd pay by cheque.

Regarding me with a suspicious state, she picked up the phone and spoke to somebody briefly, then nodded and said they would accept our cheque. I trotted back to Tinkerbelle, assured Terry I was going as quickly as I could, collected my chequebook, and hauled back to the office.

The lady had had second thoughts.

'Unfortunately, I can't accept your cheque.'

'Why is that?'

'Because we don't take English cheques.'

'But I'm going to give you a French cheque.'

'How is it,' she asked, 'that you have a French chequebook?'

She stared at me over the top of her glasses. I was reminded of all the films I'd seen of Gestapo interrogations.

'Because I live in France,' I said.

She looked as if she didn't believe me. Could I prove it, she wanted to know.

I showed her my Social Security card, the *carte vitale*, my driving licence, and an envelope from an insurance company addressed to me, and she was finally satisfied, and pushed a button to raise the barrier so that Terry could drive through. We attracted considerable attention as we installed ourselves; the 'permanent' residents walked past peering at us, and at the dogs. Dobbie had decided to adopt the role of guard dog and barked furiously at everybody who came past, and even more angrily at any impudent dogs who looked at him. His wound was still open, but clean, and Terry was swabbing it several times daily with antiseptic. It wasn't easy — he had to catch Dobbie unawares and quickly squirt the paw. If Dobbie doesn't want you to do something to him, there's little you can do about it.

Anyway, back to Lorraine, famous for its quiche, its cross, Joan of Arc, and its General Charles de Gaulle. Quiche, from the German word 'Küche', meaning cooking, was actually invented in Germany, in the medieval kingdom called Lothringen which later became the Lorraine region of France. The double-barred cross of Lorraine was adopted by the French Resistance as their emblem as a riposte to the swastika of the Nazis. Referring to his difficult relationship with the larger-than-life figure of Charles de Gaulle, a native of Lorraine, Churchill said: 'Of all the crosses I have to bear, the heaviest is the cross of Lorraine.'

I was woken from a rare comfy sleep by Terry shouting: 'Susie, it's nearly 9.00 a.m. Come on, we've got to get going.'

I leapt from the bed, and checked my watch, which read just after 6.00 a.m.

'Funny, my watch has stopped,' I said, putting the kettle on.

Except for one lone swimmer twirling around in the lake there was no sign of life, and it occurred to me that there was possibly some form of curfew in operation so that residents were assured of a good lie-in each morning. I made breakfast as quietly as possible but as fast as I could, and we started packing up. There was still no sign of life outside. When I switched on the computer to download some photos, the clock read 6.58 a.m. I looked at my watch, which gave the same time.

'What time does your watch say?' I asked Terry.

'Nine forty.'

'It's wrong,' I said. 'It's not quite seven o'clock.'

The office didn't open until 8.00 a.m., and there was no way of leaving the site until somebody unlocked the barrier, so we sat marking time for an hour, which wasn't at all unpleasant in such tranquil surroundings and gave us an unusual opportunity to sit and do nothing for a while. With a good head start on the day, we were away just a few minutes after 8.00 a.m. and in the town of Bitche by 8.30 a.m. Despite the citadel Vauban had thoughtfully built on a hill for Bitche, its situation so close to the German border meant that the town had been fairly well ravaged by wars in the past: 80 per cent destroyed in the Great War, and again in the Second World War. We followed a sign to the Garden of Peace at the foot of the citadel, where the theme of war and peace is demonstrated by collections of plants living in harmony despite their inherently antagonistic tendencies. Unfortunately the garden didn't open until 11.00 a.m., and entertaining ourselves for two and a half hours in Bitche would be impossible, so we headed off, past a roundabout adorned with brightly painted and decorated watering cans, towards Sarreguemines, through an olde-Englishe-looking and very peaceful landscape of valleys and fields dotted with rolled bales of hay, pristine small villages and neat fields of wheat and straw stubble. Like its neighbour Bitche, Sarreguemines also had an amusing roundabout, depicting a life-sized gardener working in his garden, surrounded by garden tools and a wheel-barrow, all entirely made from plants. As we were right on the German border, we decided to visit the Federal Republic, and followed a small road, dodging a red squirrel that ran in front of us, until we passed a sign announcing we were now in the Bundesrepublik Deutschland (Federal

Republic of Germany), which was the nearest thing to a formal frontier that existed. We couldn't find anywhere in that part of Germany's Federal Republic that was serving coffee. We drove through about ten villages, and all of them didn't have a café, or a bakery, so we returned to France and found in the centre of Sarreguemines a rather scruffy and friendly old-fashioned bar. It didn't look as if it had made any effort to keep up with the passage of time, or to slip into the twenty-first century, and neither did the cheery clientele, who leaned on the bar sipping alcohol and puffing cigarettes. We enjoyed excellent cups of hot chocolate and coffee, smiling at table mats made of laminated cartoons from the local newspaper.

Next town was Saint-Avold, home to Europe's largest American military cemetery. More than 10,000 American soldiers are buried in the fifty-hectare cemetery set amongst the mellow hills of Lorraine, their headstones overlooked by a large white memorial. For the rest of our journey, until we reached Brittany, we'd be driving through land that had been a theatre of war for centuries, with cemeteries of varying nationalities forming as significant a part of the landscape as the trees and hills.

Between Longeville and Zimming a metal

pillbox protrudes from a grassy mound, surrounded by conifer trees and weeping birches. Next to it stands a stone engraved with the cross of Lorraine, and the words '*Aux résistants et deportés 1939 — 1945: Leur chemin a été celui de sacrifice.*' Translations in German and English say: 'Remember, passer-by, that their way was that of sacrifice and they struggled for your liberty.' Simple, and poignant.

Unlike its frivolous neighbour Alsace, Lorraine's architecture and landscape has a more sober air. Plenty of flowers, but not the blinding displays of geraniums on balconies. The landscape is a patchwork of orderly, unspectacular wheat fields: a very stolid, sensible part of the world. Metz was our chosen town for lunch. We'd invented a silly game of looking out for funny place names, Metz being one of them because of its pronunciation: mess. Around the town we found several Sillys, a Mad, an Orny, Charly, Woippy and an Ennery. But Metz itself, capital of the Moselle *département* and the Lorraine region, is a dignified town of wide streets, pretty parks, huge churches and no-nonsense buildings. On the river Moselle dozens of swans were gliding around with their necks bent so they could see themselves in the water. We headed for an interesting-looking North African restaurant down a narrow lane, where the tables were curiously positioned on a slope so that cutlery, crockery and glassware were in danger of sliding off, and it was extremely uncomfortable sitting on a lopsided chair that was several inches higher on one side than another. The menu, when it arrived, was utterly meat-orientated, and quite expensive. We asked one of the beautiful waitresses whether there was a possibility of substituting something for the meat element, as we were vegetarians, and she said she'd ask the chef. When she returned she said no, the chef said we'd just have to eat meat. She didn't seem to think this would present any problem, because she'd come back with a carafe of water, basket of bread rolls, and the wine list, and stood with her pencil poised over her pad to take our order. We said that regrettably we'd have to find somewhere else to eat, and stood up. The other lopsided diners stared wide-eyed and open-mouthed, knives and forks still, as if they couldn't believe their eyes. After roaming around for quite a while, we came upon a truly delightful restaurant called Chez Mon Oncle Ernest, with a wonderful 1900s décor complete with an HMV wind-up gramophone. The food was excellent: roast salmon with vegetables and a potato gratin, and *pain perdu* for dessert. We asked if they could play a record on the gramophone, and were told that it made a truly awful noise, but if we waited until the last customer had left they'd try it for us. The chef placed a record on the turntable, started winding the handle, and dropped the needle on to the record, which emitted a most terrible wailing noise. He wound faster and faster, but could only produce a frenzied yowl. His sister was standing in for the regular waitress who'd been taken ill; she told us she had a teddy bear shop just up the hill, near the cathedral. When we'd finished our meal we walked up there to admire her shop which was guarded by a two-metre-tall bear, and crammed with teddy bears big and small, old and new, dressed and naked — a teddy bear lover's paradise.

Walking back to Tinkerbelle we met Metz's notorious Graouli, suspended overhead from wires, and a fine-looking creature he was. The duck-beaked, two-legged dragon with eyes bigger than its belly used to haunt the Roman amphitheatre in Metz, until St Clement came along and rather cruelly drowned it.

We'd intended driving due north up to Thionville, following the Path of Freedom, the route taken by General Patton and his troops from France to Belgium via

Luxembourg, but we made a last-minute change and opted instead to divert to Briey to have a look at Swiss architect Le Corbusier's celebrated Cité Radieuse, the apartment block designed by him in the 1960s and Briey's main tourist attraction, and from there to Valleroy to see the Russian cemetery. The radiant city was an absolute swine to find, because there were no directions to it until you were almost upon it. Maybe this was to deter visitors, because frankly this place was simply awful, a tired, ugly concrete block of flats on pillars, in a shabby area surrounded by gloomy trees, where groups of young people were drinking from bottles and smoking. It might have been a wonder of its time; personally I wouldn't have liked it even when it was brand new, and in its current decaying state we didn't even stop Tinker-belle, but turned smartly round and headed for Valleroy. Some towns were better than others at indicating where things were; Valleroy wasn't much good at directions to the Russian cemetery. Terry commanded me to keep asking people where it was, and all I succeeded in doing was attracting looks that indicated they thought I was quite mad. We saw a man on a motorbike, and I commanded Terry to do the asking this time. He was spectacularly successful, because the motorcyclist was visiting a friend in Valleroy and couldn't have been more helpful. He disappeared into his friend's house, emerged with a piece of paper with a little map on it, and was about to hand it to us when he changed his mind and indicated we should follow him. Kicking his bike into life he led us several kilometres down a country lane, to the entrance to the cemetery in a grove of trees, then wheeled away with a raised hand. Nice man.

The fifty Russians buried in the cemetery, captured soldiers who were literally worked to death in the mines, lie in graves marked with simple white crosses, each bearing a name, except for one simply engraved 'inconnu', and another which indicates three bodies buried together. A sculpture of three emaciated figures standing in a group, one with his arm raised and pointing, maybe towards Russia, watch over them, next to a post hung with wind chimes, and the only other adornment is a few clumps of lavender filled with murmuring bees and butterflies rummaging in the blossoms. I thought it wasn't a bad place to be.

Next on our list of visits was the place known as the Longwy concentration camp, the only such camp that existed on unannexed French soil. In our usual rather haphazard way we drove to Longwy, where there was no indication of where the camp might be, nor did anybody seem to know anything about it. I managed to find a brochure from which we learned that the camp was actually in a small town called Thil, several kilometres south-east of Longwy. I scored no points at all for making Terry drive miles out of our way, and by the time we'd found Thil it was too late in the day to be able to visit the camp. Consultation with the pile of books confirmed the nearest campsite was at Thionville, due north of Metz by only a short distance, so going back on ourselves we headed there, having made a largely useless detour of eighty kilometres.

The *camping municipal* at Thionville was well signposted, on the banks of the Moselle and adjacent to the Parc Napoléon, sharing its terrain with a kayaking club. A smiley lady indicated that Terry could go and park, and I waited to book in. She was dealing with a little man who looked worn out and rather desperate. He had to keep making phone calls, and standing next to him it was impossible not to hear the content, which was that he was entirely without food, or money. He implored whoever was on the other end of the line to send him some funds, and they apparently were not intending to do so. He was almost weeping. A bit uncharitably I wished he'd give me a five-minute slot so I could sort us out and go and have a drink. Twice he walked away as if he'd finished his sad business, and just as I opened my mouth to talk to the lady back he came, pulling at his hair and asking to use the phone again. When he put it down, he told the *gardienne* that money was being sent, and he would be able to settle his camping fees within two days, and she replied he wasn't to worry, just to make himself comfortable.

After he eventually wandered away, the *gardienne* shook her head and said sadly, 'Poor man. What a terrible situation.' Then she startled me by asking if she could offer me a cold drink, or a nice cup of tea. That was a first at a campsite, where, however pleasant the receptionist might be, they don't usually offer refreshments at their own expense. I declined anyway, because neither tea nor a cold drink would hit the right spot, and went to find Terry, who'd chosen an excellent corner by the park and right on the riverbank. Just opposite where we were parked, the unfortunate little man, with a dog, was climbing down out of a rather ancient camper van. I told Terry about his plight.

'Put some food together for him, and the

dog. We'll leave it beside the van.' Terry likes to pretend he's mean and hard, but internally he's as soft as an uncooked sponge. So we made up a parcel of eggs, cheese, croissants, tomatoes, fruit, milk, coffee, sugar and some dog food, and wrapped it in foil, placed it in a shopping bag and hung it on the wing mirror of the camper. Several hours later it was still there, although the man and his dog had been back for quite a while, so Terry went over and knocked on the door. He handed the packet to the man, who shook his head vehemently at first, saying he was fine, and didn't need any help. Terry grasped him by the arm, patted him on the shoulder, and said: 'Take it — we want you to have it.' So he did accept it, and we hoped he and his dog enjoyed it.

Although the campsite was well situated, it wasn't the prettiest we'd been to, but the *gardienne* made up for that by doing absolutely everything she could to make visitors welcome. Because the park attracted the town's young at night, the *gardienne* kept the campsite sanitary blocks locked to prevent the revellers from making use of them, and only residents were allowed a key. Terry and I had one key between us, so when we both needed the loos at the same time, I unlocked the gents for him and kept the key so I couldn't find myself locked in the ladies.

The inevitable happened, and while Terry was in his loo another person went out and locked the door behind him. I'd stayed chatting by the washbasins with another English lady for about ten minutes, and when I came out I could hear Terry calling patiently. Yes, he was locked in the lavatory, which caused great mirth to the surrounding campers, none of whom had thought to unlock the door for him.

When we left after a rather disturbed night because of a long, loud, late party in the park, the *gardienne* first of all asked us whether we'd enjoyed our stay, and if we could suggest anything else she could do to improve the campsite. She asked us to sign her guest book, and gave us both a hug and several kisses. If you're ever in or near Thionville and looking for a really charming lady who takes pride in her work, do visit the municipal campsite.

We went on a sightseeing expedition of Thionville, of which we knew nothing before our arrival, but it has an interesting history, amusing legends and a pleasing layout and architecture. That it was a German town between 1905 and 1914, when much of it was built to the design of a German architect from Cologne, is illustrated by wide avenues of chunky elegant houses, the sort you find in places like Kensington, and solid, tasteful buildings in the town centre. In contrast is the Tour aux Puces, the twelfth-century Flea Tower. One explanation for the name is that a princess imprisoned there was eaten alive by fleas, but we preferred the story concerning Charlemagne, who was particularly fond of Thionville, and used to stay there to indulge his passion for hunting with his pack of 683 dogs. Now, we love dogs, and once had as many as six simultaneously, but that sounds like a lot. Anyway, Charlemagne had this vast pack of animals, which stayed in Thionville while he was elsewhere. The dogs were infested with fleas which, as they ran out of space on their canine hosts, migrated to Thionville's citizens who were soon scratching as vigorously as the dogs. When the situation became intolerable, the citizenry decided to write to Charlemagne, and a messenger was despatched to deliver their letter. Like all the inhabitants of Thionville, the messenger was flea-ridden, and one of his passengers sprang on to and bit Charlemagne's nose. The emperor at once understood the problem, and ordered the building of the tower to contain the dogs and their fleas.

Five centuries later, during the French Revolution, Thionville was besieged by the

Austrian army supported by the Royalist French, including Châteaubriand, of whom more later. For two months the defenders of Thionville resisted calls by the besieging army to surrender. To underline their determination, they mounted a wooden horse upon the ramparts, with a bale of hay in its mouth and a sign reading: 'We will surrender when the horse eats the hay.'

We enjoyed our visit to Thionville, which was lively and not at all touristy. At one of several outdoor cafés in the large central square we sat trying to order drinks for nearly half an hour, but the waitress was too busy talking to her friends, and finally we gave up and found a smaller, much less attractive place where we were instantly served.

Now we turned back to that little-advertised place, the concentration camp at Thil. Following advice in the brochure, I telephoned the *mairie* to ask whether we could visit the camp, and was invited to collect the key from them. We could have a guide, if we wished, but we wanted to just wander around on our own. There were no signs in Thil to the concentration camp. The *mairie* indicated the general direction, but we couldn't find it, and asked several pedestrians, none of whom seemed to know where it was, or even that there was such a thing.

Finally we met a man who did, and we found the crypt tucked away up the hill from the town cemetery. Unlike the cemetery, which was ablaze with flowers, the crypt was a bleak place. Terry unlocked the rusty gate and we stood before a monument representing a skeletal figure tangled in barbed wire. Inside the crypt, built by local volunteers and opened in 1946, was an oven that had been installed at the camp to dispose of bodies; to one side was a notice from the manufacturers saying that they were not responsible for the use to which the oven had been put. They had installed it in the Villerupt abattoir before the war, and it had been dismantled and removed to the Thil camp by the Nazis. Three vases of roses stood in front of the ghastly thing; stone tablets on the wall bore the names of local victims. There was an urn containing ashes from Buchenwald, more flowers and ribbons and flags of various organizations, and a prisoner's suit of coarse striped material, surprisingly thick, like blanketing, not the thin fabric we'd imagined, in a glass case. There were signs that somebody was working on a scale model of the camp and factory, but it was only half finished, and a plastic bag of rubbish lay in a corner.

After the Allied bombardment of the rocket

development site at Peenemünde on the Baltic coast, the production of V2 rockets was moved to Thil, where thousands of prisoners, North African, Senegalese, Italian, and Eastern European Jews, were sent to work in the mines. They existed in appalling conditions on rations of watery soup, forced to march several kilometres to the factory from the barracks, carrying heavy rocks. While the Americans were entering Thil by road, the surviving prisoners were being shipped by train to concentration camps in Germany. There's no sign today of the subterranean factory that lies under the innocent and grassy fields populated by herds of contentedly grazing cattle. It was a sobering visit, and we thought of the despair and torment this place had witnessed, just outside a small town where nobody knew about it, and where many apparently still don't. But somebody somewhere is obviously still caring for this place and trying to keep its memory alive.

We diverted from the border again, to visit Verdun. Our trip wasn't intended as a pilgrimage, nor as a morbid itinerary visiting battlefields and cemeteries, but so much of north and eastern France is steeped in warfare that if we wanted to understand the history, we couldn't ignore these places. Just outside the small village of Abaucourt-Hautecourt is a German military cemetery from the First World War, spick and span. We'd see many more German cemeteries, all as beautifully maintained as their Allied counterparts, and the fact that they are so, in French soil, seems to recall the age of chivalry, when all the fallen were treated with equal reverence.

Because Verdun has always been synonymous with the horror of warfare — mud, blood, misery and despair — we didn't know what to expect of the vast cemetery complex there. We'd seen so many films about the battle, and read so many stories, that I thought it would be sad, depressing, unbearable, but what I hadn't anticipated was that on that bright, warm June day it would be beautiful.

Hectares of white crosses stretching over the horizon, with a red poppy at the heart of each. An ocean of crosses. Thousands and thousands of perfect rose plants, in full bloom. Birdsong, and battalions of butterflies.

During 1916, in ten months, 800,000 men died, disappeared or were wounded at Verdun. The town's symbolic importance comes from the ninth century, when the Emperor Charlemagne signed a treaty there dividing his empire between his three sons, laying the foundation of the future France, Germany and Lorraine, an event considered one of the most important in the history of Europe. The Germans believed that the taking of Verdun would deal the French a demoralizing psychological blow. They'd simply keep killing until the French no longer had the heart to fight, until their very spirit had been bled to death. But the French fought ferociously. The battle cry of Verdun was: *They shall not pass*. Unlike their enemy, the French were able to resupply and rest their troops for a few days every so often, while they were replaced by others. Eventually the two sides were simply killing each other mindlessly. France's most decorated town, Verdun was never taken.

We drove around the monuments, past the sign to the village of Fleury, which no longer exists. The sign says simply: *This was Fleury*. It was one of nine villages destroyed for all time and never rebuilt: the amount of unexploded ammunition amongst the ruins makes it too dangerous. In the ossuary are the bones of 150,000 unidentified soldiers, French and German, lying together for ever in peace in the building financed by donations from France and abroad. We went to see the Trench of Bayonets, where in June 1916 a company of the 137th Infantry

Regiment was positioned, facing German artillery. By the end of the day, they'd all vanished. After the war, bayonet tips and rifle muzzles were seen protruding from the ground. When the trench was excavated, the remains of the men were discovered beneath their weapons, and it was deduced that rather than retreat they'd remained in their positions and been buried alive. An American gentleman named C. F. Rand, from Pennsylvania, funded the building of a memorial to them. There's an imposing entrance with the inscription, in French: 'To the memory of the French soldiers who sleep upright in this trench, their guns in their hands. Their American brothers.' A paved pathway leads to a mound of earth bearing crosses and wreaths, and small bunches of flowers, sheltered by a low concrete roof on pillars. There was a deeply mournful feeling here, emphasized by the bats nesting at the eastern end of the trench.

What we noticed at Verdun, apart from the pristine condition of all the monuments, memorials and graves, was the vast network of craters and shell holes pitting the contours of the ground, from where trees and five-metre-high cow parsley grow as nature slowly reclaims the land. The mud and barbed wire have faded into a peaceful green landscape. The overall feeling I was left with was how much love remained in this place, and how, although the events commemorated here took place almost a century ago, the dead have not been forgotten. And I felt too that the ghosts of Verdun might quite possibly sleep peacefully today. It is a very, very emotional place to visit.

* * *

We went into Verdun town and were pleased and surprised to find that despite the grim associations of its name, it's a town of charm, with medieval buildings as well as many memorials like the Victory Monument and the Monument to the Dead. The entrance is through the splendid fourteenth-century Porte Chaussée, an archway within two crenellated stone towers, and Verdun's streets were hung with baskets of vivid flowers and busy with cheerful pedestrians. There's a small harbour, the eighteenth-century bishop's palace is now the World Centre for Peace, the theatre is a small-scale copy of the Paris opera house, and we found a pretty good cup of hot chocolate in a pavement restaurant.

Another wartime event took place in Verdun which was far less savage than the great battle of 1916. In 1803, the Treaty of Amiens was broken by England, who declared war on France. The treaty had only been an excuse for a short break in the irritating hostilities between the two countries. Napoléon Bonaparte ordered British nationals living in France to be arrested and detained in various areas, one of which was Verdun. For eleven years, between 800 and 1,200 English lived on parole in the city, free to lead their lives as they wished provided they gave their word not to escape. The military men amongst them received an allowance from Verdun's governor, and the poorer people were supported by charities in England. Many men had their families and servants with them. Others married local ladies. One third of the births registered in Verdun between 1803 and 1814 were British. The 'prisoners' enjoyed balls and parties, horse races and show jumping, duels and gambling. Local commerce prospered; the natives would, for the right price, help people to escape. There's a tale told of two escaped English sailors who managed to reach Boulogne, where they made a tiny boat from little pieces of wood and a fragment of sail, and with no hope of success set sail towards what they hoped would be freedom, but was almost certain to be death. They were duly captured by the French, and would have been shot if the story of their daring and foolhardy adventure hadn't reached Napoleon. He sent for the men and their waif-like vessel, and was so impressed with their courage that not only did he have them safely delivered to an English ship, he gave them gold coins as well. Ah. I've always had a big soft spot for Boney.

When the English were finally free to leave Verdun, they left a legacy of enormous debts behind, which the French government tried unsuccessfully to recover right up until the end of the Great War. But . . . in June 2003, thirty descendants of the Verdun English called on the mayor of Verdun, and one of them paid a debt of twenty-one francs, owing from his ancestor to a carpenter for the framing of a picture called *The Hope*.

Pleased to find that the town has risen triumphantly above its grim past, we turned west towards our next port of call, once more a little off-track, a small place that played a seminal role in France's history.

Although Varennes-en-Argonne is today just a sleepy village, it has two notable points of interest. The most visible is the gigantic memorial erected in 1927, in the style of a Greek temple, by the Pennsylvania Monuments Commission to honour the American troops who served in the Great War, and liberated Varennes in 1918.

A series of other more discreet memorials are dotted around the town, telling the fascinating tale of what happened there 213 years, almost to the day, before we arrived.

Imagine this: it was almost midnight on a warm June evening in 1791 when the door to the Bras d'Or tavern favoured by the Republicans was flung open, and in came breathless Jean-Baptiste Drouet, a postmaster from the not-very-far-away town of Sainte-Menehould, with extraordinary tidings: the French king, Louis XVI, and his queen, Marie Antoinette, were on their way to Varennes in a carriage trying to escape from France. M. Drouet had recognized the king because of his likeness on a coin and had ridden at top speed to arrange an ambush. The mayor of Varennes, whose name was M. Sauce, sent his children into the streets shouting, 'Fire, fire!' to awaken the dormant citizenry. By the time the royal cavalcade reached the town barricades had been set up, and after being questioned by M. Sauce the royal fugitives were invited to stay the night at his house. The next day they were returned to Paris, whence they'd been trying to flee to safety in Luxembourg. Louis lost his head in January 1793; Marie Antoinette was parted from hers in October of the same year. The king's sister, who was also captured in Varennes, went to the guillotine the following year. Louis and Marie Antoinette's ten-year-old son Louis XVII died in prison in 1795, but Madame Royale, the king's daughter, did rather well for herself and lived to a reasonable age, serving as a councillor to kings Louis XVIII and Charles X.

After what must be rated as the most sensational event in French history, many of Varennes's wealthy residents left, and the town became impoverished. The inhabitants were divided over their part in the affair, and whilst the principal players were commended by some, they were criticized by others, and received death threats. M. Drouet went on to lead a fairly exciting life until he died in Mâcon. Mayor Sauce and his wife had to leave town when he was dismissed from his post. Mme Sauce fell down a well and broke both legs running away from invading Prussians, and died several days later. Mayor Sauce's house, where the royals lodged the night before their enforced return to Paris, was destroyed in the First World War, and its location is marked by a stone plaque.

Coming to Varennes straight from Verdun, we were not greatly moved by the thought of a few royals losing their heads, but thank you to Varennes for the excellent noticeboards describing the event.

Back on the road north, we felt Dobbie should have his foot looked at to see if it was healing. Terry had been carefully cleaning it several times a day, but the wound was still gaping open. In Dun-sur-Meuse we found a veterinary surgery, and as I went through the door the vet was just off on his afternoon rounds. Very obligingly he came back and asked us to bring Dobbie in. They struck up an instant rapport, and Dobbie was happy to show his foot to Dr Gressens, a tall, fair-haired Belgian vet of great charm, who told us he owned a cottage in Scotland where he went shooting with his dogs as often as he could. I asked whether it wasn't an odd thing for a vet to go out killing wild birds, but he smiled and said he killed very few, and only did it for the pleasure of watching and working with his dogs.

Dobbie's foot was as well as we could expect, said Dr Gressens, given that it was a serious wound that would take a long time to heal. But it was clean and the best thing to do was to keep applying the antiseptic. He refused payment for his advice, and gave Terry a plastic bottle with a spout on it that might help.

8

NORTH-EASTERN FRANCE — BOOMERANGS AND BARE-ARSED POTATOES

Shortly afterwards we crossed the boundary into the Champagne-Ardennes region, and the *départément* of the Ardennes. We passed a herd of heavy Ardennes draught horses, a breed with its roots in the ice age, progenitor of all the heavy horses of the modern era. Their ancestors carried Crusaders, and the armies of Julius Caesar and Napoleon. Watching them grazing so peacefully along the banks of the river I desperately hoped their destiny was not linked to the table, like so many of the heavy breeds.

Sedan's municipal campsite sits on the banks of the river Meuse, and we settled there for the night. We found Sedan to be like the curate's egg, good in parts. Not the sinister apartment blocks teeming with mean-looking characters with pit bull terriers — this could have been the pit bull terrier capital of the world. The public gardens and parks, though, were attractive and well cared for, and there's a great monument to the dead of the First World War — a massive column with a bronze *poilu* guarded by four beautifully cast wild boars, the symbol of the Ardennes. The town centre has some splendid buildings, which could benefit from a slight facelift and a little colour. Sedan's jewel is its fortified castle, the largest in Europe, covering three and a half hectares; to stand beneath its walls is to realize just how small and insignificant one human being can be. Paradoxically, for all its size, the castle couldn't save Boney's nephew Napoleon III from a humiliating, overwhelming defeat by Bismarck's armies during the Franco-Prussian war; taken prisoner at Sedan, he was regarded as 'responsible for the defeat, ruin and dismemberment of France'. He's better remembered in France for that than as the force behind the creation of modern Paris and the demolition of the slums. He died in self-imposed exile in England, and is buried in the crypt of St Michael's Abbey in Farnborough, the church founded by his wife, the Empress Eugénie (of the lovely summer palace in Biarritz).

Sedan suffered a second mortifying defeat when the Panzers broke through the French defences there in 1940. As always, standing on the ground where such events took place was a slightly surreal experience, because in the sunshine, amid the noise of car horns and radios, it was impossible to imagine what it must have been like during battle. There were plenty of enticing restaurants at the foot of the castle walls, but it was rather early for lunch, and so we decided to go and explore Charleville-Mézières. On the way we remarked on the well-cared-for municipal flower beds and roundabouts of the small town of Donchery. What we didn't know, then, was that at the exact moment we drove through Donchery the police were digging in the grounds of a local château, and excavating the remains of two young girls murdered and buried there by self-confessed serial killer Michel Fourniret.

It was a pity that since we'd reached the Ardennes everything we'd found out about it was rather gloomy, because the wooded and peaceful countryside is very beautiful. Charleville-Mézières in appearance is solid, sensible, spacious if rather austere. There are wide avenues lined with trees and robust three-storey buildings with mansard roofs, and the central square, the Place Ducale, is absolutely gorgeous; but like Sedan, a splash of colour wouldn't have done any harm. Probably we were still under the colourful Alsatian influence, which emphasized the rather monochrome towns of the Ardennes. It was as if these large towns felt that anything as frivolous as tubs of geraniums should be frowned upon.

We ended up on one of our exasperating searches for a restaurant where we could park the van in the shade nearby, where the menu didn't consist wholly of meat, and which was open and affordable. Time was running against us, and we always panic in those circumstances: criteria give way to fear, and we're prepared to settle for just about anything. We plonked ourselves down in a pavement restaurant which didn't look particularly attractive but had plenty of fish on the menu and was willing to serve us lunch at 2.00 p.m. Although the fish wasn't great, and neither was the wine, the place was redeemed by the *crêpes* which arrived with a huge jug of Grand Marnier, with which the waiter drowned them; although they refused to ignite, they were delicious and we left the restaurant in high spirits.

Carolomacériens, as inhabitants of Charleville-Mézières call themselves, are proud their town was the birthplace of wild child Arthur Rimbaud. However, the dazzling young poet, who led a bohemian and dissolute but exciting life, did not reciprocate this affection. The town loves Arthur very much more than Arthur loved the town, and as a youth he ran away four times from the provincial ambience he despised. Abandoning poetry when he was just twenty to become a wanderer, an explorer, and possibly an arms dealer and slave trader, Rimbaud died rather horribly, in Marseille, at the age of thirty-seven from complications after having his cancerous leg amputated. Ironically, he's buried in his birthplace, when he'd probably have chosen to be left in the more vibrant and seamy atmosphere of Marseille.

Just round the corner from the Place Ducale, in the Place Winston-Churchill, is the International Puppet Institute. Every three years the town hosts the World Puppet Festival. Following tradition, we were too early by ten days to celebrate just about the most unlikely event anyone would expect to be held in this dignified town — the 2004 Boomerang World Cup. No, I am not jesting — Charleville-Mézières' staid façade seems to hide a great sense of fun. Swallowing our disappointment at missing the boomerang competition, we went next to Bogny-sur-Meuse to console ourselves with a visit to its largest resident, a fifty-tonne stainless-steel pig named Woinic.

You might believe that in a small town like Bogny-sur-Meuse, with a population of just under 6,000, a fifty-tonne stainless-steel pig would be hard not to find. It must be a fairly large creature, one would imagine, something difficult for its neighbours not to notice. With a false sense of confidence we drove into Bogny-sur-Meuse expecting to find, if not a bold sign, at least some small clue as to where the creature might be. We drove around the place for half an hour, not seeing any porcine indications, so we began asking pedestrians where Woinic was. They looked at us as if we were mad, or aliens, and hurried away.

Terry became so irritable I feared he might mow down the next pedestrian who failed to direct us to Woinic, and I was so exasperated I began to wonder just how much effort we wanted to expend on our quest. I telephoned the local tourist office for help.

'No, you won't be able to see it. It's been put away.'

How do you put away something weighing fifty tonnes, more than eight metres high and fourteen long, and why?

I explained politely that I was writing a book about interesting places in France, and we'd travelled to Bogny-sur-Meuse so as to include their pig, and it seemed a pity for Woinic to miss out on this opportunity. Would it not be possible for her to make a phone call to the owner so we could just take a tiny peep? If I rang back in five minutes, she said, she'd do her best.

But when I rang back, the answer was no: the pig wasn't available for viewing.

Terry insisted I found out where the pig we couldn't see was hidden, and so, reluctantly, the tourist office lady explained where we should go. When we arrived there was a tall iron gate, and standing inside it a splendid three-metre-high stainless-steel sculpture of a pop singer, and another of a knight in armour, but no sign of any pig. Next door to the yard there was a small garden, and a fat man sitting in a deckchair. We called out to him, smiling, and asked if he knew how we could get a glimpse of Woinic. He heaved himself out of the deckchair, spat on the ground, and said, 'It's closed. They're busy. Good-bye.' He went through a door and slammed it behind him.

And so we never did see the pig, which I think is actually a wild boar, and the man in the deckchair, rude and fat as he was, was a very poor substitute. Still hopeful that the Ardennes would reveal its better side to us, we followed the serpentine coils of the Meuse through the valley of legends, where all kinds of gremlins and ghoulies live, and the naughty *pie-pie-van-vans* lure unwary travellers into the forest where they get lost, and benevolent *nutons* will mend your shoes and saucepans during the night. We stopped just before Tournavaux to pay a visit to the four famous sons of Aymon. It was quite a hike up the side of a steep hill to where the four knights, draped in monk-like robes like Obi Wan Kenobi from *Star Wars*, stand overlooking the valley and the river winding through it, next to their magical horse Bayard, who could carry just one of them or, when required, all four.

One of the brothers killed Charlemagne's nephew in a dispute over a game of chess. Pursued implacably through the Ardennes forests by the emperor, the brothers were saved when Bayard carried them across the river Meuse in one great bound. Nothing would pacify Charlemagne or stop his pursuit of the brothers except for the sacrifice of the horse, but although he was thrown into the river with a millstone round his neck, Bayard survived, and can still be heard sometimes, whinnying in the forest.

The Meuse twists its way through the wooded, steep-sided valley between Bogny and Revin, past panoramic viewpoints. There's the seven o'clock rock, the seven villages rock, the long rock, and the Devil's château, where the lord of Thilay agreed a deal with Satan: his soul in exchange for a magnificent château for his wife, to be built and completed before cockcrow. Satan summoned all the goblins and elves, and they worked through the night, until only one stone remained to complete the château. But then the cock crowed, and Satan in a fit of rage kicked the walls down. On the opposite side of the river lounge the three Dames de Meuse, sisters married to three brothers. Whilst their menfolk were off fighting the Crusades, the hussies were disporting themselves disgracefully with some good-for-nothings, and in punishment were turned to rock.

Then there's the Dame des roches, married against her will to a man she didn't love. During his absence, the Devil changed her into a green bird so she could visit her true love. But one sad day, her mean old husband came home unexpectedly; the bird couldn't get back into her home because a grille had been overturned, and she regained her human form and fled to her lover. The husband caught her, killed the lover, fed him to the dogs, and hanged the errant lady. Sometimes, people still see a green bird that changes into the shape of a woman.

Isn't it interesting, by the way, that in all the tales and legends of infidelity, it's always the wife who's to blame? And that their crusading Christian husbands obviously didn't know that 'to err is human . . . '

Less frivolously, there's a memorial to 106 young *maquisards* who were killed on Mont Malgré Tout in Revin in June 1944. The summit of Malgré Tout earned its name in the eighteenth century, when a local land-owner wanted to build a house up there, against the wishes of local forestry folk. He insisted he would have his house, *malgré tout*. And so it was that a house appeared one morning, where the night before there had been none. The gentleman had built a demountable framework and, with the help of friends, put it into place during the night. *Malgré tout*, he had his house. Good; there was a story with a happy ending. And the countryside around Revin is ravishing.

By late afternoon we'd reached Rocroi. All we knew about the town when we arrived was that it was only one kilometre from the Belgian border, and that it had a campsite, so we were very pleased to discover that Rocroi is a wonderfully preserved, star-shaped fortified town, and the campsite was safe enough for the dogs to have the freedom to run as much as they liked. Schoolboys from the City of London school were staying at the site to do their silver and bronze Duke of Edinburgh awards. I asked one of their teachers why they'd chosen Rocroi. He said that they'd always taken the boys to the Brecon Beacons before, but when foot-and-mouth disease broke out and the Beacons were off-limits, they'd had to look for somewhere else. They'd chosen the Ardennes because it's an excellent area for walking, and having found Rocroi the previous year and enjoyed it so much, they'd returned.

Rocroi's campsite fed directly on to the grassy ramparts of its fortifications, and there were long walks and mounds for the dogs to run up and down. Dobbie's foot was still unhealed, but he needed to run, so we left him to play for an hour. Tally, who never tires, spent several hours playing football with the schoolboys while Dobbie watched, puzzled as usual.

The boys set off on one of their trials in the early evening; a couple of hours later a group of giggling local girls came looking for them, strolling nonchalantly about the site and laughing loudly. They settled down on the banks of the ramparts, turned on their radio and sat drinking beer. During the night, when the boys had returned and were asleep in their tents, the girls crept up and released all the guy ropes.

No fortified town would be worth its salt if Vauban hadn't had a finger in it somewhere. In 1643 Rocroi was the scene of a celebrated battle between the hitherto invincible Spanish army and the French, led by the 22-year-old Duc d'Enghien, from the powerful Bourbon dynasty, who came to be known as the Great Condé, and scored a resounding victory at Rocroi. Vauban began his military career when he joined Condé's regiment in 1651. When in a fit of pique Condé went to fight with the Spanish, Vauban followed him. Both men subsequently returned to France, were pardoned and went on to enjoy glittering careers. Vauban, who, as we know, was never one to twiddle his thumbs, supervised the modifications of Rocroi's defences.

It was chilly the next morning, with a sharp little breeze and rain forecast. We walked to the town centre, two minutes from the campsite. The streets of the town, which were deserted, radiate symmetrically from an old well in the centre of the square, where we had a nice hot drink with some excellent *pains aux raisins* and blue chocolate 'slates', a regional speciality. The restaurant where we were sitting proposed on its lunchtime menu the wonderfully named potato-and-onion dish *cacasse à cul nu* — bare-arsed potato stew. As far as I remember, it was the only opportunity we met on the entire journey to try a regional

French savoury dish suitable for vegetarians, and we wouldn't be there at lunchtime to enjoy it. Rocroi is interesting, and charming, but there wasn't enough there to entertain us for nearly four hours.

Aubenton lies to the south-west of Rocroi, just over the departmental border in Picardie's Aisne department, and nothing about its calm and modest appearance gives any hint that it has been the setting for famine, plague and leprosy brought back from the Crusades, and invasion by Cossacks, Prussians, and the Germans during both world wars. In 1340 it underwent a famous siege and pillage (there's a superb illustration of the Siege of Aubenton in Froissart's *Chronicles*), and the inhabitants christened two roads the rue du Sang and the rue du Sac. In 1960 the town council tried, against strong and successful opposition, to rename these sad streets.

There's a house in Aubenton which once belonged to the last of the Condé princes, who'd installed his mistress, a former London prostitute called Sophie Dawes, in the hunting lodge. When Condé was found hanged from a window in his château, suspicion fell on her, as she inherited quite a tidy sum from him, but nothing was ever proved, and she returned to London where she died in 1840.[1]

Aubenton is also home to the Jean Mermoz museum. The staff at the *Hôtel de Ville*, including the mayor, were the friendliest, smiliest and most helpful people we'd met so far on our travels when we went to ask them how we could visit the museum. The mayor picked up the phone and called the caretaker, an elegant grandmother named Mme Schlienger. She left her lunch preparations and came immediately to the town hall with her two young granddaughters, and opened up the museum.

The Musée Jean Mermoz is a shrine to France's dare-devil, record-breaking airman and pride of Aubenton. It's filled with posters and photographs, medals and certificates, newspaper articles and books, models of aeroplanes, his cradle and tiny christening robes and silken bonnet. Terry was fascinated by Mme Schlienger's tales.

Mermoz, she told us, was raised by his grandparents, just outside Aubenton. He joined the military and learned to fly, returning to Aubenton at weekends to visit. Sometimes he'd fly overhead on a Sunday morning, during Mass, to signal his arrival. People would run from the church crying,

---

[1] Jacky Billard, October 2003.

'Ah — it's Jean!' More and more people would follow until only the priest was left inside. Finally, he'd join the rest of them as they stood watching Mermoz land and taxi his plane.

Mermoz's career was the stuff of comic-book heroes — breaking records and crashing aeroplanes in deserts and mountains, being captured by tribesmen and arrested as a spy. A legendary aviator, like Saint-Exupéry and Roland Garros, Mermoz was the first pilot to fly over the Andes, shortening the route between Argentina and Santiago in Chile by almost 1,000 miles. He vanished over the Atlantic in 1936. Charming Mme Schlienger, whose husband had written two books about him, knows all there is to know about Jean Mermoz and his exploits and was happy to patiently answer all Terry's questions.

Once we'd finished admiring her museum, she asked whether we'd be visiting Mont-cornet. We'd not heard of it, and asked her its significance.

'But — it's where de Gaulle fought the tank battle!' she exclaimed, as if everybody in the whole wide world must know about this stupendous event. 'You *must* see it!' We said we certainly would.

Montcornet is about thirty kilometres from Aubenton, diametrically in the opposite direction to that which we were meant to be following, but Terry didn't get stampy-footy about the extra mileage, because even without de Gaulle he'd have been on fire to see the site, having done his National Service in the 5th Royal Tank Regiment and being rather hooked on tanks. So we set off in good spirits, through fields of wheat in varying stages of evolution from short and green to waving tall and golden in the sun. French signposting can sometimes be very frustrating, leading you along nicely to where you want to go until running out at a crossroads, so that you find yourself driving backwards and forwards ad infinitum until you feel you can hardly be bothered any more. Often local people don't know where places are, either, and look at you as if you're crazed when you ask for directions. We got lost once, but as soon as we mentioned Montcornet to a passing cyclist he replied: 'Ah, Montcornet! You want to see de Gaulle's tank, yes?' and put us on the right road.

After a rather mediocre lunch at a restaurant so jam-packed with diners that we had to perch on wonky chairs at a lopsided table almost in the gutter, we went to have a look at the monument, which in view of what was to happen shortly after the event it commemorated wasn't terribly impressive, not as impressive as one might expect. A smart 1960s tank stood on a raised platform on the corner of the main road next to the Citroën garage and outside a building belonging to a plumber. A plaque described the heroism of the French tank regiment led by a Colonel Charles de Gaulle, fighting the German invaders in the battle of Montcornet on 16 — 17 May 1940.

Colonel de Gaulle, who'd been wounded and captured at Verdun in the previous war, was a maverick, a proponent of mechanized war, and, *surtout*, a Frenchman. A month after the battle of Montcornet he'd leapfrogged the ranks to become a General, and was on his way to London to rally his countrymen to his Free French Army with his legendary Appeal of 18 June, when he called on the French people to reject the surrender signed by Pétain, and to join his army and fight for their country. In July and August he was court-martialled for treason in his absence, and condemned to death. After the war, the tables were turned, and it was Pétain who was tried and condemned to death for treason, although he was pardoned by de Gaulle, and died in prison.

We retraced our steps through Aubenton and got ourselves back en route at Hirson, where a heavy truck loaded with aggregate had toppled into a ditch and ploughed into somebody's neat laurel hedge, from where a digger was trying to extract it. The apt name on the truck was Dropsy Transport Co.

North-west of Hirson, just outside the village of la Capelle, is the Haudroy Stone, a column surmounting a platform reached by a flight of steps, and decorated with a plaque bearing a sword and the words: *Ici triompha la ténacité du poilu*. It commemorates the end of the First World War, and is where on 7 November 1918 a delegation of German politicians drove across the border from Belgium, waving a white flag and accompanied by a bugler playing the 'Cease Fire', and agreed to end hostilities. The original monument was destroyed by the Germans during their second try in 1940, and rebuilt by the French.

Terry wanted to visit Cambrai because it was the theatre for the first large-scale use of tank warfare in November 1917, when a contingent of 381 British tanks made the greatest gain in a single day ever in the history of the trenches, breaching the German lines and advancing almost eight kilometres, an event commemorated annually by the Royal Tank Regiment. On our way we passed the communal cemetery at Ors, where Wilfred Owen, English poet of the First

402

World War, was killed on 4 November, just one week before the Armistice.

Something nice had happened in le Cateau-Cambrésis — Henri Matisse was born there in 1869. In the midst of all the death and destruction that had afflicted this picturesque and unfortunately placed area of France, it was heartening to come across, every so often, an event that wasn't related to it.

Cambrai was a pleasant surprise, attractive and lively, a mixture of seventeenth- and ornate eighteenth-century architecture, with elegant squares and beautiful parks. The tourist office lives in the last remaining Spanish-style timbered building, and the clock on the town hall belfry is struck by two giant Moorish characters known as Martin and Martine. There are two legends regarding their origins: one involves somebody's being bashed on the head with a hammer, so I've chosen the second and more positive one, which tells the tale of Hakem, a Muslim Moor, and Martine, a Christian, who fell in love with each other. Because neither would change their religion, their relationship was illicit, and they were condemned to imprisonment in the clock tower and made to strike the hour, every hour, with a heavy hammer. A sympathetic priest pleaded for clemency for the pair, and the court agreed they could be released just as soon as the priest found two replacement Moors. He built two Moorish automatons who performed the striking duties with perfect precision, thus releasing the prisoners. Hakem was so pleased he converted to Christianity and adopted the name Martin. Martin and Martine were married and lived happily ever after, and produced hordes of children.

In six days' time the Tour de France would pass through Cambrai, and an orange-and-green floral bicycle decorated one of the roundabouts to mark the event. Apart from its great buildings, beautiful gardens and interesting history, Cambrai was the birth-place of another French aviation hero, Louis Blériot. And by the way — the town's citadel was designed by you-know-who.

Immediately outside the town we were back amongst tranquil wheat fields, with here and there a flowery village, like Naves, Villers-en-Cauchies and Vendegies-sur-Ecaillon, spick and span little villages of brick-built houses smothered in Picardy roses. We followed the Chaussée Brunehaut, the old Roman road named for the powerful Visigoth queen Brunehaut, up to Valenci-ennes, like Cambrai an attractive town with a lovely park, and particularly admired

Condé-sur-l'Escaut's roundabouts decorated with a flowery hare and tortoise, and a man with a horse and chain of wagons. We settled down to roost for the night at Saint-Amand-les-Eaux at a campsite in an apple orchard, which was very pleasant in the hot evening sunshine, but we woke next morning to teeming rain, and a grey and grizzly day. Our plan was to reach Dunkerque that evening, following the small roads running along the Belgian frontier.

Very soon, we didn't know where we were. There were no road signs, only spindly lanes through fields of spinach. A few potatoes here and there, but mostly spinach. An occasional field of wheat or rye, but mostly spinach. Serious quantities of spinach. We drove around admiring the spinach for a very long time, and discovered we were no longer in France, but somewhere in Belgium. Not anywhere on our map, but definitely in Belgium because the road signs were different. Through the spinach there was a network of lanes which didn't tell you where they went, or where they came from, and every so often notices signalled *déviations*, but still no indication of where to. The road surface was silver in the rain, the sky bright white above it. There was nobody around; no vehicles, no people, and no bicycles either, until we arrived in a small village. It was still raining nice and steadily, and several large metal trolleys stacked with loaves stood in the rain outside the village bakery. We found a small café/bar, where they didn't have hot chocolate. But wait a moment, the waitress had an idea. She took a bottled milky chocolate drink from the fridge, poured it into a cup and put it in a microwave. What came out wasn't the best hot chocolate I'd ever had, but it wasn't the worst, either.

We'd very easily find our way back to France, she said, it was quite simple.

In fact we didn't, and it wasn't, but we did manage to shake off the spinach fields and reach an area populated entirely by *pépin-iéristes* growing infant trees and shrubs over hundreds of hectares. The road surface here was awful, as if it had been left over from the war, and seemed to be made of rectangles of concrete glued to each other. A notice announced that the verges and hedgerows were being trimmed late in the season, to form a protective zone for wildlife.

The landscape was very flat, and we kept finding ourselves one minute in Belgium and the next in France, but we couldn't pinpoint our position because none of the road signs, in either language, corresponded with anything on our map. So we drove around, admiring the scenery, the white-painted brick houses, and some cattle grazing in the wet fields, their brilliant white coats broken by patches of grey which were almost blue. We passed the great menhir, la Pierre Brunehaut, which marks the site of the queen's frightful death.

Resisting the merrily named Café des Morts, as we were feeling very much alive, we at long last returned to France, just east of Lille, which we managed to circumnavigate surprisingly easily, through vertical sheets of rain, and into Armentières, where the mademoiselle came from. The town was virtually destroyed during the last war, and has been rebuilt, but how attractive it is we couldn't tell, because in the monsoon-like rain it was utterly dismal, the only colour provided by the shoppers splashing around the scruffy but extensive street market; there were a great many Muslim ladies, and the town is surrounded by a depressing number of military cemeteries. As we headed northwards, clinging to the small roads on the Belgian border, but managing to stay within France, we stopped to admire the splendid Flemish windmill at Boeschepe, for some reason that we did not discover called the Mill of Ingratitude, next to which was an *estaminet* where we arrived in good time for lunch. We'd never been in an *estaminet* before, nor had we ever had a typical Flemish lunch. Served on a plank, it comprised a heap of cheese slices, slabs of wonderful wholemeal bread, a wooden pot of potatoes smothered in garlic butter, a generous pot of mustard and a dish of gherkins. With a large ceramic cup of cider, it was filling, delicious and highly indigestible. The décor was fascinating: flagstoned floor, beams from which hung old metal bird cages and milk crates, antique agricultural tools, and lace-edged ladies' bloomers pegged on to ropes. The walls were covered in family photographs from the early 1900s: first communions, babies in extraordinary prams, couples getting married, the men with moustaches and flattened hair parted in the centre, the women with thick eyebrows that joined in the middle, wearing plain dark clothes and long white veils. There were proud young men, small boys with sticking-out ears, pretty little girls. Did all the pretty little girls grow up to have huge eyebrows? The background music was like an Irish jig, and if you closed your eyes you could imagine yourself in a Bruegel painting.

With the bread and cheese lodged stubbornly halfway down our digestive tracts, we drove on; although the rain had stopped, a strong wind was blowing Tinkerbelle all over the road and pushing the trees flat. Ahead, sitting calmly in the middle of the opposite side of the road, was a lump, and as we drove past I saw it was an owl. Sitting in the road is a frightfully silly idea, and what was an owl doing out and about in the early afternoon? Terry reversed, and I jumped down into the road, flapping my arms like a flying machine and leaping around to stop a car that was almost on top of the owl. The driver braked (they don't always — I've had to jump out of the way on many occasions when a driver has continued driving at me) and I picked up the owl and examined it. One eye was closed, and both feet were curled up beneath it where it sat unmoving in my hand, while we debated what to do with it. The car's occupants were intrigued and pleased; their little girl stroked the feathery head with one finger, and they wished us good luck with it before driving off with a wave.

Had it been an active healthy bird, with both eyes and both legs working, we'd have left it somewhere wooded; but in its current condition, and with the hurricane-force wind blowing, it would have no chance of survival, so I stuck it inside my fleece and we drove off to find a vet who would look after it. There isn't much in the way of urban development around this part of Flanders, right on the north-eastern edge of France, and we covered twenty-five kilometres before we found a village with any commerce. Terry went into a chemist to ask where we could find a vet, while I sat with the bundle inside my fleece. Out came the lady pharmacist and a young boy, delighted to be involved in our small drama; it didn't look as if much happened in these sleepy parts. The nearest vet, they said, was in Ghyvelde, right up on the coast. We drove along the very flat area, altitude at les Moëres two and a half metres *below* sea level, until we reached Ghyvelde and found the blue cross of a veterinary surgery. The lady vet, Dr Deliessen, watched slightly apprehensively as I delved into the fleece and tried to untangle the owl's claws from it. When I got it out and placed it on the table, she was enchanted. Both the bird's eyes had opened, but its claws were still tightly clenched so it couldn't stand. Dr Deliessen asked what we wanted her to do with it, and we explained we were travelling with two large dogs and couldn't keep the bird with us, but it needed a few days to recover its strength before being released. She telephoned a nearby animal refuge who handled wild animals, and I heard somebody shouting animatedly down the phone. Dr Deliessen replaced the receiver and pulled a face. She said the shouter was angry with us for removing the bird from where we'd found it, and we should have left it there. It's very difficult to nurse owls, he'd said, they always die. We were to take it back immediately and leave it where we'd found it. We all looked at the bird, where it sat dozily in her hand.

'Normally we would have done,' I said. 'But in its current state, and with the weather as it is, I don't think it could survive.'

Dr Deliessen nodded. 'Yes, I agree. It couldn't hunt, or avoid predators.'

'Could you perhaps keep it for a few days until it recovers?'

'It's a question of how to feed it,' she said. 'I've no experience with owls.'

Well, I had, having looked after a couple in the past, and I said I'd successfully fed them on raw liver, tinned cat food and once a mouse that the cats had obligingly caught.

'OK,' she said. 'I'll try.'

She placed the bird in a large cage at the back of the surgery, and we left it with her. I telephoned three days later.

'She's doing well. Her legs are fine, and she's eating. But I want to find a mouse, and see if she can eat it, before I release her,' the vet told us.

A few weeks later, I phoned again.

'I released her about a week after you

411

brought her in. One of the cats caught a mouse' (it's almost as if the cats know, I think) 'and she ate it straight away. That evening I took her to the woods at the back of my house, and released her. She flew straight off into the trees. That's the last I saw of her, and I'm sure she's fine.'

9

THE CHANNEL — WILLIAM THE BASTARD AND TEMPLE DOGS

We reached the Channel at Bray-Dunes in mid-afternoon. The wind blew ghostly snakes of sand over the road; inshore the sea was murky green and violent; further out the choppy grey waters were covered with white horses. It looked particularly uninviting, but the sailboarders, or windsurfers as they are also known, were happily shooting along at breakneck speed. Along the roadsides were hoardings advertising Plopsaland, with pictures of dragons and the promise of 1001 shivers for all the family. Plopsaland is an amusement park for children just inside the Belgian border, and may have a reputation as a great place to visit, but I wonder why they gave it a name that sounds like a children's lavatory.

The area around Dunkerque isn't the prettiest in the world, nor is it chic. My uncle Jim is somewhere there. He didn't make it back during the hurried evacuation of the English and French armies described by

Winston Churchill as 'a miracle', in the heroic flotilla of little boats that sailed to their rescue from England. Dunkerque's shallow beach prevented large vessels from getting close inshore, and the ragtag-and-bobtail craft played a vital role ferrying the stranded soldiers out to them. The smallest was a 5½-metre fishing boat. A theory as to why the Germans allowed this massive evacuation of fighting men is that Hitler thought the British had been taught such a good lesson that they'd be prepared to surrender, whereas an all-out slaughter would provoke a fearsome reaction. Whoops! We may never know if this was the reason, but 338,226 men were rescued from Dunkerque, and lived to fight another day.

Crossing the river Aa into the Pas-de-Calais *département* we found our way to the beach at les Hemmes d'Oye where the tide was out, the sea unpleasant, and the beach covered with a slimy carpet of bubbly green weed; but for the dogs it was heaven, the opportunity to run on sand, and for Dobbie to flop down into the salt water and start drinking it, and we thought it would be good for his injured foot. The wind was so strong it lifted the top layer of fine sand, whipping it into a fast-flowing torrent that floated like smoke over the wet sand beneath, and stung the backs of our freezing legs. Once the dogs had run themselves to a standstill, we continued along the Opal Coast through Calais and past Sangatte, now returned to just a small French coastal town, and stopped to look at the monument to the French aviator Hubert Latham, standing appropriately windswept on a large chunk of rock. A keen amateur aviator, he'd attempted to win the *Daily Mail*'s £1,000 prize in 1909 as the first man to fly across the Channel, taking off from near Sangatte, but was beaten by Louis Blériot. Latham spent most of his life enjoying himself flying aeroplanes and killing wild animals in Africa, until he was himself killed at the tender age of twenty-nine, supposedly by a wounded buffalo, although there was something questionable about the circumstances. Anyway, I hope it was the buffalo — it's always satisfying when the animals score a kill over the gun-toting great white hunter.

At France's version of the white cliffs of Dover — Cap Blanc-Nez — we looked down on to a sea so wild it seemed at any moment it could leap right from its bed and fly around in the sky, and the wind was so strong it was barely possible to remain upright. We spent the night at Wimereux sitting in Tinkerbelle reading with the heater on, buffeted by the gale. The weather was still foul next morning, the Channel ugly and mean under scudding grey clouds. In Boulogne the sea hurled great spumes of itself over the harbour wall; only a group of kite-boarders flying at great speed above the waves profited from the despicable and unseasonable conditions.

The first thing we noticed in Boulogne was the stench of fish, which is quite natural, it being France's largest fishing port, then the shriek of thousands of gulls, perching on rooftops, strutting on the harbour front, hovering over the water or dangling in the skies. Boulogne was hosting an exhibition of pharaohs, in honour of Auguste Mariette, the celebrated nineteenth-century Egyptologist who discovered the Serapeum — the tomb of the Apis bulls worshipped by the ancient Egyptians — and had tried to excavate the Sphinx before ceding to the superior tenacity of the sands. Posters of pyramids and sphinxes invited us to visit the exhibition on the dockside, but we seemed to have arrived as it was closing, because all that was left were a few traders selling plastic souvenirs and hookahs.

The street market was livelier, but the town was jampacked with shopping humanity and there was nowhere to park, so we drove on to find somewhere for the dogs to run. We stopped at Equihen-Plage where a notice said dogs were not allowed; in any case, the breakers smashing on to the beach were laden with thick brown-green scum, so we tried Hardelot, passing fields of horses and cattle appearing undisturbed by the weather, simply concentrating on munching the lush grass. No wonder it was lush if it was always this wet. By the time we reached Hardelot the wind was at near-hurricane strength: as I opened the door of the cab it was wrenched from me, and torn cleanly off its hinges. I tried vainly to hang on, as my baseball cap was whipped off and tumbled up the street. Terry gave chase, and just as it does in the movies the cap lay still until he was within a millimetre of grasping it, and then flew off again. It kept on happening, and I was a fat lot of good because I could do nothing but laugh, tears streaming down my face as the pink cap rolled and tumbled around Hardelot's streets with Terry in pursuit. Once he'd managed to outrun and jump on it, he had to fix the door back on to its hinges, and it took our combined strength to wrest it from the wind's grasp.

Unsurprisingly Hardelot was deserted apart from a few people in restaurants and bars, gazing forlornly out of windows coated with a fine layer of sand and salt. We found a modest restaurant where the food was unremarkable but entertainment was supplied by two English couples at the adjacent table. The women both wore white stiletto heels and tight white jeans, and their menfolk lots of heavy gold bracelets and neck chains. From what we could glean from their rather loud conversation one couple were estate agents who'd succeeded in selling a property to the other couple; they were celebrating with pints of beer, and a small child was eating spaghetti bolognese with its fingers. The new house-owners suddenly realized the time and had to rush to catch a ferry, and as they drove away the remaining couple looked at each other meaningfully and clinked their glasses.

After our meal we drove to the beach and tried to give the dogs a run, but the sea was too violent and the wind drove sand into our eyes; even the dogs wanted to get back in Tinkerbelle as quickly as they could. We noticed then that one-quarter of Tinkerbelle's rear bumper had vanished, and attributed it to Dobbie, who'd been hitched to it the previous evening. He'd also tipped his water bowl over on the floor so the carpet squelched.

The roads were becoming increasingly crowded, with long queues and jams building up, in contrast to when we'd set out seven weeks earlier. We pitied holiday-makers arriving this week, the first week of July, into such dismal circumstances. Even elegant le Touquet with its extravaganza of architectural styles didn't look much, seen through a windscreen battered by driving rain sloshed ineffectually from side to side by the wipers. The parks department, or whoever was in charge of the town's greenery, had been up to something odd in Merlimont, where a long avenue of beech trees had had their lateral branches nailed and roped to wooden structures so they resembled the crucified Christians in *Spartacus*. When it stopped raining, we were just coming into Fort-Mahon. Rather than risk driving further into possibly more rain, we decided to drop anchor for the night, at a mobile-home park where the *gardien* was most charming and helpful, and we could let the dogs run around freely. Dobbie's foot was finally starting to heal. The wound was dry, and we thought his dip in the sea at les Hemmes d'Oye had probably done it good.

The next morning was shiveringly cold, and the skies and seas were a uniform grey. We could have driven a few kilometres east to Crécy to visit the battlefield where the outnumbered English archers defeated the

French cavalry so soundly, but we'd seen enough battlefields recently, and Normandy's landing beaches lay ahead, so we opted for something a little cheerier, and drove round the calm, flat marshes of the Somme bay, with their air of peaceful backwaterliness, and appearance of having been unnoticed by time over the last few decades. The swans and herons seemed not at all distressed by the drizzle, weaving and winding their way amongst the reeds and marshes just as we were doing on the damp little roads. We found ourselves in the tiny town of le Crotoy, which in the drizzle was as devoid of life as the beach. Two great names in French history had passed through le Crotoy: Joan of Arc, on her way to her dreadful destiny in Rouen, and Jules Verne, who spent five years there while writing *Twenty Thousand Leagues Under the Sea*. We didn't disembark here, but clung to the comfort and warmth of Tinkerbelle's cab, and explored the Marquenterre bird reserve, until we arrived at the home of the Henson horse. This sturdy, hardy animal, perfectly adapted to life in its harsh environment, was created by God. He blew upon a handful of sand to form a magnificent mare whose coat was golden like the sands, her pride that of the great winds, and her black-and-gold mane rippling like the waves.

He ran a finger down the length of her back, leaving a long black mark, his stamp of approval. If ever the Somme bay should disappear, its image would remain for ever embodied by the Henson horse. There were many herds of these special animals grazing in relaxed groups on the rough marshland, thanks to enthusiasts like M. Bizet and M. Berquin, who'd taken over God's work and crossed some Fjord ponies with Arabs and French saddle horses to create the first man-made Henson horses. Decades of hard work and love has produced a breed that is finally recognized by the French National Stud. They are docile, versatile and handsome, and used for riding holidays in the Somme bay. At one of the riding centres a dozen small children in anoraks were scurrying around with bits of saddlery and pieces of paper, while a rather distraught young woman tried to keep them all in the same place at the same time.

We continued driving around the drizzly marshes, quite happily, until we came upon two pop-eyed white marble temple dogs standing guard at the small hamlet of Nolette, where a sign indicated 'cimetiére chinois'. We thought we should find out why there was a Chinese cemetery in this tiny backwater of northern France.

As cemeteries go, the Chinese cemetery at Nolette must rank quite highly on the desirability scale. It's just outside the village, surrounded by fields and enclosed by a beautifully built natural stone wall and portico designed by Edwin Lutyens. The atmosphere is *très, très* zen. Simple stone tablets inscribed with names and numbers, or sometimes numbers alone, stand in neat rows of flower beds jammed with flowers. The head-stones bear inscriptions like: 'A good reputation endures for ever', 'Faithful unto death', 'Though dead he liveth still', 'A noble deed faithfully done'. In the field surrounding the cemetery a group of black-and-white cows swiped up mouthfuls of grass, and along came a farmer, who leaned on the wall and was happy to pass the time of day. He told us the cemetery's upkeep is the responsibility of the Commonwealth War Graves Commission, but it's local French people who actually do the work. They usually came on Tuesdays. I thought the men buried there would probably be quite pleased with their surroundings. The inhabitants, all 842 of them, and another 42 who were never found, formed part of the 100,000-strong Chinese Labour Corps, shipped to France in 1917 to undertake building, road repairs, recovery and burial of the fallen, and general labouring, releasing

British soldiers to go and fight Germans. The Chinese mostly came from the northern provinces, lured by the prospect of earning four times what they could in their own country. They were under the command of British officers, and were kept segregated in their own camps, and even had their own hospital. Each wore an identification bracelet riveted round his wrist. They arrived in their Chinese peasant clothing, with their bamboo tools, and mostly died of cold and disease.

It was still damp and cold, but we were enjoying this very unspoilt part of the world and had no plans for the rest of the day, so we decided to take a train ride from le Crotoy to Saint-Valéry-sur-Somme, on the little Somme bay steam railway. We shared a carriage with an elderly lady and her small grandson, seated on hard, polished wooden seats. The heavy windows were raised and lowered by sturdy leather straps. The old lady told the little boy how she'd travelled on these old trains sixty years ago, and how uncomfortable they were for long journeys. The engine chugged through the marshes and flat fields of wheat and corn, blowing its whistle frequently, and emitting clouds of steam and smoke, attracting stares of mild interest from cattle and indignant glares from geese. We stood on the platform of the carriage, holding the wrought-iron railing as the train rocked and rolled, its wheels feeling as if they were square by the way they thumped over the rails. Sometimes the old, long-remembered whiff of dirty coal smoke floated around us. It reminded me of the train that used to deliver me to boarding school. We disembarked in Saint-Valéry and followed our fellow passengers up the main street in search of food. The first restaurant, the Drakar, was jammed with diners, which indicated that the food there should be good, so we joined a long queue of other damp people. A few lucky ones were led to spaces as they became vacant, and others were turned away and wandered off despondently. When we reached the head of the queue, the *maître d'* asked whether we'd booked. We shook our heads, and he suggested we returned in fifteen minutes, which we did. When we reached the head of the queue a second time, again the *maître d'* asked if we'd booked. This time we said yes, which wasn't really true, but we didn't want to be sent away for another fifteen minutes, and won a tiny table just inside the door next to a couple with lank wet hair and dressed in old sacks. The staff ran around as best they could through the crush, trying to keep up with the ever-changing customers; the windows ran with condensation and personal clouds of steam rose from the moist customers. A party of four old people came in, with a small white poodle on a lead, and as they followed the *maître d'* another small dog shot out from beneath a table, where it was tied to the leg, and tried to kill the poodle, which stood its ground. The table was jerked about on the end of dog No. 2, as the two set about each other snarling and yelping, and a waitress laden with a heavy tray had to leap over them. It was a wonderful scene straight from *Fawlty Towers*. The food was excellent, and we sat smugly watching hopefuls queuing up outside for the chance of a table. We did know a momentary guilty pang, but crushed it, and concentrated on enjoying our meal, and watching the antics of one of the waitresses. For no apparent reason she dropped a tray piled with dirty plates and glasses, which crashed to the floor and made a spectacular mess. A lady appeared from the kitchen with a mop and bucket and cleaned it up, while the waitress stood red-faced and almost in tears. She vanished into the kitchen and five minutes later came out with another large tray containing two buckets of *moules marinières*, which she managed to empty all over the head and shoulders of a small boy at the table next to ours. The poor little chap was drenched, with mussels in his hair and clinging to his woolly jumper; slices of onion and fragments of herbs were draped over his ears, and he was saturated with hot liquid. An adult carted him off into the washroom, while his mother berated the clumsy waitress and the rest of us sat and stared. The bewildered child reappeared a few minutes later in a jumper far too big for him, and the *maitre d'* arrived and presented a bottle of bubbly to the diners and a large ice cream to the boy.

Feeling that the Drakar had given us good value for money, we surrendered our table to a wet couple and went to walk around the town, to which we took a strong and immediate liking. Even on such a dreary day it had a great deal of quiet Picardy charm, embellished by a host of marching bands, from the Rexpoede brass band dressed in black smocks and caps and red kerchiefs, and the bagpipes of the Premier Val de la Somme from Pont-Rémy, to the local Boy Scouts (scoots, as it's pronounced in French), magnificent in scarlet tunics, and led by a scoot who was seventy if he was a day, with a ferocious moustache and heavy spectacles.

Just beside the harbour a stone plaque commemorates the noteworthy event that took place in Saint-Valéry-sur-Somme nearly a thousand years earlier, when a Norman noble charmingly known as William the

Bastard assembled an army and fleet to go and bash up the English. A storm damaged the ships after they'd sailed from Dives-sur-Mer, forcing the fleet to take shelter in Saint-Valéry-sur-Somme where they spent several weeks repairing the vessels. Once ready to set sail again, the Bastard declared a day of worship to St Valéry, whose relics were paraded through the streets for an entire day. The following day, 29 September 1066, the wind changed, and the fleet of over a thousand ships and around 50,000 men sailed to England, where the Bastard's army gave the English a thorough thrashing at Hastings, and killed their king, Harold. After that, they didn't call William the Bastard any more. Wey hey! they called him William the Conqueror. Quite why he'd felt compelled to undertake this aggressive venture was something we'd never really considered, but shortly we'd find out, thanks to the continuing precipitation.

Amongst the modest streets and neat houses, one building stood out, because it was painted in tangerine and lime green and managed to look absolutely delightful. Walking around the medieval part of town we met troubadours and knights, queens and jesters, and the significance of the sack-clothed diners became apparent. Nine hundred years after William's death, in 1987 the town of Saint-Valéry-sur-Somme, now amicably twinned with the town of Battle near Hastings, built a giant William. The giant is paraded through the streets each year during the Fêtes Guillaume at the beginning of July, which by pure and unusual coincidence happened to be taking place the day we were there.

We climbed aboard the pretty red-and-turquoise train for our return journey. It stopped momentarily on the swing bridge, and as I stared idly out of the window into the canal, where the yachts sat obediently side by side at anchor, I found myself gazing into a pair of limpid eyes over a fine set of whiskers all capped by what looked like a German helmet. It took a few seconds for me to recognize it as a seal, and by the time I'd squealed to Terry, who was looking from the opposite window, it had slid beneath the water and vanished. On the way back we saw swans, geese, ducks, herons and egrets in the wetlands, and decoy ducks floating on ponds beside hides. I've always thought what an unsporting and sneaky way it is to kill birds, luring them with decoys. We clattered, thumped and tooted our way back to the terminus at Noyelles, where we had a narrow shave with another train with which we only just avoided colliding, because somebody named Gérard hadn't switched the points in time, and he earned a loud and irate reprimand from our driver. The other train was occupied by several dozen very old people, sitting with their chins on their chests, or heads tilted back, open-mouthed. They were all asleep and happily unaware they'd been within seconds of being involved in a train crash.

Back at le Crotoy the dogs were happily sleeping in Tinkerbelle. We drove to Cayeux-sur-Mer to give them a run. What an odd place this was: a pebble beach lined with bathing huts, and concrete ramps to reach the water. On the outskirts of the village there were mountains of shingle in different colours and calibres: big, medium, small, grey, white, brown, and huge boulders. If you need shingle or pebbles, Cayeux is the place to go. The dogs were unimpressed; after walking halfway down the ramps and sniffing over the edge, they came back and stared at us reproachfully, saying this wasn't at all what they had in mind, and where was the sand? They couldn't be persuaded into the grey foamy water that crept furtively through the pebbles and trickled back out again, so we drove on to Mers-les-Bains, where there's a rather strange campsite where the buildings, including holiday homes for rent, are designed like bunkers; troglodyte structures with grass growing over them. We thought it might be a converted wartime facility, but the *gardien* said no, it had actually been built like that.

10

NORMANDY — BLOWN AWAY BY BAYEUX

We crossed into Normandy at le Tréport, one of France's largest fishing towns and a lively holiday resort, where you can visit the Delgove fish smokery, if you wish. In the tourist-office brochure it translates to become a red-herring factory. I'd have liked to visit it, because I'd never seen a red herring, and who knows when one might come in handy, but Terry was adamant he wasn't prepared to go, so instead we headed for Dieppe in search of lunch. Dieppe was very lively indeed, and the sun was properly out as it should be in July. A round-the-coast-of-France yacht race was in progress, and the harbour front was crowded with stalls selling marine clothing and nautical gadgets, and the blood collectors were looking for new donors. English people can no longer donate blood in France, because of the risk that we could be carrying mad cow disease. Terry looked rather longingly at a catamaran simulator for children, but I towed him off to the free

431

Internet access facility generously set up by the town, where we caught up with our e-mails from the past month, both pleased and simultaneously slightly disappointed that there was absolutely nothing of importance in them.

Dieppe being a major fishing port, we felt certain of having a good lunch there, and were spoilt for choice for restaurants. However, we managed by some uncanny talent to find on the harbourside what might be the worst restaurant in France, or even the whole of Europe. We both ordered freshly grilled sardines, and about twelve seconds after he'd taken our order the waiter returned with two plates of microscopic cremated skeletons. Hairthin ribs poked through gaping wounds from beneath a blackened coating, and sad white eyeballs gazed blindly at the ceiling from small charred faces. I pushed a forkful of one of these things into my mouth, because I was famished. It was a gastronomic experience unequalled by anything I could remember. The sardines were not scaled, and it was like chewing and trying to swallow a mixture of burned straw and flakes of crisp plastic. Somewhere in the middle was something soft and slimy and extremely bitter. I think it might have been a liver or a spleen. Terry's sardines seemed to have fared slightly better than mine, and he said he'd enjoyed them, but I gave up after the first mouthful and ate the lemon slice and a hard bread roll. A seagull came to our table and stared at us in a meaningful way. It accepted the first morsel of bread politely, refused the next piece, spat out the piece of sardine I offered it, and wisely waddled away to the next restaurant. Despite the shocking food, we enjoyed sitting in the sun watching the yachts and their crews bobbing around in the harbour. After we'd seen as much of Dieppe as we wanted to, we walked back to Tinkerbelle, and a man fell into step beside us. He was tattooed on his neck and wearing a loose and violently patterned shirt; he was patently off his head, but apparently harmless. As Terry said, I always attract maniacs. Without invitation, our new companion struck up conversation, asking whether we were English, German or Dutch. He seemed satisfied, even pleased, that we were English, and said, 'Yes, I thought so!' What made us look so specifically English, I wondered.

He pointed to the TransManche ferry sitting just outside the harbour, and warned us never to go on it, because the captain, he said, was a drunk. He made the characteristic French gesture of a fist twisted on the end of his nose to illustrate his point. You should see the ferry if it leaves port after lunch, he said. Weaving from side to side, and one of these days, just wait and see, there'll be a frightful accident. We thanked him for the tip, discouraged him politely but firmly from climbing into Tinkerbelle with us, and set off down the Alabaster coastline, where the sea was calm and beautiful in shades of green.

Via a narrow and peaceful road through a tunnel of overhanging trees, we arrived in genteel Varengeville-sur-Mer, perched on the cliffs. The dogs were unimpressed by the narrow strip of noisy shingle calling itself a beach. The beauty that has attracted artists from both sides of the Channel had absolutely no impact on them. I persuaded Terry that we might have a walk through the Parc des Moutiers, several hectares of gardens created by Gertrude Jekyll around a house designed by Edwin Lutyens for a local banker in 1898. It was relaxing strolling about the formal box-hedged gardens near the house, with their pergolas, fountains and stone benches, and giving on to wide green lawns leading into wooded glades of rhododendrons. There was a stunning panorama over the aquamarine sea from a wooded spot, and with its bog areas, ferns and exotic specimen trees the place was very beautifully designed, and peaceful, and a pleasant change from sitting in Tinkerbelle's cab or being bashed about by the wind on stony beaches.

The landscape around here was ravishing, with the sea to one side and lush hedges and beautifully kept gardens on the other, and an air of smug contentment emanating from the elegant houses. The villages were separated by fields of flax, and although the flowers were on the wane it still made a very lovely sight. Veules-les-Roses, despite taking a bashing in 1940, has managed to retain a chocolate-box prettiness, and is home to France's teeniest river, the 1,100-metre Veules, which pops up magically from its source just outside the village, and wends its way to the sea between fields of cress, ancient thatched cottages and big old mills.

Saint-Valéry-en-Caux is another enchanting seaside town of *colombage* and narrow shuttered houses, with wrought-iron balconies overhanging the harbour, and pot plants dangling in the sunshine over sleeping yachts, peaceful except for the plaintive wailing of gulls. Next is another gem, les Petites Dalles, off the beaten track and exquisite. Little wonder this coastline and these small towns so attracted the Impressionist painters. The beaches were still shingle, and out of bounds to dogs in les Petites Dalles, but it had become very hot and they needed to cool down, so we let them out to explore at the feet of the cliffs. Tally disdained the water but Dobbie threw himself down and lay with gentle waves sweeping backwards and forwards over his head.

The very small village of Sassetot-le-Mauconduit has a château where in 1875 the intriguing and tragic Empress Elisabeth of Austria (Sissi), wife of Franz-Joseph, came to spend the summer with her small daughter and an entourage of seventy. She used to descend to les Petites Dalles to bathe in the bracing air and water of the Normandy coast, and she may, or may not, have later returned to Sassetot to give birth to an illegitimate child, according to the *Secrets of a Royal House* written by her niece, the Countess of Larisch. It was Sissi's son, the Crown Prince Rudolf, who died at the hunting lodge in Mayerling, Austria, in an apparent suicide pact with his young mistress, Marie Vetsera. He seemingly shot her through the head, and then killed himself, although there were rumours that he had been killed for political reasons. The official version of his death claimed at the time that he was mentally unbalanced, so that he could be buried in the imperial tomb. Poor Sissi was stabbed to death in Geneva. According to one critic, the only thing worth seeing in Sassetot was the château, and 'inside is not that nice, nor is the food'.

We stopped at a superbly located campsite at Yport, on a terraced hillside looking straight down on to the glorious seascape that has inspired so many great painters. I was gripped by an urge to set up my easel and dig out pots of paint and brushes and capture the shades of blue of sea and sky, the white of the cliffs, and the houses of Fécamp just along the coast. Then I remembered that I don't have an easel, or any paints, because I can't paint, so instead I meandered down to the sanitary block at the bottom of the hill to find a shower. They were all occupied, and another person was waiting ahead of me, a man carrying a red umbrella. I thought it was odd to take an umbrella to the showers, or indeed to be carrying one at all on a day when there wasn't the teeniest hint of cloud anywhere in the sky, with the temperature pleasantly in the mid-70s. Although we were standing side by side at quite close quarters, his body language indicated that he wasn't receptive to any kind of social intercourse, and although I was bursting to know what the umbrella was for I didn't ask, in case it was for whacking or stabbing nosy people. The shower outside which we were standing became vacant, and he marched in, hooked

437

the umbrella on to a rail, looked at it for a couple of seconds, removed it and walked a little way to stand outside another occupied shower. I gratefully took the one he'd rejected, which suited me well as I didn't have an umbrella to worry about, and to this day I haven't been able to think of a single reason why anyone should take an umbrella into a shower.

The next day the beautiful weather was holding; the sea was very, very blue, and it would be hard to find a prettier part of the world. We went to Etretat, intending to lunch there, which seemed a modest and simple project until we reached the town and drove into one of those traffic jams where nobody can move. The streets were very narrow, blocked with vehicles coming from every direction. We were trapped behind a butcher's delivery vehicle; the back door opened and a youth dressed in a white cloak and hood, like a monk, and with white boots, clambered in and emerged with half a pig, neatly sliced from snout to tail, slung over his shoulder. He delivered it to the *boucherie* next to where we were stuck, and returned for the second half. His white outfit was by then streaked with blood and he looked like a surgeon who'd cut through somebody's artery. Absolutely disgusting, and I can say with certainty that there was nobody in Etretat that day who could have been more revolted than we were at being stuck next to a shop full of dead animals in bits and pieces, or hanging by their feet from hooks.

We were imprisoned there for a long time, and once we escaped we shot towards a newly vacated parking space and found ourselves going the wrong way up a one-way street, into a line of aggressive people hooting and waving us back to where we'd come from. But in the meantime other vehicles had followed us, and we all had our heads stuck out of the windows shouting to the person behind telling them to reverse into the main street which was still at an impasse. Charming as Etretat is, and it's very charming indeed, we'd just about had our fill and were going to abandon our planned visit when Terry by some superhuman means spotted and somehow snaffled a parking place just about long enough for a Mini, before anybody else could get it. Smiling apologetically at the queue of drivers all around us, we explored the town that has been home to painters, presidents and writers, amongst them Guy de Maupassant who wrote a particularly disgusting story entitled 'The Englishman of Etretat' in which the hero is reputed to eat nothing but monkeys. Etretat is touristy, with a wealth of old, timbered properties, and resisting the *hôtel tout confort* enticingly named le Donjon we found a table at a simple hostelry where the *moules marinières* in cider were quite acceptable and we could sit and watch the frantic tourist world go by the window in its never-ending search for a parking space.

We went to admire the cliffs at Etretat, immortalized most famously perhaps by Monet, although my favourite is by Gustave Courbet. The cliffs are a miraculous work of nature, where over the centuries the tides have scooped great arches through the chalk.

Just a short distance from Etretat is the le Valaine goat farm, where they produce caprine products including goat's-milk chocolate and ice cream. A guided tour in French was starting as we arrived, and our choice was to tag along, or miss the visit completely because there wouldn't be another tour that day. So we joined the ten other people and followed our guide Bernard into a large barn where we all had to wipe our feet carefully on a mat just inside the doorway. Being an organic farm le Valaine doesn't use disinfectants, but the special mat would destroy any bacteria on our shoes, and we were not to touch the goats, please, because we could pass germs on to them. The tour began with an explanation of hygiene, and the difference between a virus, a bacterium and a protozoon. Bernard wasn't only an expert on his subject, he was also a skilled entertainer, punctuating his talk with frequent jokes.

We learned that the goats are fed on an assortment of foodstuffs including barley, corn, straw, hay and lucerne, which is also known as alfalfa and was first introduced into Europe by the Moors, and has as high a sugar content as chocolate, which is why goats enjoy it so much. With our new knowledge of hygiene and nutrition, we moved into the airy barn where the female goats pass the time of day when they're not out at pasture. Two of them obligingly approached Bernard when he invited them to, and searched his pockets for pieces of dried bread, a delicacy to them. They were completely docile while he moved them around to display their salient points. Some had horns, and some didn't. This is purely down to nature — he hadn't cut any of their horns off. Back in the mists of goat-time, their horns served as cutlery to help them break branches and strip bark. As they evolve through the centuries, becoming increasingly domesticated, they are losing the need for horns, which are slowly disappearing. Likewise the strange dangly things beneath their necks — these are vestigial remains of tusks, Bernard said, used for self-defence and, like the horns, becoming obsolete. In time, apparently, goats will have neither horns nor danglers.

The next thing we learned about goats is that every herd has a dominant female who tells the rest what to do. We were introduced to her, and then we met her little daughter, the only baby amongst the herd. When the kids are born, they stay with their mothers for a few short weeks before being separated, the females to grow on until they're ready to supply milk and replace the older goats, and the little males — here Bernard rolled his eyes and rubbed his hands together — to be made into pâté. We all grimaced. Recently female goat No. 2 had challenged the dominant female, and, having not the benefit of tusks, stuck her knife and fork into her foe's tummy, which caused goat No. 1 to lose her kid. She'd been mated again and successfully produced the baby we were now seeing, who, because she was much younger than the other kids, and so small, and because her mummy was top of the tree, had been allowed to remain with the nannies. Maybe one day, said Bernard, she'd take over her mother's crown.

We moved to view the cheese-making room through small windows.

Did any of the ladies in our group make cheese, asked Bernard.

We all shook our heads.

He pointed at a woman with two young children.

'When your children were babies, did you feed them on milk?'

'Yes, of course,' she replied.

'And afterwards, did you put them against your shoulder and bounce them up and down?'

She nodded.

'And did they then spew up sour white stuff all over your clothes?'

She agreed.

'Well, then — you made cheese! That's what it is — curdled milk.'

There were trays of cheeses in various stages of ripeness, and the discussion turned to spores and mushrooms. I admit I got a little lost here, because my French has its limitations, but it was something to do with the dusty black stuff that built up on the outside of the cheeses. Bernard took a dusty-coated cheese from a tray, wiped his finger over it, and smeared it over the eyelids of an embarrassed teenage girl.

'*Et voilà!* The original eyeshadow, as used since the days of Cleopatra. Non-allergenic, waterproof, and free of heavy metals, unlike modern cosmetics.'

From now on, I thought, I'm going to smear spores from goat's cheese on my eyelids.

'It won't come off with water,' he continued. 'The only effective way of removing it is' — he pulled out a clean white handkerchief, and licked it — 'saliva!'

He reached towards the girl's eyelid with the spitty handkerchief, as she shrank back in horror which we shared, and then laughingly replaced the hanky in his pocket, and herded us outside to meet the ram, a handsome bearded animal tethered on a patch of long grass.

Bernard explained that he and this fine male goat had something in common, a little thing that was special to them, and would we like to see what it was? The crowd shuffled their feet nervously as Bernard's hand seemed to hover at the front of his trousers. Then he grabbed the goat's beard, and stroked his own.

'The goat urinates on his beard. Me, I don't! But let me explain why the goat does.'

By peeing on his beard, and rubbing it on the neck of the nannies during mating (and a nanny goat can produce eight different smells to encourage him), he leaves his distinctive odour on their necks, to remind himself if he has or hasn't mated with them. Although I personally love goats, and we have two, I don't find the smell of a working ram, or his urine, appealing in any way. But, according to Bernard, goat's musk is one of the ingredients in 4711 *eau-de-Cologne*. Who'd have thought it?

We treated ourselves to some of le Valaine's excellent cheese and chocolates, carefully not looking at the jars of pâtéd kids, and continued on our way, avoiding running over a large khaki-coloured snake that chose to cross the road in front of us, and agreeing that the tour of the farm had been very informative and entertaining.

A monument in Sainte-Adresse marks the fact that during the First World War, the Belgian government in exile based itself in the town. We'd only ever driven through the ferry terminal of le Havre, France's largest commercial port, where the cross-Channel ferries ply in and out all day, and had never spent time actually looking at the town. So it was a pleasant surprise to see rows of bathing cabins on the beach, a flotilla of yellow yachts in the harbour, and the promenade crowded with holidaymakers licking ice cream and strolling about, apparently unfazed by the strong winds whipping the flags: All around the port was neat and tidy; fishing boats dozed at their moorings before their next shift, and only the rather sorry state of the potted palms indicated that this was very much a northern seaside resort. There was a large commercial complex calling itself the World Trade Centre.

We crossed the Seine estuary by the Pont de Normandie, and meandered around pretty, dozy villages of thatched cottages topped with irises to bind the thatch and draw up the moisture, and found our way to Berville-sur-Mer, the Seine-Maritime's only coastal village. Two rotting hulks on the esplanade reminded us that Berville was once a thriving port; the last fisherman retired in 1994. The dogs had a good run while Terry inspected the construction of the fifty-year-old boats. Berville has a very pretty church, l'Eglise Saint-Melain — Melain was the bishop of Rennes. Apart from more orthodox forms of decoration, the walls have graffiti scratched on them by long-gone sailors, entreating God and the saints to protect them at sea. From there we followed the Seine to Honfleur, exquisite, hot and very busy, the harbourfront houses looking as if they're straining to reach the sea. Samuel de Champlain sailed from there to discover Quebec.

In Trouville-sur-Mer and neighbouring

Deauville, watering hole of poseurs and horse-racing fans, we shared with several thousand other motorists an hourlong traffic jam trying to get from one side of the town to the other during the afternoon rush hour, past well-watered lawns and trees smothered with climbing red roses. It was far too hot to be sitting in a van with two large panting dogs, and I felt some sympathy for a blonde woman in a green hat, who was obviously completely mad, trying unsuccessfully to cross the road and screaming abuse at scooters and bicycles weaving through the traffic.

In Villers-sur-Mer, a life-sized and benign dinosaur (a brachiosaurus, I think) composed of greenery stands on a roundabout with her elephant-sized baby, signifying that this is a particularly rich palaeontological area. People scour the sands of the Black Cow cliffs collecting fossils. I haven't the slightest idea where we settled that night, because we drove for miles and miles and miles trying to find somewhere that wasn't full, and eventually succeeded, by which time we were quite dizzy from driving and too tired to worry about where we were. We showered in modern, claustrophobic cubicles like vertical plastic coffins, ate a snack, and talked for half an hour to our neighbours, a Canadian girl and a Dutch man who'd met in China and were going back there to work. Then we slept the sleep of the righteous and exhausted.

The next morning the excessive heat of the previous day had been washed away by absolutely torrential rain, propelled horizontally by a saw-toothed wind. The calendar said the first week of July, the weather said February. We went back to Villers-sur-Mer from wherever it was that we were, to take a better look at the dinosaurs, and also the Greenwich meridian, which is marked by a line of dots painted on the road, leading to a blue stripe on a low wall looking out to sea, with a telescope pointing across the Channel to Greenwich.

On the windy, rain-battered beach a man in a black baggy tracksuit was entertaining a group of small children, playing happily and apparently unaware of the weather. He had them jumping up and down, raising their arms above their heads and stamping their feet in the sand. Two little girls played on a trampoline; one was cautious, just bouncing a few inches, but the other leapt higher and higher, kicking up her heels as she flew into the air. Old people sat on benches in raincoats, huddled under umbrellas; wellied pedestrians tucked *baguettes* into fleeces, anoraks or raincoats. Water flowed in streams along the gutters and down the shop-front canopies, and dripped from peaked caps. We squashed into an already crowded restaurant, steamy from wet clothes, and sat sipping hot drinks, wiping condensation from our spectacles. More drenched people tried to get in; people squeezed even closer together at tables to make room for other refugees from the weather; yet again it was raining so hard it was funny. The drumming noise on the roof was loud enough to make conversation impossible, and then it grew even louder, as if somebody was physically turning up the volume. We all started laughing; what else was there to do?

We stayed for lunch, a plate of piping hot *galettes* followed by strawberries and cream, washed down with a pitcher of cider. We'd been in there for three hours, and the weather didn't show any sign it would improve, so back we sploshed to Tinkerbelle and drove off along grey roads beside a grey sea under a grey sky, until we reached Bénouville, home of the historic bridge that was the first objective captured on D-Day by airborne troops landing in gliders. In recognition of their extraordinary coup, the bridge would be renamed Pegasus after the winged-horse insignia of the British Airborne division. When it had been condemned as being no longer suitable for modern traffic, the original Pegasus bridge was bought by British veteran associations for the symbolic price of one pound, and now lies a few metres from its previous situation over the river Orne, near its successor. Parked alongside the bridge is a replica of the Horsa glider, bearing the black and white invasion stripes that identified it to Allied aircraft spotters, which has all the elegance of a garden shed, but did such a first-rate job. Various components of the Horsa, which was made almost entirely of wood, were built in furniture factories around London. Another glider named the Hengist was manufactured as a back-up for the Horsa. In a rather neat little twist, the Horsa and Hengist gliders were named after two German warriors who invaded England in the fifth century.

Beside the legendary bridge is the equally historic Café Gondrée, the first house in France to be liberated after the invasion. It's still owned and run by Mme Arlette Gondrée, a little girl at the time of the liberation, whose parents were members of the Resistance, supplying vital information to the British regarding the German forces on the bridge. Every inch of the tiny café's walls is covered with memorabilia: photographs, medals, letters, helmets, flags, certificates.

Mme Gondrée doesn't seem to have made any concessions to the twenty-first century in her café, which happily looked as if nothing had changed in the last sixty years. It's the modest, scruffy simplicity of the place that gives you the wonderful sense of stepping back in time when you sit there. We queued at the counter for a cup of coffee, and forced ourselves on to a table occupied by an old English couple who reluctantly moved their paraphernalia to allow us space. Soggy bikers queued with helmets slung over their arms, ahead of a group of debonair French air force officers in creaseless khaki raincoats.

The wintry conditions hadn't deterred the sailboarders skimming at breakneck speed over the scummy foam whipped up on the murky, green-grey sea of the Côte de Nacre. There was almost nobody on the roads, or in the village streets. It was the sort of weather in which you'd like to be tucked up in front of a log fire with a book, a plate of crumpets and a nice warm drink.

We arrived at the eight kilometres of beach stretching from west of Ouistreham to Lion-sur-Mer and codenamed 'Sword' during the Normandy landings. This was the first British objective. The sands cowered beneath pouring rain, and many of the seafront properties were sad examples of immediate-post-war architecture at its ugly worst. Adjacent to Sword on the western side is Juno beach, which was the target of Canadian forces. During the Allied landings sixty years and one month previously, the weather had been as unseasonably miserable as it was today; this was a major factor leading to their success, because the Germans could not have expected the Allies to attempt the landings in such adverse conditions. 'Operation Overlord' had already been delayed by twenty-four hours due to bad weather; had they waited any longer it might never have been launched: the worst Channel weather for twenty years was on its way. Now, just as the sixtieth anniversary celebrations of the event were in full swing, the weather was thoroughly detestable. Visiting the landing beaches for the first time, we thought the weather couldn't have been better. In the lashing rain it was possible to imagine something of what the troops had experienced in their journey from the landing craft to the beaches, struggling through cold, rough waves, beneath cumbersome loads, in saturated clothing, and under fire.

At the appropriately named Graye-sur-Mer, we took advantage of a sudden break in the rain to let the dogs on to the beach; two hundred metres from Tinkerbelle the grey skies began again emptying their grey load on to the grey waters, the sodden sands, and us, so we all returned to the vehicle frozen and drenched to the skin and shivering, even more able to understand, in a very minor way, what it must have been like on 6 June 1944 — the longest day.

In almost-deserted Courseulles-sur-Mer a brave carousel was spinning anoraked children astride horses, fish and aeroplanes. There are many monuments and memorials there, including a Sherman tank recovered from the sea in 1970 and restored; the *La Combattante* stone in memory of the Free French Forces' destroyer of the same name, which delivered General de Gaulle to France on 14 June, and an eighteen-metre-high cross of Lorraine marking the spot where he set foot back on French soil after the liberation; and plaques commemorating the Canadian regiments who took Juno beach. You can't visit these places, especially on a miserable day, without being chilled by the thought of all the lives lost in the immediate area. You look at the choppy waves and think of the landing craft and the men they spewed out; you think of the midget submarines that had lain on the sea bed, gathering information and guiding in the landing craft; the whole enormous task of planning Operation Overlord. The French holiday guide books, holiday snaps and sailing books that gave vital information to the planners. Colonel Sam Bassett, landing secretly at night to test whether the sands could bear the weight of the tanks. The building of the 'funnies' — tanks designed to do strange tasks. And the delicate question of how much information about the planned invasion could safely be given to the Resistance, whose cooperation was critical, but whose ranks contained suspected traitors. That an operation so vast could be successfully launched and accomplished, without word reaching the enemy, was beyond belief. And we imagined the mutual euphoria of the locals and their liberators when they met in the shattered villages, and shared pots of cider and calvados. On an old, thatched, timbered windmill a short distance back from the beach a cormorant sat upon one of the sails, preening itself, oblivious of the significance of the monuments around it.

We continued along the coast, passing through the oddly named Ver-sur-Mer (ver means worm in French). Gold beach, the middle of the five landing beaches, and the British troops' second objective, extends from west of Courseulles to Arromanches. We cast anchor in Arromanches, where the campsite *gardien* assured us that although Normandy is France's wettest region, it almost never rains for two consecutive days, and we could expect seasonal weather next day. This was up-lifting news, because travelling in a small camper van with two big dogs is very much more enjoyable if you can all get out of the vehicle from time to time without getting frozen and soaked.

The following morning brought something unusual for Normandy — a second consecutive wet day. Contrary to the *gardien*'s assurance, we were treated to intermittent heavy showers punctuated with periods of icy drizzle. We went to visit Arromanches's 360° cinema, to watch a film of the events of D-Day from the perspective of the people who were there, taken from original war correspondent archives, and interlaced with colour film taken of exactly the same spots now, in peacetime. The eighteen-minute-long film is projected on to nine screens encircling the auditorium; there's no commentary, just background sound and music, and the noise of the guns is deafening. Men run through collapsing buildings; tanks rumble; men fall; and on a pile of rubble a soldier binds a dog's injured paw. When the film ended we left in silence, feeling that for those few minutes we'd personally experienced this momentous event.

Out in the sea the remains of the Mulberry harbour are visible. It's one of the things my mind always has difficulty in getting to grips with, the concept of floating concrete. I realize it works, because I've seen the result, but despite Terry's patient explanations I still don't truly understand it. When you consider that more than 150 of the concrete caissons, some of which were 60 metres long, 15 metres wide and 18 metres high and weighed up to 6,000 tonnes, were manufactured in England and towed across the Channel by tugs, you have to marvel at the ingenuity and optimism of those who believed this thing could work. It had to: to supply the Allies with the reinforcements and equipment they would need following the landings, there had to be some means of unloading supplies on to the beach whilst the ports were still in German hands. The Mulberry harbour at Arromanches, known as Port Winston, would do its job for ten months, but its brother at neighbouring Omaha Beach was destroyed by the violent storms which raged between 19 and 22 June 1944, like the one raging today.

Emerging into the familiar rain, we did something unusual, being not very good at museums: we went off to visit Bayeux. It was

Terry's idea, which I agreed to, expecting to be bored but prepared to endure that if it meant being able to walk without getting any wetter. By the time we'd fought our way into a parking space in Bayeux, and to the front of the queue for tickets to see the tapestry, we were advised of a wait of up to an hour before we could get in, and so we devised a cunning plan to go and have an early lunch, then double back to the Centre Guillaume le Conquérant and have the place to ourselves whilst everybody else was eating. The town was awash with sixtieth-anniversary flags hanging sodden from their poles. In a quaint street of timbered buildings we found a restaurant making the transition between morning coffee and lunch, where the staff were having a sit-down and a chat and weren't absolutely thrilled to be disturbed by us. But they installed us at a table and asked us to wait, which we did patiently, until the chef arrived.

An American family took the table beside us. There were mum and dad, an auntie, a grandma, and two engaging teenage girls bursting with vitamins, perfect skin, excellent teeth and manners, and an overwhelming desire to see grandma eat snails which they were certain she was going to love. Although she wasn't convinced, she obligingly agreed.

The girls and their father spoke French reasonably well; mum, grandma and auntie didn't speak it at all, but they were all enthusiastic about French food and France in general, which was encouraging after the general breakdown in relations between the two countries over the Iraq war. With more than 66,000 Americans dead on French soil during the Second World War, nearly 11,000 in Normandy, it seemed a great tragedy that the old allies had subsequently fallen out so bitterly, and it was encouraging to see that not all Americans were boycotting France. I could in one way understand the Americans' resentment at the outset of their assault on Iraq, and that they felt France owed them a debt of allegiance that should override its own sentiments. But I hoped fervently that fifteen months after the Iraq invasion, able to see the appalling débâcle created there, the Americans might no longer feel so sure France had been wrong.

While we ate our lunch I discreetly watched granny battling with the snails. The girls showed her how to clasp the shells in the miniature forceps and prise the inhabitants out, and she put one in her mouth. After a lengthy chewing and a gulp, she said they were very nice, but she thought she'd just eat the sauce. She endorsed what I've always believed: snails are just an excuse for mopping up lashings of melted garlic butter with a bread roll. As fish-eating vegetarians, we're confused about snails: while they're clearly not a fish, they're not really a meat, either. We've probably eaten them twice in the last twenty years, and I don't really know why, because they wouldn't be anything without the garlic butter.

Our crafty scheme had worked, and when we returned to the exhibition we only had to queue for five minutes before being handed an electronic guide rather like a large mobile telephone, and allowed through the doors into the darkened room where the original Bayeux tapestry lives. For a moment I panicked, feeling claustrophobic, but the moment I saw the first panel, I forgot my surroundings. I'd been expecting a gigantic, gloomy woolly picture, like those hanging in the dining hall of Pierre Loti's house, but this was really something else. It wasn't a tapestry at all.

No. This is what it is: an absolutely mind-blowingly wonderfully crafted cartoon, of simple stitchwork on a linen strip seventy metres long, but only fifty centimetres high, telling the story of why William the Bastard had gone off to England to whack Harold and become a conqueror. It wasn't an act of wanton aggression at all, but to claim the throne that Edward the Confessor had intended William to have, and Harold, perfidious creature that he was, tried to steal from him. The text on the not-tapestry is in crude Latin, and the electronic guide explained the words and actions so exquisitely depicted in simple stitches. The problem was that the queue ahead moved at a much slower pace than the guide, which couldn't be turned on and off. So while listening to an explanation of panel No. 11, we were stuck in front of panel No. 7, trying to store up all the information to correlate it with the pictures when we eventually reached them. Behind us were people even more distant from what they were listening to. But it didn't matter, because as we edged along in the darkness watching the scenes unfolding in the glass case that houses the embroidery, we were lost in time, sailing with William's fleet across the Channel. What is extraordinary is how a few threads of wool perfectly convey the emotions of the characters. They weren't anonymous people, but soldiers and sailors, farmers, dogs and horses, sometimes mythical animals, fleets of ships, Normans and Saxons. We heard the snort of the horses, the ribald shouts of the soldiers, the lapping of the waves on the sides of the boats, and the shooshing of arrows and clashing of sword and axe. And for heaven's sake — there's Halley's comet making one of its periodic appearances, shortly after Harold's coronation, a foreteller of doom if ever there was one! You're not looking at history — you're living it!

And the amazing thing is, this work of art was created more than nine hundred years ago! Could the people who made it have ever imagined it would last so long? They were not going to leave the battle of Hastings to word of mouth, they wanted it chronicled so that every man could see why and how it took place. Even more amazing is that it has survived through the centuries, almost intact apart from the two final missing panels. And it's come so close to disaster several times. After resting in obscurity for four hundred years following its creation, it was noted on an inventory of Bayeux cathedral in 1476. Another three hundred years passed before very much interest was shown in it, when the French Revolution was about to break out. If it hadn't been for the actions of a gentleman named Lambert Leonard Leforestier, the cloth would have been used as a cover for munitions wagons. Lambert managed to retrieve it and replace it with something more suitable. Bayeux's burghers established a council to protect it, which was just as well, because not many years later somebody suggested chopping it up and using it for decoration. This unthinkable idea was thwarted, then along came Napoleon who carted it off to Paris, where he wanted to study it to see if he could pick up any tips from William on how to successfully invade England. Failing to do so, he returned it to Bayeux, where it would be displayed in between various wars, and locked away for protection during them.

Its craziest adventure must be that recounted in Andrew Bridgeford's book *1066: The Hidden History of the Bayeux Tapestry*. At the outbreak of the Second World War, the cloth was treated with insecticide and locked away beneath Bayeux cathedral. Once the Germans arrived, it wasn't long before they found it, and like Napoleon they hoped it would help them emulate William's successful invasion of England. The French suggested that it should be moved for safe storage to Sourches château at Saint-Symphorien, west of le Mans. The Germans agreed, but the only vehicle the French could lay their hands on for the transport of this invaluable treasure was a lorry fuelled by charcoal, which really wasn't up to the job being asked of it. It needed pushing to start it after the driver's lunch break, and very soon conked out completely, and had to be shoved up the many hills along the route. Reaching the crest of a hill, it careered crazily down the other side, with the pushers chasing frantically after it until its impetus was halted by level ground. It took ten hours to cover the 115-odd miles, but at least its priceless cargo remained safely in Sourches for the duration of the war, until the Allies landed. At this time it was ordered to be delivered to the Louvre by Herr Himmler, who had it in his acquisitive eye. It was due to the deliberate prevarication of German commander Dietrich von Choltitz, whom some called the 'Saviour of Paris' because he obeyed his heart and not his Führer's spiteful orders to destroy that city, that Himmler didn't get his avaricious hands on the cloth. Once the war was over, it was returned to Bayeux, where it has been undisturbed for the past sixty years.

I felt I could sit and look at it for a whole day, and was disappointed when we reached the final panel, an explanation of which we'd heard five minutes before we arrived there. You can't go back, you have to keep moving onwards, rather like sheep queuing for the dip, as more and more people move up behind you. Upstairs in the Centre Guillaume le Conquérant, you can visit a replica at your own pace, and I think without charge. The last thing I'd expected was to enjoy this visit, because I'm a self-confessed philistine whose idea of hell is wandering around a museum looking at bits of pots and obscure relics of past ages. It's just the way I am. But in Bayeux I found something I could look at again and again and again. I wanted to buy it and pin it up all round the walls of our house. It did for me what all the tedious hours of droning teachers with their dry, meaningless facts and dates never could: it put passion, excitement and life into history. In the brochures and leaflets handed out by the French tourist offices I found the drama that had escaped my school history textbooks.

How accurately does the not-tapestry tell the tale? Is it biased, having been told from the Norman perspective? Who sewed it? William's wife Mathilde, having nothing better to do than to sit stitching with her ladies in a draughty castle? Or was it worked by accomplished English hands? Because not only were the English talented needlewomen with all the requisite skills to create such an embroidery at the time of the Norman invasion, but over eight hundred years later a group of Englishwomen, the Leek Embroidery Society, would actually *make a replica*!

A lady named Elizabeth Wardle had seen photographs and drawings of the Bayeux tapestry, and made up her forceful mind that England must have its own version. So she formed a group of thirty-nine embroidering ladies, one of whom would use the photographs to trace the pictures on to linen. Elizabeth was married to Thomas Wardle, whose family business was fabric dyeing, so she was well placed to have the threads coloured to match the originals. Within a year of starting their work, the industrious ladies had completed it, more or less true to the original apart from an understandable desire on their part that their labours should not go unsung: each of them embroidered her name on to their section of the tapestry.

The other differences between the two cloths are certain omissions. When you see the original, albeit there is a great deal to take in visually at the same time as trying to retain the audio information, you will quite likely have time to notice the well-defined distinction between male and female horses, and also the fact that amongst the naked figures frolicking and crouching in the border some of them are emphatically masculine, as can be seen because they are also stark bollock naked. Imagine how this could have affected the Victorian embroidering ladies, especially if there were *maidens* in their midst. But they circumvented this distressing situation by simply disregarding the offending appendages, except for a Miss Margaret Ritchie, who seems to have been something of a rebel, and less sensitive than her fellow embroiderers. The lady who laboriously traced the original design on to the linen had pencilled in little pairs of shorts to protect the modesty of the ladies and their subjects. Miss Ritchie, however, refused to dress her model in this garment. Imagine the blushful tuttings, whisperings and comments that must have gone on behind her back! Would those masculine parts that discomfited the English ladies have been a reason for giggling and sly jokes by their French counter-parts all those centuries ago?

By the time we reluctantly came to the end of this splendid visit, it was still raining. It had been raining ceaselessly for nearly forty-eight hours, but as we reached Omaha beach the sun finally broke through. 'Omaha' was the ten-kilometre stretch of beach where everything went so horribly wrong during the invasion. Aerial bombardment designed to weaken the German defences was ineffectual. Specially adapted floating tanks didn't float

— they sank and never reached the beach. Unhelpful currents and winds landed the American troops everywhere but where they should be; they were easy targets for the well-entrenched and numerous German artillery emplacements overlooking the beach from the cliffs above. Trapped on the beach without the tank support they had expected, it was only by super-human determination and effort that the Americans succeeded in their objective, scaling the cliffs, at the cost of 2,400 casualties. The event was graphically depicted in the film *Saving Private Ryan*. It was difficult to visualize now, on a peaceful day, in the sunshine.

At Saint-Laurent-sur-Mer's American cemetery are 9,386 graves, all in perfect alignment and immaculately tended, a list of 1,557 names of people who disappeared without trace, and a truly beautiful seven-metre-high bronze sculpture *The Spirit of American Youth rising from the waves*. All American cemeteries in France have been given to America by France, in perpetuity, free of any charge. A few kilometres down the road is the German cemetery, a reminder that it wasn't only Allied soldiers who died: 21,500 German soldiers are buried there, among them the German hero and Panzer ace Michael Wittmann, commander of the Tiger tank Bondesquely numbered 007, killed in August 1944, at the age of just thirty.

Tally and Dobbie ran on the narrow sandy beach, and people strolled around in the sun among the pillboxes and memorials on the grassy hillside. While it was impossible to see this peaceful, pleasant strip of sand and grass as a bloodied battleground, the seafront houses were mostly bleak and sullen-looking, unadorned by even a single plant. They overlooked the beach drearily, as if afraid to offend the ghosts of the past by any frivolous decoration. I found this place unbearably sad. To the rear were older properties that had survived the war, charming old buildings covered with ivy and climbing roses.

We stopped at Pointe du Hoc, the strategic site which had to be neutralized before the landings, because from there German cannons could dominate both Omaha and Utah beaches. The American Rangers tasked with knocking out the cannons had to land on the narrow beach, which was becoming ever narrower as the tide came in, and scale a thirty-metre perpendicular cliff. They did this with extending ladders supplied by the London Fire Brigade, mounted on amphibious vehicles called DUKWs, and rocket-fired ropes fitted with grapnels. A British commando with the Americans, Colonel Travis Trevor, strolled around on the beach encouraging the men. Somebody asked whether he wasn't afraid of being shot. He replied that he took two short steps and three long ones, so the snipers always missed him. Actually, no sooner had he spoken than a bullet hit his helmet and knocked him down, after which he stopped taking short and long steps and crouched down on the ground like everybody else. When the Rangers succeeded in scaling the cliff despite the Germans' trying to cut their ropes and drop grenades on them, they found the cannons they'd been sent to destroy had already been removed from the casemates for safety and replaced with telegraph poles. The Rangers found the guns and put them out of action, but were cut off from support and had to hold out for forty-eight hours, sustaining 75 per cent casualties before reinforcements arrived.

At Pointe du Hoc we found a hilltop pitted with craters up to 15 metres wide and 3 metres deep, surrounding dozens of concrete bunkers and casemates, some intact, and some in ruins with fingers of twisted metal pointing out of them. In one we discovered a swallows' nest in a dark corner, the fledglings hanging over the edge with gaping beaks as the nervous parents delivering food to their young skimmed the heads of the sightseers. The craters serve as playgrounds for children who slide or roll down to the bottom and heave themselves back up by clutching handfuls of grass. Looking down from the cliff's edge, by the tall dagger-like obelisk erected by the French to honour the Rangers, I tried to imagine what it was like for the men hauling themselves up there, under fire, and having the strength to do so and arrive fighting at the top. I think that of the battlefields we visited, this is the one which portrayed most vividly the actuality of warfare: the sheer size of the bunkers and the craters brought home what the men on both sides were faced with. We left Pointe du Hoc in a rather contemplative mood, and didn't have much to say until we reached the outskirts of Grandcamp-Maisy, where pale sunshine reflected from a ten-metre steel sculpture in the shape of a young girl releasing a dove from her upraised hands, a gift to France from Chinese sculptor Wen Yaoyuan. The original of this sculpture, which symbolizes world peace, stands in a square in Beijing; Wen Yaoyuan was forced into factory work during the Cultural Revolution, and now devotes himself to working for world peace, giving statues to different countries. It was heartening to see something which had a positive significance rather than a memorial to the dead: we'd seen so many memorials, so many graves.

★ ★ ★

We were approaching the last lap of our odyssey, and had very mixed feelings. On the one hand we wanted to see our home and the animals, and we were both tired from the constant travelling and living in a confined space. On the other hand, though, each day had brought new and wonderful experiences, forming a kaleidoscope of memories, and we felt that we would like to travel ad infinitum until there wasn't a nook and cranny that we hadn't visited and learned about.

On les Veys bay stands Isigny-sur-Mer, home of the great Isigny-Sainte-Mère cooperative dairy, formed by the amalgamation of the dairy farmers of Isigny-sur-Mer and Sainte-Mère-Eglise, the first village liberated on D-Day. Here the Normandy milk generously provided by the cattle who graze the luxuriant greenery is transformed into the AOC (Appellation d'Origine Controlée) dairy products, including the incomparable buttercup-yellow butter. The temperate climate and generous rainfall in Normandy means, they say, that the grass grows so quickly that you can actually see it doing so,

471

although with Tinkerbelle's wipers contending with a new downpour we might have missed a few blades. Isigny-sur-Mer's second claim to fame is that it was the home of Walt Disney's forebears, Disney being a corruption of 'd'Isigny'.

The westernmost of the landing beaches, 'Utah', was a particularly bleak stretch of coastline; mean houses along the seafront stood dourly taking the brunt of the hateful weather, and trees bent like bows beneath the driving rain and the spiteful wind whipping off the sea. Colin Bruce, from the Department of Printed Books at the Imperial War Museum, told me there was no significance in the code names given to the beaches, which were chosen to be deliberately meaningless to anybody unaware of them. He said too that a sixth landing area for the Allied invasion, code-named Band, was designated to the east of the river Orne, but was never used.

At Quettehou, we passed a man sitting in the rain in a field on a low three-legged stool, milking a cow into a galvanized pail, watched by another man and a small boy. A solitary rainbow-sailed dinghy bobbed just off the exotically named Île de Tatihou, and fishing boats lay tilted on their sides in the mud in pretty Barfleur, where the air smelt deliciously salty and seaweedy. You wouldn't be any wetter or colder out in the sea that day than you were walking along the streets. The weather here on the Cherbourg peninsula seemed to be getting worse by the day. You'd need a sturdy heart to pretend it was a good place to be at this time. Unripened wheat looked as if it had been flattened by a steamroller; the fields, still fallow, were saturated oceans of shiny mud, with the ploughs lying idle on the boggy land. Rows of people in coloured rainwear stooped under their hoods, diligently picking lettuces. A woman with glowing, fluorescent crimson hair walked beside the hedgerow, towing a wet, bewildered-looking little boy in a hooded anorak. The backwoods were peppered with pretty properties, and the hydrangeas were splendid; how could they be otherwise here where they could gorge themselves to their hearts' content on the eternal rain?

Normandy's most beautiful crop is horse-flesh. It seemed every field, every garden held at least one burnished beauty grazing apparently unfazed by the appalling weather. The Gatteville lighthouse peered through the gloom as we followed narrow little lanes winding past small granite cottages and wild, rocky land smothered in deep-pink heather, and the tide was coming in rapidly, gaining inches with every sweep.

We chose to give the uranium processing plant at Cap de la Hague, and the nuclear plant at Flamanville, a miss, and cut down from Cherbourg to the western coast of the Cotentin, where we arrived at a beautiful sandy bay surrounded by grassy dunes and smooth chunks of cushion-like black and blue-green stones. The dogs raced around while we tramped the damp, tightly packed sand, whirling our arms and stamping our feet to keep warm in the glacial wind. To Tally's great delight we met a group of people playing with a ball, and off he ran to join in. Unfortunately they weren't inclined to play with him, and one woman snatched the ball and clutched it possessively to her chest. Tally stared at her and wagged his tail hard, and was very nonplussed by her unusual behaviour. Normally people playing ball were delighted to have his help.

We lunched in the teeny toytown-by-the-sea village of Carteret, then went to Lindbergh beach, named after the American aviator because he'd overflown it on his record-breaking New York to Paris solo flight. The dogs helped a couple of young men flying stunt kites in the icy wind; the sun came out and the skylarks sang, and clumps of wild orchids and patches of wild thyme grew along the roadside. On the road we came up behind a boat being towed by a tractor. Within the boat stood a very old man directing the traffic. He signalled vehicles past energetically and with no reference to the oncoming traffic. Despite almost causing a collision, he continued merrily waving people on. Avoiding an accident not-withstanding his best efforts, we saw a sign to the Château de Pirou, and as it was quite some time since we'd visited a château, we thought we'd go and have a look. Pirou is very picturesque, quite small, in fact rather like a large toy castle. Built in the twelfth century on an artificial island surrounded by a moat, when we visited it was in the throes of a restoration project started in 1968, after falling into ruin over the centuries until it had become a simple farm. We strolled on the battlements in the sunshine, looking out over the marshes towards the Channel Islands, then went to admire the Pirou tapestry, made during the 1970s in the same style as its more famous Bayeux relative, and relating the tale of the Norman conquest of Sicily and southern Italy.

In ancient times, the château of Pirou had been under siege by Vikings for some time when the assailants became aware there was no sound coming from within the walls. They stormed the castle, but found only one old

475

man. All the inhabitants and the garrison had vanished. They promised to spare the old man's life if he'd tell them how the people had escaped. He said they'd used a magic spell to transform themselves into geese, and had flown away, and the enemy recalled seeing a large flock of geese overhead the previous evening. In time the geese returned, but were unable to find the spell needed to return to their human form, because the spell-book had disappeared. They still return, each year, in the hope of finding it. The château's present owners tried to introduce non-migrating geese, but sadly they were poached.

We continued meandering along the coast, exploring small lanes until we found an empty sandy beach in a place that seemed to have no name. We parked Tinkerbelle behind the dunes and spent several hours enjoying a respite from the weather. The dogs ran through the water, over the sands, and up and down the dunes. Tally was inexhaustible, but Dobbie returned every so often and flung himself down to recharge his batteries. With his recent forays into the salt water, his paw was at last healing well. Because where we were was so sheltered and peaceful, and ideal for the dogs, and as there was nobody around, we decided we'd do some 'camping *sauvage*' just for the one night, instead of going to a campsite. At nightfall, we put the dogs into the cab with their beds, and drew the curtains around them, then settled down in the back with a DVD and a bottle of wine.

We were enjoying *Master and Commander*, and I was trying to rationalize how a rather overweight man with a Cupid's bow mouth and long hair could be as devastatingly attractive as Russell Crowe, when at 11.00 p.m. a car drew up nearby and we heard men's voices. I was reminded of the warning we'd been given all those weeks ago about being careful where we stayed at night. There was a rap on the door, and Terry opened it cautiously to find himself face to face with two *gendarmes*. They were friendly and polite, but said we couldn't stay there for the night. Not just for one night? No, *désolé*, not even one night, but there was a designated place for *les camping-caristes* just one kilometre down the road. They gave us directions and drove away.

'Well,' said Terry, 'we'll have to move. You stay where you are and I'll hop into the front and drive us round there.'

So he climbed into the cab, and followed the *gendarmes*' directions until we reached a car park on the edge of a small village, where several other camper vans were parked. When the vehicle halted I heard a brief exchange between Terry and someone else, and when he re-joined me he was almost crying with laughter. As he'd driven into the parking area, the *gendarmes* had signalled him towards a vacant place. As he halted Tinkerbelle, one *gendarme* walked up to what he thought was the driver's side. But Tinkerbelle was an English vehicle, and instead of finding Terry sitting there, the man found himself face to face with a huge black dog, and his expression froze in shock as he struggled with the thought that the dog had driven the vehicle. Terry said he'd never forget the *gendarme*'s momentary open-mouthed amazement, nor Dobbie's look of puzzlement at being stared at in such horror.

Terry was still laughing the next morning. It was a blue-sky day, with clouds on the horizon, and armies of scarlet poppies patrolling the coastal road. We drove through Granville, which we'd last visited about fifteen years previously on a grey drizzly day, when it had seemed a small and rather dull town, despite being the birth-place of one of the great *couturiers*, Christian Dior. Now, though, under benevolent sunshine, Granville seemed sturdy, animated and reliable. The tide lay far out beyond a vast expanse of golden sand dotted with small pools and beds of seaweed, and the blue, red and yellow sails of flotillas of small boats bobbed in the distance.

This part of France's coastline might not show too many signs of warfare, but our old friend Vauban hadn't overlooked it in his tireless quest to fortify his country. At Carolles a stony and uneven path leads from the car park to la Cabane Vauban, one of several lookout posts built under his direction at the end of the seventeenth century to keep an eye on the English enemy across the Channel. Sentries watched shipping movements and signalled to each other by means of fires, smoke or sirens. The Vauban cabin is a stocky single-roomed building of thick stone walls beneath a stone roof; there's a chimney and fireplace, and spectacular views across the bay of Mont-Saint-Michel. It's a great bird-watching site, too, and on our way back to Tinkerbelle we detoured through a field smothered in flocks of singing birds stripping seeds from the plants.

Hoping to see the famous fast tide incoming to the bay of Mont-Saint-Michel, we parked on the cliff top at Genêts, but although we sat there for what seemed like ages the tide didn't appear to be in any hurry, so we went on to Avranches for lunch. Avranches is where Henry II of England crawled around on his knees in penance, to obtain absolution for the rash words that led to the murder of Thomas Becket in Canterbury. The town is renowned for its beautiful medieval manuscripts, and an enterprising Avranches *chocolatier* advertised in a brochure that they created chocolate manuscripts. I thought what fun it could be to produce a 100,000-word manuscript in chocolate and send it to Transworld Publishers by refrigerated pantechnicon. I had a vision of the editorial department sitting around eating their way through it, and somebody saying: 'Gosh — did anybody ask Susie if she has a hard copy?' Disappointingly, the advertised manuscripts were simple chocolate tablets with a single fancy letter engraved upon them, and they'd be too laborious to assemble and impossible to read.

We arrived when the market was in full swing, with displays of fruit and vegetables burnished and shining like jewels in a treasure chest. After loading ourselves with punnets of blackberries, raspberries, strawberries, blueberries and gooseberries we walked through the back streets of the marketplace and found the humbler traders, old people with simple trestles displaying small bunches of their home-grown fruit and vegetables, and regretted having no room left to buy their produce. Although Terry might disagree, I felt the meal we had in Avranches was the most enjoyable of our trip. After trying half a dozen restaurants which all rejected us because they were full, we found a tiny place called le Pouc in an alley. When we arrived, although it was empty of people, there wasn't a square inch of it that wasn't wonderfully decorated. A stunningly slim, pretty girl swathed in exotic silken clothing explained it had previously been an Indian restaurant belonging to a Briton, which explained the elephants and Himalayan mountains, the minarets, tigers, jungles and palm trees painted on the walls, even in the loos. The girl and her partner had retained the original decoration when they bought it — and I agreed it would have been sacrilege to destroy such wonderful work — and added to it in their own style, which included fairies diving into the lakes and hovering over the mountains. The whole effect was quite enchanting. The girl had done all the fairy painting herself, as well as making lamp-shades from feathers and paper. Not only was the décor delightful, the food was excellent. While Terry sat digesting and savouring a coffee or two, I skipped round the corner to the church of St Gervais to have a look at St Aubert's skull.

481

St Aubert was the bishop of Avranches in the eighth century. He was visited by the Archangel Michael who told him to build a church on the rock known as Mont Tombe, where a Christian settlement had existed since the fifth century. The bishop failed to react. Michael reminded him. When Aubert still didn't start building, St Michael, his patience and normally good temper exhausted, poked the dilatory bishop in the head with his finger, leaving a large hole in the cranium. This encouraged St Aubert to undertake the building of an oratory where the Archangel had suggested. Over the centuries it grew to be a Benedictine monastery, and between the thirteenth and sixteenth centuries the stupendous abbey, called 'la Merveille', was built. Used as a prison during the late eighteenth and nineteenth centuries, today it is France's most popular tourist attraction. Although Brittany seems to claim Mont-Saint-Michel, geographically it's in Normandy, although its bay does extend over the two regions.

The bishop's holey skull was meant to repose in the treasury of St Gervais's church, and as I'd never seen a skull pierced by a finger, I wanted to have a look. You have to pay to visit the treasury, which houses a collection of ecclesiastical riches in gold and statuary, religious clothing, and the relics of St Suzanne, an unfortunate maiden from Rome who refused the marriage proposal of an emperor's son, and had her head cut off instead.

St Aubert's head, or what's left of it, lives in a glass cage, and the extraordinary thing is this: when I saw it, although the skull certainly had a finger hole in it, it wasn't made of bone like yours or mine, but gold-plated copper! Now how do you explain that?

Pondering this miracle, I collected Terry and we walked round Avranches's public gardens, a collection of manicured lawns, tapestry-like flower beds, towering trees, ponds and a magical view of Mont-Saint-Michel across the serpentine estuary. Two local heroes are commemorated there: Général Roger Valhubert, a son of Avranches and much-decorated soldier, who died of his wounds at Austerlitz; and a Resistance leader named Désiré Lerouxel killed during the bombardment of Avranches. In the park stands a large sinuous sculpture which looks as if it's made from metal, until you get close and read that it was carved from a giant sequoia tree felled by the great storm that ravaged France in 1999. It's called very appropriately *La Fille du Vent*, and was made by a local sculptor named Fabienne Campelli. The great monument to 'the Glorious American army of General Patton', and the restored Sherman tank named Thunderbolt are displayed on the way out of Avranches, from where revolver-toting Patton (whom Hitler referred to as the 'General-cowboy') began his victorious tramp across France to the German border. Very unfairly, General Patton was killed in a car crash just after the end of the war, and is buried in Luxembourg.

Heading for the coastline where we'd first begun our journey, we made a brief detour to Ducey, to see the château there that was the family home of Gabriel, Earl of Montgomery, captain of the Scottish guards of King Henri II of France. (You'll remember how Henri III of Navarre became Henri IV of France after Henri II and all his sons had died.) Montgomery was unfortunate enough to be responsible for the monarch's death during a joust when, precisely as Nostradamus had predicted, a splinter from his lance found its way into the king's eye, causing him a lingering and painful death. Probably served him right: Henri had a nasty way with Protestants, having them burned alive or cutting out their tongues. Banished in disgrace, Montgomery converted to Protestantism — could there be a better example of adding insult to injury? — and fought with the Prince de Condé (father of the Great Condé) in the Wars of Religion. Subsequently he was captured and executed on the orders of Henri II's widow, Catherine de Medici. Nostradamus predicted all that, too. There's every possibility the Château Montgomery is wondrous to behold inside. However, it was closed when we went, and the exterior didn't do one little bit to entice us to explore it further. I suspect it might rate as one of the ugliest châteaux of all time, a tall, grey and foreboding granite building patched in places with brick, with insufficient and far too narrow windows. It looked like the ancestral home of the Addams family.

11

FULL CIRCLE — CREEPY CASTLE, AND FINALLY HOME

Ahead, on an 85-metre-tall granite rock, sat the incomparably beautiful abbey of Mont-Saint-Michel. We drove past numerous souvenir shops until all that separated us from it was the causeway, several thousand cars and teeming ant-like sightseers marching to and from it. We agreed this time we'd enjoy the scene as a whole rather than struggling around the streets, so we sat happily in Tinkerbelle, gazing at this beautiful jewel of France, bathed in a sunshine that made the stone glow. We could have happily sat there round the clock watching the changing colours of la Merveille, perched on the rocks like an elaborate cake decoration.

This breathtaking view of Mont-Saint-Michel was the cherry on the cake of our journey, and we were ready to head for home. Driving slowly along the flat landscape edging the bay, where an occasional horse cropped the grass, and people were selling garlic and onions by the roadside, we arrived back at le

Vivier-sur-Mer where we'd begun our journey more than 10,000 kilometres ago. Le Vivier-sur-Mer had begun farming *bouchots* — cultivated mussels — fifty years ago, in 1954. The original method was discovered by a shipwrecked Irish sailor who noticed that mussels attached themselves to pieces of wood stuck in the water. The mussels at le Vivier-sur-Mer are produced by attaching spats from the Atlantic coast to ropes wound round stakes planted in the sand. The little mussel babies hang round for about eighteen months, growing nicely and contentedly, until along comes one of the special wheeled boats which enable the mussel farmers to reach the breeding grounds at any time, tide in or out, and they're picked off, boxed up and end up on our plates.

We said our definitive *au revoirs* to France's outer limits here, at the point where we completed our perfect circle around the entire perimeter of the country, and turned towards home.

Although technically our trip was over, other places and points of interest chose to pop up along the way, like Mont-Dol, the granite mound where St Michael and Satan fought a violent battle, and the Devil's claw marks can be seen on the top; and at quaint, medieval Dol-de-Bretagne the menhir of

Champ Dolent, almost ten metres high, with another seven metres below the ground. One legend tells that it fell from the sky to stop a great battle between two brothers, and another says that every hundred years the stone shrinks by one inch because the moon nibbles a tiny piece each night. When there's no more left of the menhir, it will signal the end of the world. To work it out, you could convert the current height into inches, and see how many centuries it will take . . .

We debated whether to just keep driving until we reached home, or to spend one last night in Tinkerbelle, and when we arrived in Combourg we decided to cast a final anchor. We sat beneath the awning sipping wine, looking back at all the places we'd been and the people we'd met.

Next morning we drove into Combourg, home town of Romanticism, for a last leisurely morning cup of coffee and choco-late. By chance there was a guided tour of Combourg's château just starting — we were in the right place at the right time for one of the very rare occasions on our journey. Terry proclaimed himself all châteaued out, but I jumped at the opportunity of visiting Châteaubriand's childhood home. The ticket-selling lady said I must se dépêcher with the speed of light to catch up with the tour, so I sprinted along the curving path between neat lawns and up the stone stairs leading to the central part of the building, which is guarded on either side by circular towers topped with witches' hats. The guide launched into her script, and after establishing that I was English and not German handed me a translation, for which I was most grateful, as it meant I'd understand far more than I normally did when the commentary was in French.

I didn't notice whether there was a motto over the front door, but if not I'd like to propose 'Abandon Hope All Ye Who Enter Here'. Combourg Château is the very embodiment of gloom.

In the hallway a bust of François-Réné de Châteaubriand stands below the family coat of arms given to one of his forebears during the Crusades, with its cheery slogan: 'Our blood stains the banner of France.' When the crusading knight returned, his wife was so overjoyed she died of happiness. I'm sure we heard the same story at the Château de Joux. Crusaders' wives seemed to be either shameless hussies or faint-hearted ninnies. A graphic, jolly painting depicts Cardinal de Richelieu's siege of la Rochelle when he starved 18,000 people to death. In what is now the lounge, there are portraits of

Lamoignon des Malesherbes, grandfather of Châteaubriand's sister-in-law: both of them went to the guillotine. There's also a portrait of Marie Leszczynski (remember her from Wissembourg?).

A bust of the defiant Countess of Châteaubriand, who was the mistress of François I, stands in the dining room. When he dispensed with her services, he asked her to return the jewellery he'd given her (not only was he fickle, but a cheapskate too). She returned it as soon as she'd had it melted into ingots. Bravo. There are also various items of furniture and *objets d'art*. The only thing I could find to like in the château was a silver tea service ordered by Châteaubriand during his stint as ambassador in London in 1822. The beauty of the set lies in its absolute simplicity, which is a pleasant contrast to the other ornate, depressing paraphernalia. It was in this room that Châteaubriand, in his *Memories from Beyond the Grave*, described his father pacing around by dim candlelight, casting ghostly shadows.

Leaving the dismal dining room we moved on to the archive room, a small museum housing personal items such as documents, family portraits, souvenirs from foreign travels, his deathbed and an inkstand in the shape of a black cat on his desk; Châteaubriand commissioned the piece to remind him of the cheery legend of the long-dead count of Combourg whose wooden leg tapped itself up the staircase, followed by a black cat.

What a fun place this was turning out to be!

Moving on to the east and south battlements there are views over the town and the lake, and the fairground where once a year 'something resembling joy' could be seen in Combourg.[1]

In the Cat Tower we could admire a mummified cat, exhibited in a glass showcase. The animal would have been walled up alive, according to tradition, when the château was built, to ensure good luck to the inhabitants. The writer described the room he occupied as a child at the top of the turret, where flitting owls, rustling winds and creaking doors convinced him of the presence of ghosts, until he was immune to fear. He wrote: 'I could have slept with a corpse.'

We traipsed on to the western battlements giving views on to the gardens, and a stone cross marking the favourite spot of the writer's melancholic sister, Lucile. According to Châteaubriand the château boasted secret

---

[1] *Memories from Beyond the Grave.*

passages and dungeons 'and everywhere silence, darkness and a face of stone: such was the château of Combourg.' Indeed it was. For the rest of his life he'd suffer 'a vague sadness', and who can be surprised? Most of us would probably have gone stark raving mad had we had to endure the horrors of Combourg. Nevertheless he did very well for himself both as the founder of Romanticism in French literature and as a career diplomat. And for the gourmets, it was in his honour that the recipe for Châteaubriand steak was invented.

This really was our last stopping place, and once I'd joined Terry for a final hot chocolate we pointed south and headed home. Surprisingly, as we left Brittany behind the flourishing greenery we'd become so accustomed to over the last few weeks gave way to hectares of pale-beige grass withered by drought. The nearer we got to home, the drier became the terrain, and we returned to a dusty landscape of wilted plants and weary trees.

Frequently in the places where we'd stopped, we'd trawled estate agents' windows, discussing idly what we could afford in a particular area. It had been easy to succumb to quaint stone cottages, modern apartments overlooking the sea, alpine refuges, narrow houses in colourful city back streets. Almost everywhere we'd been had held the hint of new pastures. But driving up the lane to our home we knew that for now this is where our hearts lie.

Vivien had done a magnificent job. The garden was spick and span, without the hint of a weed. The animals were all there just as we'd left them: Leila, Tuppence and Thruppence; two hens; two cats; two parrots and a whole load of fish and frogs in the pond. Before Terry had switched off Tinkerbelle's engine, Vivien was shooing me down to the stable. The floor had been dug out and the foot-deep old bedding removed; it was swept clean and the straw neatly piled round the edges. Thrusting pitchfork, rake and broom into my hands, she explained exactly what I was to do thereafter, in perpetuity, without fail.

I was taken to the kitchen for directions on how to be tidy. The kitchen carousel cupboard, which I often couldn't open because it was so jammed with odds and ends I couldn't find a home for elsewhere, was neatly organized. That was how I was to keep it, said Vivien sternly. I promised I would, and I have. There was a tour of the linen in its new order.

What an extraordinary person she is. All

we'd wanted was to know the animals were being fed, watered and kept safe. She'd taken upon herself the entire management and reorganization of house and garden, and we will never be able to adequately express our gratitude to her. Vivien and Tinkerbelle made our journey possible; without both of them we couldn't have done it.

* * *

For the first week, Tally and Dobbie sat beside Tinkerbelle every day, nearly all day, wanting to know if we were going anywhere. On the sixth day, Terry asked casually: 'Where do you fancy trying next time?'

That's the big question. France is a huge country, and every corner and crevice holds something of interest. So far, we'd only skimmed the surface.

We do hope that you have enjoyed reading this large print book.

Did you know that all of our titles are available for purchase?

We publish a wide range of high quality large print books including:
Romances, Mysteries, Classics
General Fiction
Non Fiction and Westerns

Special interest titles available in large print are:
The Little Oxford Dictionary
Music Book
Song Book
Hymn Book
Service Book

Also available from us courtesy of Oxford University Press:
Young Readers' Dictionary
(large print edition)
Young Readers' Thesaurus
(large print edition)

For further information or a free brochure, please contact us at:
Ulverscroft Large Print Books Ltd.,
The Green, Bradgate Road, Anstey,
Leicester, LE7 7FU, England.
Tel: (00 44) 0116 236 4325
Fax: (00 44) 0116 234 0205

Other titles published by
The House of Ulverscroft:

BEST FOOT FORWARD

Susie Kelly

Why would an unfit, fifty-something Englishwoman embark on a solo walk across France from La Rochelle on the west coast to Lake Geneva over the Swiss border? With no experience of hiking or camping, Susie Kelly found out the hard way that it is possible to be overloaded and ill-prepared at the same time. Scorching days, glacial nights, perpetual blisters, inaccurate maps, a leaking tent and an inappropriate sleeping bag were daily vexations, but as she hobbled eastwards, the glory of the French landscape revealed its magic and the kindness of strangers repaid her discomfort in spades.

TWO STEPS BACKWARD

Susie Kelly

Susie Kelly and her husband Terry dreamed of a home in France. With their dogs, parrots and horses, they moved to a farmhouse in the Poitou-Charentes region. While Terry worked in England, Susie had to contend with a homicidal gas cooker, burst pipes and a biting guinea fowl. The enormity of what they had taken on seemed overwhelming, and when Terry came close to death, the dream threatened to turn into a nightmare. But the kindness of the local community inspired them to make a new life for themselves in the place they now call home.

A CHILD CALLED FREEDOM

Carol Lee

Carol Lee returns to Africa, the country of her childhood — and to Soweto, the place where hundreds of protesting schoolchildren were killed in 1976. She meets one hungry boy called Freedom. As the links emerge between Freedom's story today, and the Children's Uprising thirty years ago, Carol begins a personal quest. Her journey brings her to the leaders of this event, revealing how their courage helped change a nation — and why speaking the truth mattered more than their lives. This inside view of South Africa's struggle to meet its past as well as its future brings together the remarkable stories of two very different African childhoods.